# ANATOMY *of a* HAUNTING

## ABOUT THE AUTHOR

Lee Strong lives with his wife and son in Rockford, Illinois. Lee has been a freelance writer for nearly two decades.

THE NIGHTMARE
ON BAXTER ROAD

ANATOMY *of a*

HAUNTING

LEE STRONG

Llewellyn Publications
Woodbury, Minnesota

First Edition
First Printing, 2013

Cover art: Clouds: iStockphoto.com/jkitan
        Hell and fire: iStockphoto.com/Eva Serrabassa
        House: iStockphoto.com/Shaun Lowe
        Wolf eyes: iStockphoto.com/Joel Jensen
Cover design by Ellen Lawson
Editing by Andrea Neff
Interior photographs supplied by the author

Llewellyn Publications is a registered trademark of Llewellyn Worldwide Ltd.

**Library of Congress Cataloging-in-Publication Data (Pending)**
ISBN: 978-0-7387-3552-8

Llewellyn Worldwide Ltd. does not participate in, endorse, or have any authority or responsibility concerning private business transactions between our authors and the public.

All mail addressed to the author is forwarded but the publisher cannot, unless specifically instructed by the author, give out an address or phone number.

Any Internet references contained in this work are current at publication time, but the publisher cannot guarantee that a specific location will continue to be maintained. Please refer to the publisher's website for links to authors' websites and other sources.

Llewellyn Publications
A Division of Llewellyn Worldwide Ltd.
2143 Wooddale Drive
Woodbury, MN 55125-2989
www.llewellyn.com

Printed in the United States of America

## ACKNOWLEDGMENTS

I'd like to express my sincerest appreciation to the following people, for if it weren't for them, Carlie's story would remain a fading memory, encased in wooden crates and a paper box packed full of notes and recorded conversations.

First, I'd like to thank my editors, Amy Glaser and Andrea Neff, for understanding the nature and complexity of Carlie's story, and taking the time to nurture my sow's ear until it became a silk purse.

Last, but by far not least, I need to thank author Annie Wilder, for if it weren't for her insistence and guidance, this story would never have seen the light of day.

Dedicated to the memory of two
of the most courageous women
I have ever known:

Mrs. Carlie Summers
*September 1937–July 1999*

Mrs. Loretta Heinz
*May 1924–January 2000*

# CONTENTS

*Foreword . . . xi*

*Prologue . . . xiii*

***Book One:*** **The Arrival . . . 1**

***Book Two:*** **The Haunting . . . 51**

***Book Three:*** **Nowhere to Run . . . 219**

*Epilogue . . . 333*

# Foreword

In order to tell the terrifying story of the McPherson house haunting, one has to tell Carlie Summers' story. On a beautiful spring day in 1992, I met Carlie for the first time. Sitting across the kitchen table from me, she rolled up the sleeves of her flannel shirt to expose withered, disfigured arms covered in long, thin white scars and discolored patches from burns that had healed years earlier. Their cause *is* Carlie's story.

The events behind the insanity and depravity that created the haunting in the first place, and ultimately culminated in Carlie's story, encompassed a time span of over 150 years. Unfortunately, due to space constraints, many of the violent events that occurred during Carlie's four-year nightmare have been left out, others condensed, and still others depicted as they were described in police, accident investigators', and coroners' reports.

Many of the names and locations depicted in this book have been changed at the request of Carlie Summers out of respect for the privacy of the residents of the small Iowa town. To prevent the spirits of the McPherson house from drawing unwitting victims into their violent and demented history, the exact location of the house will remain unidentified.

# Prologue

### THE MCPHERSON HOUSE

Two years earlier, as her bedroom filled with flames and dense, black smoke, Grace Baxter passed away, and she wasn't the first person to die under mysterious circumstances in the house on Baxter Road.

For nearly 150 years, the old house has sat isolated. From the top of a small knoll, it vigilantly protects and conceals the terrifying secrets of the restless souls that roam its halls.

The question is, *Would Grace Baxter be the last to die?*

*The McPherson house, circa 1951. Photograph taken by William Baxter.*

Book One

# THE ARRIVAL

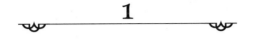

# 1

### THE SUMMER OF 1981

It was July 14th, 1981, two years after the death of Grace Baxter, when Jonathon and Carlie Summers pulled into the drive of the silent and foreboding two-story house.

Carlie had inherited the house from her late aunt, and it had been more than twenty years since she had last set foot on the property. Carlie was amazed to find that, after so many years, not a lot about the old house had changed.

Jon, on the other hand, felt there was something very eerie about it. The old house appeared to be permanently under a deep shadow. The sun was out and there wasn't a cloud in the sky, yet the vacant house remained dark and ominous. He also couldn't shake the feeling that something inside was watching him.

The second-floor window stood in stark relief to the rest of the house. Scorched black and hastily boarded after the fire that had taken the life of Carlie's aunt, the window drew Jon's attention. He couldn't take his eyes off it.

The thought of what had happened behind that boarded-up window chilled his spine.

The fact that the house had been on the market for two years without a single interested party wasn't lost on Jon either.

Carlie didn't seem to notice any of this, not even the window. Something else about the house captivated her. It wasn't something tangible; it was more a feeling. To her, the house emanated a sense of desolation and abandonment, as if it were lonely—as if it were waiting for her.

When Carlie opened the front door and stepped inside, the passage of time simply melted away, leaving her with the feeling of returning home—to where she belonged.

Walking from room to room, she tenderly caressed every hand-sculpted, wood-and-stone-inlaid surface that the original owner had created nearly a century and a half earlier.

Walking through the enormous kitchen into the eat-in breakfast area, she remembered Grace telling her the story of the original owners designing and building each room—how every board, nail, rock, stone, and ounce of mortar had gone into fulfilling their lifelong dream. As she stood in the center of the room, Carlie was reassured to find that, even after sitting vacant for two years, the house still carried the fragrant aroma of freshly baked bread and Aunt Grace's sugar cookies.

Jon wandered three paces behind Carlie as she explored each room, describing not only its history but also the legends behind every little detail. As hard as he tried, Jon still could not summon the same euphoric feeling for the old house as Carlie had.

To him, the interior was dark and oppressive; the air was stagnant and heavy and reeked of burnt wood and electrical wiring. In the kitchen, a hole in the roof had allowed access for a family of raccoons or some other creatures into the rest of the house. Their musky urine scent permeated the raw wood surfaces of the floors, countertops, and cabinets.

The combination of these odors was so prevalent and overpowering, it made Jon's eyes water.

Jon followed Carlie down the central hallway until she abruptly stopped at the end. She tenderly ran her fingertips over the brass trim on the heavy oak door. Turning the handle, she pushed the door open and waited for her eyes to adjust to the darkness.

As the door swung inward, Jon recoiled from a rush of frigid air and the putrid smell of death and decay.

The icy touch of an unseen hand—something invisible yet all too real and physical—grabbed him by the front of his shirt, held him at arm's length, and threw him, flailing, into the far wall. Sliding to the floor, Jon involuntarily gagged at the overpowering stench as it settled into the confined space of the narrow hallway.

Jon felt the need to find a reasonable explanation for what had caused the putrid smell before abject terror overrode his ability to reason.

Possibly a diseased animal had found its way inside the sealed room, where it had died and decomposed.

Whatever it was that had thrown him against the wall, however, was an entirely different story; everything about it was incomprehensible.

Looking up at Carlie, he realized that she hadn't noticed the smell or any of what had happened to him.

After their tour, Jon wanted to run, to get Carlie as far away from the house, as fast as humanly possible.

Taking one last look at the house, Jon could feel the icy glare of someone or something watching him; whatever it was, it had given him a warning that he would never forget.

~

During their drive back into town, Jon kept his eye on Carlie. She sat in her seat perfectly still, slack-jawed and glassy-eyed. She was lost in her own world—a world that excluded everyone and everything else. Something was horribly wrong with her, and he was positive it had everything to do with Grace's house.

They were just outside of town when she finally began to shift in her seat; she looked over at him and smiled. Carlie was back.

In town, they met with Dexter Simmons, Grace's attorney. Handing Carlie a document from the state titled "Execution of Eminent Domain," Dexter explained that substantial repairs needed to be made to the house immediately, or the state would confiscate and demolish it.

It was Dexter's responsibility to sell the house and give the proceeds to Carlie. However, the time to do that had run out.

Without giving it a second thought, Carlie told Dexter that she would take the house; she would make the necessary repairs and some improvements of her own, and then move in.

Jon's jaw dropped. He waited for the punch line—but one never came. Carlie was dead serious.

At that moment, it really didn't matter what Dexter or Jon thought. The house needed *her*.

When Dexter reached across the desk, taking Carlie's hands in his, he told her that what she was proposing was a bad idea and he hoped she would reconsider.

Carlie couldn't. Her decision was far too important. When he told her that he would rather see the house demolished than have her live in it, she became livid.

Jon couldn't believe what he was hearing, nor could he understand Carlie's unshakable determination. After witnessing Dexter's efforts to dissuade her, Jon was sure that the old man knew something was wrong with the old house, and hoped that maybe his insistence would persuade her to change her mind. Jon knew it was useless for him to try to change her mind.

Over the next two hours, the couple listened as Dexter explained what a huge decision it was to even consider moving into the house. Carlie appeared to be completely aware of the pitfalls she and Jon would face. The more they talked, the more animated Carlie became. She described the feelings and impressions she had gotten while in the house. She conceded that these were not the same feelings Jon had experienced. She addressed Jon's concerns by admitting that he was right: they hadn't experienced the same things, but quite possibly she had experienced what the house used to be—what it was supposed to be and would be again—and not necessarily what it was at that moment.

Carlie had been considering the idea of moving away from Chicago for some time. She felt that a complete change was something both of them needed. Their life had become little more than an endless circle of days.

Maybe new scenery, new people, and a slower pace were what they needed.

Not at all sold on the idea of moving into the house, Jon did, however, understand that time was of the essence in starting the repairs. Dexter had already taken the liberty of hiring a local contractor.

After Carlie signed all the required documents and construction agreements, Dexter said he would set up an appointment for them to meet with Paul Jacobson, the contractor.

It had been a long, trying day, and Jon faced a minimum eight-hour drive back to Chicago. Checking his watch, he saw that they had only an hour or so of daylight left, so after saying goodbye to the attorney, he asked Carlie if she wanted to stop at the edge of town and get a motel room rather than drive through the night.

Checking into the tiny motel, they dropped off their few travel items. After settling in, Jon suggested that they go into town and eat before the county rolled up the streets for the night.

~

The town consisted of one main east-west highway, which offered very little in the way of restaurants. After dismissing the two fast food places at the west end of town, Carlie suggested they go back to the café with the semis and pickup trucks parked in front.

"If it's good enough for truck drivers and the locals, it should be good enough for us," she told him.

As the tinkling little bell over the door announced Carlie and Jon's arrival, the clanking of glasses and loud, boisterous conversation immediately stopped. All eyes shifted toward the front door and the newcomers. Even dressed in their most casual clothes, the two of them looked completely out of place.

When the silence became almost palpable, a raspy female voice—attached to a waving, disembodied arm—chimed in from the back of the room, "Y'all just sit down anywhere you like. I'll be with you in a minute."

Choosing an empty booth at the front of the room, Carlie slid in and Jon followed across from her. Before they could even adjust their clothing, the waitress was dropping two menus and two glasses of water in front of them. "Take your time, folks. When you're ready, just holler."

"Hey, Loretta," a booming voice came from the far corner of the room, "you got any more pie back there?"

Without even turning around, she yelled back, "Yeah, Cecil, I got pie. Just hold your horses, old man! You ain't wasting away."

When the room erupted in laughter, the waitress made an apologetic gesture. "I'm Loretta, folks, and I apologize—some of these old farts think they own the damn place," she said. "Don't pay them no mind. Y'all just relax and take your time. I'll be back to check on you in a few minutes."

Smiling, Jon looked across the table at his wife. "Well, Dorothy, we made it—welcome to Oz."

Carlie looked briefly over her shoulder. The animated crowd behind her had already returned to their normal conversations.

It took fifteen minutes or so for their meals to arrive. Neither of them had eaten a thing since breakfast, and Carlie ate as if she hadn't eaten in a week. Jon couldn't believe his eyes. Carlie was always an incredibly fussy eater.

Tonight she ate like a farmhand.

Her platter-size dinner plate was piled high with a piece of deep-fried meat the size of a small frying pan, green beans, mashed potatoes, and enough gravy to classify the meal as an inland sea, and she wolfed down every last bite. She then proceeded to soak up every drop of the remaining gravy with a basket of homemade bread.

After Carlie was finished splashing around in her gravy, the two returned to their motel room. Jon was at a complete loss for words. He pulled out a clean pair of underwear and his pajama bottoms from Carlie's overnight bag and headed for the shower. As the steam and hot water beat down on the tight muscles in his neck and shoulders, he replayed how strange Carlie had acted while they were in the old house.

Even as he silently hoped he had seen the worst, his evening—and hers—was about to get much stranger.

Jon lay in bed for hours watching Carlie sleep. There had been far too many firsts that day, and Jon wasn't comfortable with any of them.

～

That night Carlie dreamed that she could see the old house off in the distance and she desperately needed to get there. Running toward it, Carlie felt very real pain. The sharp rocks of the gravel road poked deep holes and cut ragged gashes in her bare feet.

In the looming darkness, the vacant house stood silent—alone—a silhouette set against a sea of weathered husks and barren trees. It felt so real. She could literally see and smell the white billows of her hot breath as they evaporated into the night air.

Standing on the cold wooden porch, she slowly turned the handle and opened the front door. Stepping inside, she heard a baby crying in the dark. She recognized the cry immediately as that of her own child.

Standing alone in the pitch black, she turned toward where the sound seemed to be coming from. Every step felt as if she were walking in molasses.

A sense of desperation took hold of her as she tried to make her way down the hall. Struggling with each step, she couldn't manage to reach the source of the crying. The closer she seemed to get, the farther away the baby's cries moved—compelling her to follow.

At the end of the corridor was a massive oak door. She knew that her baby was just on the other side, and time was running out.

Expecting to find the door locked, she was surprised at how easily the brass handle turned. She pulled open the heavy door and stepped out of the darkness into a brilliant moonlit night; at her feet, she felt a tiny mound of dirt. Running her hands across the loose dirt, she found a simple polished granite stone.

Carlie knew that the crying was coming from the grave directly beneath her. Dropping to her knees, she felt the cold, damp earth against her exposed skin. As she twisted and turned in her sleep in an attempt to unbury her sobbing infant, a strong, gentle hand caressed her face and hair.

The foreignness of the touch and the unfamiliarity of the cool hand against her warm skin brought her fully awake and straight up in bed. Confused and disoriented, Carlie swung her arms through the darkness in search of the source of the touch.

All she found was her husband sleeping soundly in the bed next to her in the empty room.

## 2

### FIVE MONTHS LATER

As heavy snow ushered in the first day of winter 1981, Carlie and Jon watched it through their motel room window. Staring at the vacant field across the road, Carlie felt extremely apprehensive. Her gut told her that something had happened to Dexter.

He had called the night before and insisted that the couple make the trip from Chicago to Iowa to meet with him to discuss the house. It just wasn't like him to be late for anything. Picking up her purse, Carlie said that they couldn't wait any longer; they needed to drive out to the house.

As they turned off the main highway onto the narrow drive, an ambulance with its lights flashing roared past them, forcing Jon to hit the brakes on the frozen gravel, sending their car sliding sideways.

Carlie's anxiety increased as they finished driving to the house.

Parked at the end of the drive, two cars and a red pickup truck waited in the snow for their arrival. Paul Jacobson, of Jacobson Construction, and Daniel Herrera, of the Lake County Inspector's Office, introduced themselves to Carlie and Jon. They apologized for the inconvenience, but said Dexter had insisted on meeting the two men on site. When he arrived, Paul found Dexter lying face-down on the driveway. The paramedics believed Dexter had suffered a stroke.

When Carlie asked why Dexter had even been out there, the two men looked at each other and shrugged. Neither had any idea.

Paul offered to take them on a tour of the property.

Jon accepted their offer, but Carlie hesitated.

Concerned about Dexter's health, Carlie wondered what had come over the old man. Why had he ventured out to the house alone?

Before she knew what was happening, something came over her and her whole attitude changed. She no longer cared what had happened to Dexter; he had no right coming out here, and he deserved what had happened to him. This was her house.

Unable to hide her feelings of contempt for the old man, she was afraid that Jon would notice.

Grasping for an excuse to get away, she lied to Jon, telling him that she would rather wait to tour the house until the next morning when the light was better.

As the voices of the men faded into the distance, Carlie sat brooding alone on the cold front steps when a quick movement in her peripheral vision caught her attention—then there was another one. What she perceived more than saw were darker shadows darting swiftly within shadows. There was nothing definitive about the movement; it was just an unnerving impression.

She tried to ignore it, but her uneasiness quickly grew into dread—she was positive someone was staring at her. It gave her an almost sickening feeling, one that caused the hair on the back of her neck to stand straight up. The uneasy feeling quickly moved to her bowels as she thought about Dexter lying helpless in the back of an ambulance. She wondered if she would be next.

Carlie tried her best to shake the overwhelming sense of terror. It was a feeling she just couldn't fathom; since she was a small child, this house had always been a source of comfort for her.

In hopes of regaining some semblance of calm, Carlie stood and turned to open the front door.

As she turned, the curtain slowly closed across the window. Carlie caught a glimpse of an old woman—who disappeared just as quickly.

When she opened the door, a peaceful feeling of being welcome— not only *in* the house but also *by* the house—came over her. A feeling of comfort and serenity drew her deeper into the front room.

She was standing in the middle of the empty room when she heard the voices of the men returning. She hurried out and met them as they walked across the drive.

*The ghost (woman) in the window, circa 1949.*

After Daniel informed them of how well the construction was coming along, the two men left Carlie and Jon standing alone in the drive. The couple watched as Paul and Daniel's tail lights disappeared onto the main highway.

As she took one last look at the house and Dexter's snow-covered Mercedes, Carlie sensed the movement again; something in the shadows was watching her.

"Jon, we're being watched," she whispered.

"I know," Jon whispered back. Pointing across the snow-covered lawn, Jon indicated a small patch of raised ground. "I saw a scarecrow in the corner of Grace's garden. I think he's got the hots for you."

Carlie glared at him. "Jon, sometimes you can be such an insensitive yutz." Then she punched him on the shoulder hard enough to make his arm go numb.

"Yeah? Well, you hit like a girl."

As Carlie pushed him toward the car, Jon turned away and grimaced at the pain coursing down his damaged arm.

Hoping to lighten Carlie's mood—even a little—Jon attempted to discuss how well the construction was coming along, but Carlie offhandedly waved him off before he had barely started.

As the couple rode in silence back into town, Carlie couldn't shake the feeling that something other than a scarecrow had been watching her. She wondered if what she had experienced had anything to do with Dexter.

She thought back to how shocked she had been by the directness of Dexter's statement—that he would rather see the house demolished than see Carlie and Jon move into it. She could still hear the concern in his voice when he said, "I wish you would reconsider."

She wanted to tell Jon about her experience, but no matter how hard she tried, she couldn't put into words the depth of the terror she had felt.

Carlie and Jon agreed that they couldn't leave town without checking on Dexter's condition, so they ate a quiet meal at the café and returned to their motel room. Sitting at the tiny table in front of the window, Carlie watched the snow fall. Finally, she turned to face her husband. "Jon, I need to talk to you about something."

Lying on the bed reading, Jon folded the corner of the page. Sitting up, he spun around until he was facing her and said, "Sure, not a problem."

"I know you're going to think that I've lost my mind, but I saw my Aunt Grace tonight at the house. I think it was because I was so scared. Someone was watching me—I know it—and I was scared to death. The minute I needed someone the most, there she was peeking out the window, just as she used to do when I was a little girl.

"I went inside the house, and it was exactly how I remembered it. It was warm and comfortable. It was security. It gave me protection from what was outside—does this make any sense?"

The general air of violence emanating from the house had more than likely prompted Carlie's fear. Jon couldn't be sure that someone or something had actually been watching her; he hadn't been there at the time. After his own experience, though, he couldn't discount the idea either.

Jon's motivation was purely self-serving. He didn't want to move into the house—and if he could use Carlie's terrifying experience that evening to help create doubt, he had to exploit it.

"Carlie, I've told you from the beginning that something is horribly wrong with that house. Even Dexter tried to warn you."

"Actually, what happened tonight just reinforced my desire to move in. Jon, I believe more than ever that I belong in that house, and I believe that this was Aunt Grace's way of telling me that she feels the same way."

Carlie's answer was far from what Jon wanted to hear. At least she had finally experienced to some degree the same gut-wrenching fear that he felt every time he thought of moving into the house.

"Do you believe for a moment that what happened tonight was an isolated incident? I don't. I'm afraid that not only will it happen again, but that this was only the beginning of something worse if we do move in."

"I don't know, Jon."

With that, she sat down next to him and let out an audible sigh.

～

The next day, Jon and Carlie were both up early, and after breakfast, they drove to the Lake County Hospital. They found Dexter resting comfortably in the cardiac intensive care unit. His complexion was horribly pallid, and there were dark circles under both eyes, but his eyes were still bright and very much alert.

He tried to speak, but his mouth pulled down on the right side. His speech was slurred, and spittle ran down his chin. Placing her hand on his left shoulder, Carlie gave Dexter a gentle squeeze and told him not to exert himself, but his light blue eyes danced wildly around her face, then over to Jon. Dexter needed to communicate with them, but before he could, a nurse rushed into the room. Turning to Carlie and Jon, she told them that it would be best for Dexter if they left.

As she finished her speech, a silver-haired doctor entered the room. Dismissing the nurse, he introduced himself as Doctor Tremmel.

The doctor quietly explained to Dexter that if he couldn't remain calm, then Jon and Carlie would have to leave. Dexter nodded in passive agreement and began to speak very slowly and deliberately. His heart monitor beeped at a steady rate as he asked Carlie if she was still planning to move into the house.

She nodded, and Dexter continued. "I—nee—you—wor—fo—me." The confusion in Carlie's eyes forced Dexter to repeat himself. "YOU—work—fome."

"Are you sure?" Carlie asked.

Dexter nodded emphatically. "*Yes!*"

"All right," she said. "I'll give my two weeks' notice. We'll have to find somewhere to live until the house is ready."

Dexter shook his head. "*No—you—say—my—hoss.*"

"We can find an apartment or a rental house," Carlie said. "There's no need to inconvenience you. We'll be fine."

Dexter shook his head emphatically. "I—nee—you. You—nee—unerstan about—hoss."

With that, the monitors beeped faster. Dexter closed his eyes and laid his head back. Once the monitors slowed to a normal rhythm, he started again. "I—pomise—Gase—tke—ca—you. Pease—don't—ague."

Carlie looked at Jon, and he made an imperceptible nod of his head, so Carlie reached down and touched the old man's hand. "Okay, we will."

Dexter watched as the doctor handed Carlie a set of keys. Then, completely exhausted, he closed his eyes and fell into a deep sleep.

～

On the drive home, Carlie was deep in thought. *What did he mean, we need to understand about the house?* What could he possibly know that she didn't? She worried again about the shadows and wondered if Dexter's presence at the house had created them.

Finally, Jon broke the silence. "I guess it's settled. I was really hoping we would have a little more time to discuss it."

"Everything will be fine, Jon. I promise."

# 3

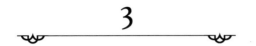

SPRING 1982

In the late spring of 1982, over a year after deciding to move into Grace's house, Carlie and Jon were finally settling into their newly reconstructed home. Carlie was still working for the slowly recuperating Dexter Simmons, and Jon was teaching pre-law at a nearby state college.

Paul Jacobson was finished restoring the house and had done a magnificent job. This was Paul's last day on the job, and Carlie left work early so she could express her gratitude for all his hard work.

Since her very first meeting with Paul Jacobson, Carlie had found something very threatening about the man. It was a feeling she couldn't explain, but he scared the living hell out of her. A great deal of her trepidation was due to Paul's appearance. He was solid muscle, packed onto a six-foot-five-inch frame. His most striking features, however, were his eyes: pale gray and intensely alert, predatory and as feral as a wolf's.

Carlie surveyed the house and the grounds. The restoration had brought the century-old farm back to a state of near perfection. Paul had accomplished so much in just a few short months.

"Paul, you have done a magnificent job on this old house, especially the grounds," Carlie said.

The pleasant conversation she had envisioned quickly turned confrontational.

"Mrs. Summers, I'm positive you don't have the slightest idea what I've been through, but seeing as how you brought up the subject, I'll tell you. Over the last six months, I've lost two of my best men and some $4,000 worth of material. I assumed you took it. It was your material. You could do whatever you wanted with it. After a month or so, it started reappearing. Someone used part of it on the old barn and the tack room. Actually, I appreciated it when they used it to repaint portions of the house. What I didn't appreciate, though, was when we would paint a room, and the next morning we would come back to find someone had painted the words 'Leave my house alone' in red paint all over our white walls."

"I'm so sorry, Paul! I didn't know."

"I figured it had to be kids messing around, so I hired a security guard.

"The next morning we found twenty-seven sheets of newly hung drywall torn off and broken into a million little pieces. Cost me a full day, and the security guard never heard or saw a thing."

Carlie was at a loss for words. She just stared at him.

"We kept our materials and equipment in the barn. On the first Friday morning after we started, we went to get ladders and scaffolding and found the words 'Get away from my house' actually *dug* almost a quarter of an inch deep into the wood panels on one wall.

"Someone replaced every board by the following Monday morning.

"As funny as it may sound, we actually got used to coming in and finding things torn up. We just quit fixing them. The next morning or the day after, we would find the damage repaired and could go on with what we were doing. We worked around it for almost a month. Then whoever was doing it just quit.

"Then…my electrician was running that main electrical junction."

Paul hesitated long enough for Carlie to follow his finger, which was pointing toward a series of wires connected to a three-inch power line running from the transformer on the main highway. "Those thick black lines carry nearly one hundred kilovolts of electricity. Those other lines break it up so you can use it on the property and in your house. Imagine his surprise when he connected the house to the main line only to find someone had flipped on the circuit breaker box. That much electricity in a continuous circuit will turn someone into a bloody puddle of goo in less than a second. He was fortunate; he only suffered a few minor burns and a broken hip."

"God, Paul, I'm so sorry."

"Me too—he quit. Rumors start quick in this business, and they started flying fast and furious that day. It took quite a while before I could find another electrician willing to set foot on the property, let alone fix the damage and finish the job."

"I don't know what to say. Do you have any idea what happened?"

"At that time I didn't. Three days later, my roofer was pushed off the roof."

"That's horrible! Who would push him off the roof?"

"No one—Charlie has been doing roofs alone for twenty-six years. There was nobody on the roof with him that day either. But he was lifted off his feet and physically thrown off the roof all the same; ten men watched it happen. It's something you don't forget. He broke four ribs and a collarbone. That delay cost me almost three weeks.

"What I'm trying to say is we didn't have time to do any extra work on the grounds or the outbuildings. I appreciate your kind words, but we didn't do it."

That queasy feeling returned to the pit of Carlie's stomach as she listened to Paul. It had been a while since Carlie had experienced the unsettling feeling that someone was watching her. Nevertheless, the feeling was back. As Paul talked, Carlie caught a glimpse of a shadowy figure standing inside the barn. After Carlie turned toward Paul and then back again, the shadow was gone, or at least she could no longer see it.

Handing Carlie a massive roll of drawings and documents, Paul turned to leave, but changed his mind.

Stopping abruptly, he turned to face her. "What in the hell possessed you and your husband to move into this house in the first place?"

Evidently, the question was purely rhetorical, because he quickly changed the subject. "You know, when Grace and William moved in here, I did a lot of work on this old house. She wanted to turn the addition on the back of the house into a sewing room. I always thought it was stupid that someone would build an addition with no windows and then not run electricity into it for light. It made even less sense to not have a way in or out, except for one external doorway. So I started checking the connecting wall to the house and found a hollow spot. There actually was a door into the house, but someone had boarded it up and plastered it over.

"This house has a bad history, and I'll bet even money that it has something to do with that room back there."

Leaving Carlie standing in the driveway, he slid into his pickup and slammed the door. Turning, he looked into her eyes, and in a brief moment of uncharacteristic concern he said, "Listen to me, lady, and listen well. If I were you, I'd take my husband and literally run from this house. Not tomorrow—today. And I'd never look back."

As Paul Jacobson drove back to the main highway, he couldn't see that Carlie's lips had pulled taut against her teeth, or that the expression in her eyes had changed from confusion to one of contempt.

With a hint of a smile on her lips, Carlie and the shadowy figure standing at the edge of the house silently watched Paul as he drove away for the last time.

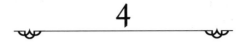

## 4

Jon returned from work to find Carlie sitting with her back against a tree. With her head resting on her knees, she was quietly rocking, oblivious to Jon or her surroundings.

As Jon watched his wife, he remembered coming home from school one afternoon and finding his mother sitting exactly the same way and doing exactly the same thing. Three weeks later, she committed suicide.

This was not like Carlie at all. Squatting down in front of her, he reached out and placed his hands on top of hers. He started to ask what was wrong, but before he could, she waved him off. Pushing him out of the way, she stood and brushed off the seat of her pants. She picked up the roll of drawings and walked past him toward the house.

"He tried to warn me about something. He was *so* pissed."

Looking up from his newspaper, Jon asked, "Okay, I'll bite. Who was pissed? Who are we talking about?"

"Paul—Paul Jacobson. I came home early today and he unloaded on me."

"Geez, Carlie, can you be any more vague?"

"I'm sorry. What part of this don't you understand?"

"Probably most of it. Let me see if I have this straight. We have Paul Jacobson—he was pissed, and he unloaded his frustration on you. Is that pretty much the sum of it so far?"

"Yes."

"Then I guess I'm up to speed. Go ahead."

Carlie had to bite her lip to keep from laughing; Jon could really get right to the heart of the matter. That was what made him a terrific teacher—and an extraordinary lawyer.

After bringing her impulse to laugh under control, she turned, walked across the kitchen, and sat down across from him. "He was trying to tell me something—besides just being frustrated about everything that went wrong during the construction."

"What did he tell you?"

"He rambled on about the addition on the back of the house. The way he made it sound, that doorway is the entrance to hell itself."

Jon couldn't help but flash back to the day he and Carlie had inspected the house—how she had opened that door and that horrible stench had emanated from the room. More importantly, he still firmly believed that something from inside that room had physically attacked him.

Jon recognized the old Carlie returning as she talked. "Mmm, sounds ominous."

"I know."

"Did he say anything else of importance?"

"I think what bothers me the most is that after everything was said and done, he left me with more questions than answers."

Carlie stood and walked back to the counter. "He really was trying to tell me something that he felt I should know or at the very least be made aware of."

Jon didn't want to push her, but he wanted to find out more of what Paul had said; he half-expected Paul's words to confirm his own feelings about the house. "Why don't you tell me exactly what happened that got his knickers in such a knot?"

Carlie set the salad bowls on the table, pulled out her chair, and sat down. Over the next forty-five minutes, she retold Paul's story of sabotage, accidents, and frustration.

"The last thing he said was what really bothered me. He told me that we should run from this house—abandon it—and never look back."

Jon knew she was leaving something important out of her story but decided not to pursue it. Instead, he pointed to the roll of paperwork on the counter. "What's all that stuff over there?"

"Oh, those? I'm not sure. He just handed them to me. I assume they're our blueprints and permits."

Carlie remembered the shadows and decided not to mention them.

~

Carlie excused herself after eating and headed upstairs. The shower felt wonderful, but the softness and warmth of the comforter felt even better. Within seconds, Carlie fell into the deepest sleep she could remember having in years.

Carlie awakened to the screaming of a heavily accented male voice and the tortured cries of a young child. It sounded as though the man was beating the poor kid to death. While the man screamed incoherently, the child begged and pleaded for someone—anyone—to save him.

Carlie knew that if she didn't act, the man would surely kill the child.

Running out the back of the house, Carlie slammed the screen door and ran down the steps. She felt the wet grass and soft mud between her toes as she raced across the yard toward the sound of the child's screams. She smelled the pungent odor of fresh cow manure and newly mown hay as she swung open the heavy barn doors.

In the dimly lit building, she made out two silhouettes in the far corner. The smaller of the two hung suspended from a rope tied to a rafter, while the other was swinging what appeared to be a long, flexible whip.

Screaming "STOP!" at the top of her lungs, Carlie woke herself from the nightmare.

Jon turned on the bedside light and gently ran his hand across the small of her back. "Are you all right?" he asked.

Sitting on the side of the bed, she saw that her feet were wet and caked with dirt and bits of straw. "I don't know—I don't think so."

# 5

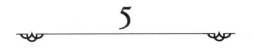

When Jon came down the stairs for breakfast, he found Carlie brooding at the table over a cup of coffee.

Deep in thought, she stared out the kitchen window. She didn't seem to notice her cardinal as it landed on the windowsill. It whistled, chirped, and pecked at the glass to get her attention; she had not missed setting out a handful of birdseed for it since they moved in.

She slowly turned and watched Jon enter the kitchen. She looked like death warmed over. Her eyes were dark and sunken, her face was pale, and her cheekbones were festooned with bright red patches.

"My God, Carlie, you look sick as a dog."

"I'm all right. I didn't sleep very well last night."

"You're not going in to the office today, are you?"

"No, I think I'll just go back to bed."

Jon walked to the coffee can that held the birdseed and scooped out a handful. Opening the kitchen window, he set the seed inside the planter box. As soon as he closed the window, the cardinal returned and began to eat.

It took Carlie almost a full minute before she realized what Jon was doing. "My poor baby," she said as she walked to the window. "Did Mommy forget your breakfast?"

Looking back at Jon, she appeared dazed and confused. Jon took her arm, which was hot to the touch; he turned her around and set her back down in the chair. Without a word, he fixed her breakfast. When it was finished, he slid the plate in front of her and suggested she eat.

Shaking two aspirin out of the bottle, he handed them to her and poured her a glass of orange juice to wash them down.

Carlie took the pills and began eating. In a matter of minutes, she cleaned her plate.

"Sweetheart," Jon said, "maybe you should go back to bed."

Turning, she looked at Jon as if she didn't recognize him.

In a few seconds, recognition returned to her eyes. "Oh, I will later. I have so much to do this morning."

"Like what? Your office can't possibly be that busy."

"Office? Oh yes … the office." She felt like she was walking out of a heavy fog. "Oh God, no, I'm not going to the office today. I need to go back to bed."

"That's a good idea. Why don't you go to bed now?"

"You don't mind?"

"No, I don't mind at all. I'll clean up here and be right up."

Turning, she walked out of the kitchen and up the stairs to the bedroom.

Jon finished rinsing the dishes and placed them in the dishwasher. After pouring himself another cup of coffee, he headed up the stairs.

Stepping into the room, he found Carlie already gently snoring.

He took a quick shower and changed clothes, and while he tied his tie, he watched Carlie as she slowly turned in her sleep. He could see that a little color had returned to her cheeks, but there were still dark circles beneath both of her eyes.

～

As Carlie slept, the temperature in the room began to fall and a light coating of frost formed on the inside of the windows. She barely stirred when her side of the bed compressed under the weight of an unseen presence.

A movement as gentle as a breeze shifted her hair from in front of her eyes. She moaned softly as the invisible hand brushed her cheek.

She opened her eyes to find herself running across an open field, but she was evidently running too slowly. Someone took hold of her arm, forcing her to run faster. When she looked over, she saw a young boy.

"Come, you must hurry," he said. "If you don't, he'll catch us and beat us again."

Carlie was running as fast as her legs would carry her; they felt like rubber. Her mouth was dry and her lungs burned.

Then out of nowhere, something grabbed her by the hair, yanking her off her feet. The ghostly hand pulled her backward into the dirt.

Lying on her back, she gasped for air. Staring up at the clear blue sky, she saw a face suddenly appear. It was the face of a man with long, greasy black hair. She stared into his eyes—eyes filled with loathing, eyes she had seen somewhere before. The eyes were light gray and feral, like the eyes of a wolf.

Screaming, she sat straight up in bed.

As groggy as she was, it didn't register with her at the time when the smoky black shadow melted into the darkest recesses of the bedroom.

Spinning around on the edge of the bed, Carlie hung her head and ruffled her hair. She sat quietly for a few minutes before finally mustering the energy to stand up.

As the temperature began to rise, the frost on the windows dissipated into droplets of water. Her exhaled breath came in a single billow of white vapor. Shuddering from the chilled air, she pulled her heavy robe from the back of a chair and slipped her arms into the sleeves.

Her legs quivered and the muscles in her thighs cramped as though she had just run a marathon. She remembered having a nightmare, but was only able to remember clearly the eyes of the man staring down at her.

As she walked into the bathroom, she could already feel the stress and ache in her body starting to fade. Dropping her robe to the floor, she stood in front of the waist-high mirror. "Jon was right," she said out loud. "I do look like death warmed over."

Turning to walk toward the tub, she saw what appeared to be deep scratches on her left shoulder. As she ran her hand over the red, swollen area, small particles of dirt fell to the floor—and the wounds burned as though she were rubbing them with sandpaper.

Carlie filled the tub with hot water and poured in a capful of lavender bath oil. Soon the room was steamy and humid and smelled of fresh-cut flowers. Stepping into the water, she slowly lowered herself and stretched out. Laying her head back against the white porcelain, she closed her eyes and breathed in the soft fragrance of the lavender.

Carlie opened her eyes about halfway as she sensed a shadow passing in front of her. The old woman kneeling at the side of the tub reached up and gently pushed back Carlie's hair from her face. Carlie could feel her Aunt Grace's unique touch. The old woman's withered fingertips ran gently across Carlie's forehead. "Shhhh," a soft, hollow voice whispered in her ear.

# 6

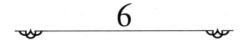

Carlie didn't think she had fallen asleep, but the tepid water in the tub had wrinkled her fingertips and the palms of her hands. Standing, she wrapped herself in a towel and stepped out of the tub onto the cold stone floor.

Picking up her hairbrush, she stopped as she looked at herself in the mirror. Her eyes were bright and full of life; even the dark circles were gone. As she ran the brush through her hair, it flowed and danced with multicolored highlights. She not only looked better, but she actually felt better.

Turning slightly to her right, she looked to see if she had imagined the scrapes. She hadn't—they were still there, only they were smaller now and no longer the angry red color they had been earlier. Reaching over her shoulder, she gingerly touched the afflicted area, remembering how painful it had been. But there was no pain. She had no idea where the scrapes had come from, but it seemed to be close to a miracle that they were nearly healed.

Slipping into her robe, she turned to examine her reflection in the mirror one more time. As she watched the wall behind her, a brilliant blue-white light began to appear. The light slowly transformed into the misty, translucent shape of a person. Carlie couldn't believe what she was seeing. In the blink of an eye, the form was now hovering directly behind her, less than three inches behind her left shoulder.

She stood transfixed as the image of her Aunt Grace manifested itself behind her left ear. She could feel the warmth through her heavy robe as her aunt placed her hand on Carlie's wounded shoulder.

Carlie was on the verge of fainting when the apparition suddenly dissolved into the afternoon sunlight.

After returning to the bedroom, Carlie straightened the covers and put on a flowered cotton housedress and her most comfortable tennis shoes. When she finished dressing, she made her way down the stairs and back into the kitchen.

The clock showed that it was a little after eleven in the morning. Jon would be home soon; she had to hurry.

She prepared an early dinner and placed it in the oven. Once she was finished, she hurried out the kitchen door and down the steps into the back yard.

~

Standing in the brilliant midday sun, she shaded her eyes. There it was: a slight incline in the contour of the surrounding property.

Rushing across the grass, she kicked up swarms of gnats into the warm afternoon air. She glanced back at the house. She had to hurry; she had so much to do.

This area was much larger and more remote than she had originally anticipated. The oblong patch of ground was weed-choked and overgrown with grass. How was she ever going to find what she was looking for?

She crawled on her hands and knees, running her fingers frantically through the grass in front of her.

As she systematically dragged her fingers through the dirt, she hooked a fingernail on something flat and hard. Her fingernail snapped off, leaving her nail bed exposed to the air and bleeding.

Ignoring the pain, she began ripping at the grass and pushing the dirt away with the palms of her hands. There it was: black granite veined in silver, pink, and gold. She wiped harder—it was exactly as she remembered it from her dream. The granite grave marker gleamed in the afternoon sun.

She uncovered it completely and sat back on her haunches. Sweat trickled down her temple, and she wiped at it with the back of her hand. Torn and caked in dirt, her hands began to swell. The tip of her finger where her nail had been was bleeding harder now.

She stood and walked to the front of the house. Oblivious to the pain in her finger or the scratches caused by the thorns, she broke off dozens of multicolored roses and carried them back to the granite marker. She caught a fleeting glance of a shadowy figure watching her every move from the darkest recesses of the barn, but she was so intent on what she was doing that she completely ignored it. What she didn't see, though, was Jon standing in the driveway, also watching her every move.

*Burial plot in the garden, circa 1982.*

Jon thought seriously of intercepting his wife as she headed for the house, but when he saw the blank, faraway expression in her eyes, he changed his mind.

Checking his watch, Jon saw that it was only 12:20; he was home almost three hours early.

He watched Carlie as she walked up the back steps into the house. Once she was out of sight, he got back in the car and slowly drove back to the highway.

~

Jon found Dexter sitting in the living room watching television. Dexter was finally mobile again but needed the assistance of a wheeled walker. Dexter pushed his way across the living room and answered the door.

Jon followed the old man into the house.

After Dexter dropped into his overstuffed chair, Jon sat down on the couch across from him. "So, how have you been, Dexter?"

The old man looked Jon up and down before he answered. "Probably a little better than you."

"Why do you say that?"

"Simple—you're still living in that house."

"I came over to ask you about the house. I need you to tell me everything you know about its history."

"Can you be more specific?"

"Not really."

"I don't know what I can tell you, Jon."

"Dexter, I don't understand what's going on, but I'm sure that what's happening to Carlie has something to do with her being in that house."

"Yeah. Grace reacted exactly like Carlie did when she first saw the house. Everything seemed fine until after William's death."

"Something about that house scares me."

"After the original owner, at least seven families tried to live in it before William and Grace."

"What happened to them? Where did they go?"

"I don't know for sure. I've heard a lot of rumors, but I don't deal in rumors. I do know this, though.

"About three years before Grace and William moved in, a local family put a deposit on the house. After spending the day out there, they took off and never came back. They never returned any of my phone calls, nor did they ask for their deposit back.

"I tried to talk William and Grace out of buying it."

Jon could see that their conversation was starting to take its toll. "I know we've never really discussed it before, but Carlie and I have always wondered why you went out to the house alone on the evening you had your stroke."

"One of the neighbors called and said they had seen someone on the property. I called Paul and Dan and asked them to meet me out there instead of at the office. We've had problems in the past with vandals. I assumed that it was kids."

"Was it? Kids, I mean?"

"I don't know; no one was there when I got to the house. I was going into the barn when my chest tightened up. It was as if someone were squeezing my lungs, shutting off the air. Then I lost control of my right arm. It started jerking and twitching uncontrollably."

"God—was there pain involved?"

"I don't remember any pain, just the tightening in my chest and lungs. I couldn't take a breath, and I got dizzy and lightheaded, so I tried to get back inside the car. I never made it."

"Do you remember Paul or the ambulance getting there?"

"I only remember how cold the dirt was, and there was a distinct smell of decay. Then someone whispered in my ear, 'Leave my house alone, or next time you will die.' The voice in my ear was kind of swimmy and in an echo. It had to have been an oxygen-deprived hallucination. I'm grateful that Paul showed up when he did.

"Speaking of Paul, have you read this?" Shuffling through a pile of newspapers on the footstool next to his chair, Dexter pulled one out and tossed it across to Jon.

Jon looked at the old man inquisitively.

"Section two, 'Local and State,' second page, midway down."

Jon turned the paper to section two and opened it to the second page. The headline read, "Local Man Killed in Single Car Accident." Jon continued to read:

A vehicle belonging to local contractor Paul Jacobson was discovered in the woods off Route 175 late Monday evening. According to Patrick Hemmings, the spokesman for the state police, Mr. Jacobson's automobile, a red 1980 Chevrolet pickup, was traveling west on Route 175 at a high rate of speed. Apparently, when Mr. Jacobson rounded the curve at the junction of Highway 71, he veered off the roadway into the woods. At this point, it appears that alcohol was not a contributing factor to the accident, so we speculate that Mr. Jacobson may have swerved to avoid hitting a deer in the road.

Mr. Jacobson's pickup traveled approximately 200 feet after leaving the roadway before it collided with a tree. Mr. Jacobson died on impact. Officer Hemmings went on to say that the investigation was still open and ongoing.

Jon looked up at the old man. "Holy crap, I can't believe he's dead. Carlie talked to him that day."

"I can hardly believe it myself. I called his wife when I read it in the paper. She thought he was on his way home, but he was going the opposite direction when he had his accident."

Remembering the conversation he had had with Carlie the day of Paul's accident, Jon felt the need to get home and give her the news of Paul's death. Looking at his watch, Jon realized the two had been talking for almost two hours. "Geez, Dexter, I need to get going. Can I hang on to this newspaper?"

"Sure, not a problem."

Insisting Dexter stay where he was, Jon let himself out.

～

It was only a twenty-minute drive back to the house, but it seemed like it took forever. The meeting with Dexter had left Jon with more unanswered questions and an uncomfortable knot in the pit of his stomach. He couldn't get a grasp on the fact that Paul Jacobson was actually dead. It wouldn't have bothered him half as much if he weren't absolutely positive that Carlie had been the last person to see him alive.

As Jon pulled into the drive, he could see that a heavy shadow had once again settled over the house. The closer he got, the more he felt the same oppressiveness he had felt when he and Carlie had first inspected the property. Something was watching him.

Jon had converted part of the barn into a garage and a workshop during the reconstruction, but today he couldn't bring himself to park inside. He could see Carlie's BMW, but the massive old building was much too dark and had too many unexplainable shadows. Pulling onto the grass, he parked in the bright sunlight near the back door.

Shutting off the engine, he stared at the barn. He was positive someone or something was waiting for him inside. It took a couple minutes before he pulled himself together enough to walk to the door. Stopping, he turned back and noticed a fleeting movement in the barn's deepest recesses. It had to be his imagination.

Determined not to let his overactive imagination get the best of him, he took a deep breath and opened the door. As Jon walked into the kitchen, he found Carlie sitting at the table reading a magazine. She turned and greeted him. "Hi, sweetheart. Did you have a good day?"

"Uh, yeah, I did. How are you feeling?"

"Feeling? I've never felt better, why?"

"Because you were sick when I left."

"I was? I think I was just tired. I had a nice nap. I feel great now."

# 7

Standing, Carlie walked over to Jon and threw her arms around him. Jon hugged her back and then held her at arm's length. She looked refreshed. Her eyes were clear and bright, and they no longer had the dark circles he had seen earlier.

She had also changed her clothes. She was wearing a different house-dress now, a purple one, but she was still wearing the same pair of black and white tennis shoes he had seen her in earlier. Jon didn't even know Carlie owned a housedress, let alone a pair of tennis shoes.

"Nice dress. Where did you find that?"

"What, this old thing? I've had it for years."

"Funny, I've never seen you wear it before."

"Where would you like me to have worn it? To the office, or court—maybe the bar association's annual dinner? Jon, I've never worn it because I've never found an appropriate place *to* wear it—until now, that is. Don't you like it?"

"Of course I like it; it's just so different."

"Well, it's comfortable—and I like it."

Changing the subject to avoid an argument, Jon said, "My God, Carlie, something smells incredible."

Pushing him away, Carlie headed for the stove. "I almost forgot. Go shower. Dinner will be on the table in about fifteen minutes."

As Jon showered, he couldn't believe the difference in the way Carlie looked since this morning. She was actually acting differently, as if she were enjoying life again.

While Jon pulled on a clean pair of jeans, he couldn't help but think that he actually preferred his wife this way, and before he upset the applecart, he would keep all these inexplicable changes to himself.

As he walked into the kitchen, he couldn't believe his eyes. There was enough food on the table for a small army.

"Carlie, are we expecting the 5th Fleet?"

Pulling out a chair, Carlie pointed to it and laughed. "Of course not, silly. This is all for you. Sit down and eat."

Carlie served up dinner, and they both ate in silence. As she filled Jon's plate for the second time, he took her hand in his; that was when he noticed her finger with the torn nail. The tip of her finger was red, swollen, and caked with blood where her fingernail had been.

"My God, Carlie, what happened?"

"Oh, I was gardening today; actually I was weeding the garden."

Jon just looked at her; he didn't know what to say. Her smile was radiant and she was full of life, something he had not seen in her in years. He couldn't find it in his heart to bring up what he had seen earlier when he came home or to go into his discussion with Dexter. He just couldn't.

# 8

When dinner was over, Jon helped Carlie clean up the kitchen and put away the dishes. After they finished, she took Jon by the arm. "It's a beautiful evening. Why don't we go sit on the front porch and watch the sun set? I'll pour a couple glasses of wine and we can spend some quiet time together. What do you think?"

"That sounds like a plan."

It was a cloudless night, and the stars stood out in brilliant relief, like millions of hand-tossed diamonds on black velvet. Carlie spun around on the swing and rested her head against Jon's shoulder.

"Jon?"

"Hmm?"

"Are you happy?"

"I'm happy we're together. I'm happy to see that you seem to be happy."

"But are you happy that we moved into Aunt Grace's house?"

"To be honest, I still have my reservations. It's not what I'd call an overly friendly house. Something about it feels evil, and it scares the living shit out of me sometimes. Why do you ask?"

Sitting up, she turned to face him. "Really?"

"Doesn't it scare you?"

"Not anymore. I think the house is protected by the spirit of Aunt Grace."

A cold chill ran down Jon's spine at Carlie's answer.

"Sweetheart, can I ask you a question?" Jon started.

"Of course you can."

"Since we've been here, do you feel different?"

"I'm not sure I understand what you're asking."

"It's just that I've noticed a lot of changes in you since we moved in. Actually they started before we moved in, but they are much more pronounced since moving into the house."

"Really? Like what kinds of changes?"

"Well, the way you dress, and your appetite. It's as if this house has had an effect on you. You are definitely the not the same old Carlie that you used to be."

Carlie smiled for the first time since Jon started talking. "That's exactly what I'm trying to say, Jon; I'm happy—truly happy—maybe for the first time in my life. I've finally found a place where I feel like I really belong."

Pulling her close, Jon closed his eyes and leaned back in the swing. Carlie didn't even realize something was changing her. Maybe it had to do with the house, and maybe it didn't, but either way, he was getting a little concerned.

Leaning her head against Jon's shoulder, she looked up in time to catch a shooting star race across the heavens. As she watched its trail dissipate into the night sky, she felt someone watching them. It was slowly becoming a regular part of her life, so she pushed the feeling aside.

# 9

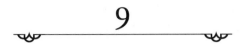

Lying down next to Jon, Carlie curled up against his side. He wrapped his arm around her and pulled her closer. Within seconds, they were both snoring softly.

Carlie felt sharp pain as the gravel and rocks bit deep into her shoulders and backside. Twisting and turning, she managed to catch a glimpse of the man's contorted face as he dragged her across the open field. Stopping to switch hands, he bent over her. Raining spittle into her face, he cursed her very existence.

A swift, punishing kick beneath her left breast sent pinpricks of light flashing before her eyes, starving her lungs of air.

Unable to fend the man off, Carlie rolled into a fetal position, which seemed to infuriate him even more. Digging his nails painfully into her scalp, he grabbed a handful of hair and began dragging her again.

Stopping, she heard the screech of metal against metal and then the audible thud of something heavy as it dropped into the soft dirt. Opening her eyes, she watched the sky above disappear and everything turn black. She found herself suspended in midair. In shock, she took a quick breath, only to have it knocked out a moment later as her head and back slammed hard against wooden steps.

Falling and tumbling backward, her body finally came to an abrupt stop, slamming her already injured head painfully against the hard-packed dirt of the cellar floor.

As she struggled to maintain consciousness, the heavy door above slammed shut, enveloping her in an impenetrable darkness. Then someone locked the door from the outside. Lying helpless on the cold, damp earth, Carlie began sobbing uncontrollably, not only because of the pain, but also because of the isolation and rejection she felt.

"Carlie? Carlie! Are you all right?"

Opening her eyes, Carlie found Jon leaning over her.

As her eyes adjusted to the darkness of the freezing bedroom, Carlie could see the concern on her husband's face.

"It was just a bad dream, sweetheart. I'm all right now."

Touching her cheek, he quickly pulled his hand away. "My God, you're freezing."

Wiping the tears from his wife's cheek, Jon pulled her close and began rubbing her back and arms vigorously to warm her. He stopped when she involuntarily winced in pain. Running his hand gently under her top and across her shoulder blade, he felt dampness against his fingertips.

He turned on the bedside light and looked at his hand under the diffused glow. Blood covered the tips of three fingers. He looked down at Carlie for some kind of explanation.

"Carlie, what in the hell is going on? What happened to your shoulder?"

Looking at Jon's bloody fingertips in disbelief, she sobbed, "I don't know."

# 10

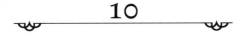

Carlie was still pacing the kitchen floor as the sun rose the next morning. She had been there since she had awakened from her nightmare. Jon was sitting at the kitchen table watching her, concern etching deep lines in his forehead.

"Carlie, why don't you sit down, sweetheart. You're wearing a rut in the floor."

"I'm glad you think this is a time for levity, Jon."

"Oh, believe me, I don't think this is in any way funny, but you do need to sit down."

"Why?"

"I went to see Dexter yesterday."

"Your point?"

Pulling the newspaper from his briefcase, he opened it to the story about Paul Jacobson. "He showed me this story in the newspaper."

Carlie stopped pacing and turned to face her husband.

"It's about Paul Jacobson—he's dead. He had an accident."

The expression on Carlie's face never changed. "That's terrible. What happened?"

"According to the article, he ran his truck into a tree sometime after leaving here on Monday."

Turning her back to Jon, she placed both hands on the edge of the kitchen counter and gripped it tight enough to turn her knuckles white. Her reflection in the kitchen window showed a combination of excitement at the news and pure contempt for the man. As Carlie slowly turned to face her husband, her expression of mock concern was back.

"God, Jon, that's terrible."

"According to this, you might have been the last person to see Paul alive."

"I'm sorry to hear that he's dead. His wife must be devastated."

"Did he say anything to you about where he was going when he left?"

"He didn't give *me* any idea; after he unloaded on me, he left in a cloud of dust."

"Well, I had to ask."

"He just drove away."

"It's just that there have been so many things. These nightmares you're having—they're becoming an every night occurrence. And now Paul's accident; I'd like to know what the hell is going on."

Waving her hand through the air as if to assure him it was nothing, Carlie said, "Last night was a bad dream, nothing more."

Looking at her curiously, Jon knew better, but conceded. "Yeah, that's probably it. Do you remember what you were dreaming about?"

"Not really; it's all fuzzy now. I do remember being somewhere intensely dark. I felt that someone had buried me alive, then you woke me up."

"Are you all right now?"

"I'm fine *now*. You don't need to worry about me; people have bad dreams all the time."

"Yeah, but no one person has them *all the time*. I guess what I'm asking is, *is something wrong?*"

Carlie gave Jon her most endearing smile. "Of course not, sweetheart. There isn't anything wrong with me at all. It's probably just a combination of everything. You know—new house, new job, new surroundings."

"I hope that's all it is."

When Jon finished his cup of coffee and headed up the stairs to get ready for work, Carlie opened the cabinet door and pulled out the roll of plans Paul had left with her. Unrolling them on the kitchen table, she flipped through the first four pages before she found what she was looking for. She pulled out that sheet of paper, then rolled up the rest and put them back under the counter.

After Jon left, Carlie ran upstairs and changed into a pair of old work jeans, one of Jon's old flannel shirts, and a pair of Grace's heavy work boots. After she was dressed, she rolled up the piece of paper and headed out the back door.

In the barn, she found the crowbar she was looking for hanging on the wall and a shovel right below it. With the heavy tools in hand, she walked back to the house.

Setting the tools on the ground, she unrolled the plot map and situated it on the back porch according to the north-south direction at the top of the page. Picking up the shovel and the map, she measured off approximately seventy-five feet.

Holding the shovel handle with both hands, she jammed the steel tip into the soft dirt, moving both left and right in small increments. She repeated this process for what seemed like over an hour when the shovel slid a few inches into the dirt and hit something solid.

Dropping to her knees, she pulled the dirt away by hand until her fingers scraped across what felt like wooden planks. She'd found it! Standing, she began to dig in earnest.

Finding the door boarded shut and padlocked, she pried the boards free with the crowbar. When she was finished, she turned the crowbar over and, with the hooked end, ripped the padlock's hasp loose from its mounting.

It was exhausting work. After breathing through her mouth for so many hours, it felt as dry as the Sahara, and her tongue was sticking to the roof of her mouth. A five-minute break was all she needed. Her shoulders ached, and blisters covered the palms of both hands. Dropping the crowbar in the dirt, she walked to the house.

After pouring herself a glass of iced tea, Carlie took a deep breath and began to relax. She wondered exactly what she would find once she finally made her way down the cellar stairs. She remembered being thrown down them in her dream. She was still a little apprehensive after the experience, but she knew this was something she had to do.

Jon would be home in a few hours. She had promised him something special for lunch, so she quickly put the ingredients together for a pot of chili. Once it was simmering, Carlie finished her tea and headed back outside.

She almost missed the first step; something was wrong. The door to the cellar was now lying wide open. She was positive that she had left it closed when she went inside the house.

Carlie looked around the back yard, expecting to find Jon leaning against the side of the barn waiting for her. But he wasn't. No one was there, just her.

Cautiously she walked to the cellar entrance. The gaping hole beyond the door was black as pitch. The first two wooden steps reflected the outside light, but after the second step, the darkness was impenetrable.

She remembered seeing a kerosene lantern hanging on the wall in the barn. After picking up the shovel and crowbar, she returned to the barn and took down the lantern. She located a book of matches on the workbench and tried to light the lantern. It wouldn't light. Shaking it, she found it was out of kerosene.

She located a gas can marked "Kerosene" and shook it. There was still liquid sloshing around in the bottom, so she poured it into the fill tube. She lit another match, and this time the lantern sparked, sputtered, and, with a hiss, flickered to life.

The pale yellow light illuminated the steps just enough to keep Carlie from falling down the stairs and breaking her neck. At the bottom, she found two more lanterns hanging on wooden pillars. After a few minutes, she had all three lanterns lit, which bathed the cellar in a warm yellow glow. The musty room was at first glance empty, and it reeked of mildew and mold.

With the lantern outstretched in front of her, Carlie found the dirt floor in front of the farthest wall stacked with at least fifteen wooden crates. The light wasn't good enough for her to see exactly what was inside them, but she instinctively knew they were for her.

# 11

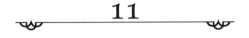

Carlie dropped the last two crates on the living room floor and bent over in sheer exhaustion. With both hands on her knees, she stood in the crowded room panting and wheezing like an old dog.

The chili cooking in the kitchen smelled delicious, but she couldn't stop to eat—not yet.

The thought of moving the heavy crates one more time was daunting to the point where she almost started crying.

Her arms were weak and her legs were still quivering from carrying them up the stairs, across the yard, and into the house—and now she had to move them again. But where? she wondered. Where the hell could she possibly hide all these boxes so Jon wouldn't find them?

Walking across the living room, she stopped in front of the grandfather clock. She couldn't believe her eyes; the clock showed that it was only 12:45. Jon wouldn't be home for at least another two hours. Looking at the crates scattered across the living room floor, she wondered how she had accomplished as much as she had in just a little over an hour.

She had a few extra minutes now; she had to take a break. Settling into Jon's overstuffed chair, Carlie lifted her sore and swollen feet onto the ottoman and rested her head against the back. Closing her eyes, she fell asleep almost immediately.

~

She opened her eyes in the darkness of the dank, foul-smelling cellar. She could barely breathe from the beating inflicted upon her. The tip of his massive work boot crashing repeatedly into her side had broken at least two ribs just below her left breast. She had a deep gash in the back of her head and a mind-numbing concussion.

The pain in her head and side was excruciating, but she was no longer crying. Her feelings of abandonment and desolation gave way to anger. Her anger—as with any pre-adolescent child—manifested as threats. *They'll be sorry. When I'm old enough and big enough, I'll kill them all for what they've done to me.*

~

When Carlie did finally open her eyes, she was back in her own living room, safe in Jon's chair. The grandfather clock had just finished its four smaller chimes and was beginning its deep, resonant bongs. Carlie sat and listened to the clock's striker as it reverberated three times against the walls of the room.

The sound of Jon's car on the gravel drive brought her straight up in the chair. In a panic, she looked around at the mess that she had left on the living room floor. But it wasn't there.

Looking at the empty floor, her immediate fear was that she had dreamed it all. There was no cellar. There were no crates. Then she saw them, in the far corner against the staircasing wall, neatly stacked in rows of five boxes wide and three boxes high.

The back door to the kitchen opened, and Jon shouted into the empty room. "Carlie, I'm home."

"I'm in here, Jon."

Jon laid his briefcase on the counter and crossed the kitchen toward the sound of Carlie's voice. He was halfway across the kitchen when Carlie entered from the living room. With a warm smile, she wrapped her arms around him and gave him a huge, powerful hug.

She had no alternative now; she had to show him the crates—and hope for the best. "I'm so glad to see you. I'm really happy that you're home."

"Uh…I am too?"

"I have so much to show you."

"Does it by chance have anything to do with that gaping hole in our backyard?"

Taking him by the arm, she pulled Jon into the living room and pointed toward the stack of boxes against the far wall. Leaving him in the center of the room, Carlie walked over and pulled a leather-bound book out of one of the crates. Opening it, she turned toward her husband.

"Look, Jon. See what I found today?"

His eyes widened, and in a soft whisper he said, "Wow! What the hell is all of this?"

"They're journals—and there are hundreds of them."

"What exactly do you mean by journals?"

"You know—journals—they're like diaries. This is what people did before the advent of cable television."

"Okay.... Where did all these journals come from?"

"The storm cellar."

"I didn't know we had a storm cellar."

The events of Carlie's dreams from that afternoon and the night before passed through her mind just long enough to make her feel guilty when she answered, "I didn't either. I found it marked on the plot maps Paul Jacobson gave us."

"Then am I correct in assuming that the gaping hole in our yard is the entrance to this cellar?"

"Yep."

"Great. Is there any possible way to cover it up, or do I have to worry about breaking my neck?"

Book Two

# THE HAUNTING

# 12

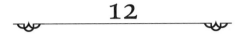

After Jon came back up from inspecting the empty cellar, he and Carlie walked over and sat down on the porch steps.

"I really think having a functional storm cellar is a good idea," Jon said.

"You're probably right."

"I'll fix the door instead of sealing it shut."

Standing, he took Carlie's hand and pulled her to her feet.

As he walked toward the barn, Jon again felt that someone was watching his every move. Turning to Carlie, he could see that she was again in her own little world.

Leaving Carlie at the door, Jon walked inside the barn. In the workshop, he found all the tools he would need to fix the door. With these in hand, he headed back outside to Carlie.

As he passed her, he stopped, expecting her to follow, but she didn't. Her eyes were dark and transfixed on something deep within the shadows of the barn. She was staring into the far corner as if she were remembering a long-distant memory.

Jon reached out and tugged on her sleeve. "Are you coming, Carlie?"

As he touched her arm, she recoiled and spun away from him. With her hands balled into fists and her teeth clenched, she hissed, "*Get your fucking hands off me! If you ever touch me again, I'll kill you.*"

Bowel-loosening terror gripped at Jon's stomach. In their eighteen years of marriage, he had never seen Carlie act like this before—she was one of the most non-aggressive people he had ever known. He was positive that if Carlie were holding the tools instead of him, he would be dead right now.

Her crystalline emerald eyes were as dark and haunted as a stormy sea. They expressed no recognition of who she was talking to or of her surroundings. All Jon could do was stand perfectly still—and pray he wouldn't have to defend himself.

Minutes passed, but it felt like an eternity. Neither of them moved. Slowly Carlie's eyes began to change. They softened—and recognition of Jon and her surroundings began to return.

Her hands unclenched, and the muscles in her jaw relaxed. It was like watching someone wake from a hypnotic trance.

Carlie finally looked directly at Jon and smiled. "Well, did you find what you were looking for?"

"Yeah...I did. Are you all right?"

"Of course I'm all right." Concern flashed in Carlie's eyes. "Why do you keep asking me if I'm all right?"

"Tell me what happened in the last...let's say ten minutes."

Carlie looked at Jon as if he had two heads. "What the hell are you talking about?"

"Just humor me. Tell me what you remember about the last ten minutes."

"You walked into the barn and picked up some tools to fix the cellar door. You came back out, and I asked if you had found what you were looking for."

"That's all you remember?"

"Of course that's all I remember. That's all that happened.

"Jon, I love you, but don't fuck with me today. I'm really in no mood for it. Why don't you go fix the cellar door by yourself. I'm going in the house."

Jon stood in the driveway watching Carlie as she stormed off. He wasn't alone and he knew it. In his peripheral vision, he caught the slightest movement on the second floor of the house. The fine hairs on his arms stood straight up as he caught a fleeting glimpse of a woman as she disappeared behind the curtains.

# 13

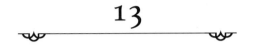

As the shadows of dusk crept across the living room floor, Jon found Carlie curled up on the couch reading one of her newly found journals. She had pulled out about a half dozen of the thick leather-bound books and stacked them neatly on the floor in front of her.

Watching her as she read, Jon was beginning to be concerned about Carlie's sanity—and his own, too.

He wondered if Carlie was suffering from a nervous breakdown. This was so unlike her. Carlie was the most mentally *and* emotionally stable person he had ever known.

Jon felt it was best not to mention what had happened that afternoon, especially if she couldn't remember any of it anyway, so he opened his briefcase and pulled out a stack of papers. He had enough papers to grade to keep him out of Carlie's line of fire.

He had been working on the papers for almost an hour when Carlie set down the journal she was reading and turned to him.

"Are you at all interested in what I'm reading?" she asked.

Setting down his papers, Jon looked directly into Carlie's eyes. "Of course I am. Is it interesting?"

Carlie was acting as though she hadn't had a meltdown in the driveway at all. Jon was still very leery of her, although he was becoming cautiously optimistic with the change he could see coming over her.

"Are you sure? I see that you're busy and I don't want to bother you, but this is fascinating reading."

"It's not a problem. I could use a break. Remind me whom these journals belonged to."

"Her name was Edith, Edith McPherson."

"And that would be?"

"Edith and Ian McPherson originally settled this land and built this house in the early 1800s."

"Wow, all of those belonged to this Edith McPherson?"

"To be honest, I don't have a clue. I doubt it, though; they look to be a collection from a bunch of different families. From what I can see, it's a written history of this house."

"Oh goodie, that's just what we need—a written history—and of *this* house."

Jon could see Carlie's eyes growing dark again and her jaw beginning to clench. He made a mental note: until he found the underlying cause of why Carlie was acting so strange, he was going to have to walk on eggshells around her.

"I'm only kidding. Don't get your knickers in a knot. Can I get you something to drink? I'm going to get myself a glass of iced tea."

"A glass of tea would be nice, thank you."

When Jon returned, Carlie continued. "You need to listen to this," and she began reading Edith's elegantly handwritten entry.

*Today was the happiest day of me life. Tonight Ian asked Da for me hand in marriage. Of course, Da had to burden the poor boy by asking him a million questions. I felt so bad for Ian. There he was, cleaned and pressed, dressed in his Sunday finest and sweating just like a pig in the summer sun. The more uncomfortable Ian got, the more Da seemed to enjoy it. In the end, Da did give Ian his consent, but to be sure, it is true he made the poor lad work for it.*

*Mum cried, and Emily danced around the room at the news.*

*In four more months, I'll be fourteen and I will finally be **Mrs. Ian McPherson**. I can hardly wait!*

"My God, Jon, she was just a baby."

"They got married much younger back then, Carlie. I wouldn't read too much into the age factor. Besides, their life expectancy was so much shorter back then than it is today."

"I guess you're right, but it is mind-blowing to even consider being married that young."

Yawning, Jon stood and picked up his briefcase. "Are you coming to bed? I'm exhausted."

Carlie ran her fingers over the soft leather cover. "I'll be up in a few minutes."

# 14

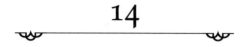

Jon awoke to a gentle, feminine touch on his right arm. Opening his eyes, he expected to find Carlie standing by the side of the bed; instead, he found the room black as pitch. Even the radiant light from the starry sky seemed unable to penetrate the darkness. The room was also completely empty—except for Carlie, who was sleeping soundly in the bed next to him. The clock on the nightstand showed that it was 3:00 AM. Although the room was empty, not three feet from his side of the bed was a radiating, bluish light.

The bright blue light quivered slightly but hung suspended just above the floor. Jon blinked several times and rubbed his eyes, but the light was still there. It hovered in front of him, perfectly still—as if it were watching him, gauging his reaction.

Without taking his eyes off the strange blue orb, he reached his right arm under the covers and across the bed until he found Carlie's hip. Shaking her slightly, he whispered her name.

"Carlie? Carlie, wake up!"

Carlie didn't move, so he shook her a little harder and called her name a little louder.

"*Carlie!*"

Carlie rolled over, snuggled up against his right side, and draped her arm over his stomach.

"Hmm?"

"Carlie, wake up!"

"Not tonight, Jon. I'm too tired."

The light began to pulsate. Slowly and as if suspended on strings, it moved across the room closer to the bed. Jon instinctively tried to push himself away, but he couldn't; Carlie was too tight against his side.

The area next to the bed surrounded by the light was becoming increasingly colder. He could feel the cold radiating against his exposed arm and face as the light came closer.

Jon stared directly into the brightest spot in the light. He felt that he was making eye contact with someone—or something. He wasn't afraid of it at all. He should have been—that would have been the only logical reaction—but he wasn't.

Jon instead grew more fascinated with each moment. Exerting a substantial amount of effort to avoid disturbing Carlie, he pushed himself into an upright position. He kept staring at the light, and waited.

Jon noticed that although it was in reality a light, the space surrounding it remained oppressively dark. Whatever it was didn't radiate light, it simply was light. Jon found this phenomenon amazing. He wished he could wake Carlie so she could see it too.

Jon had never been a believer in the supernatural or paranormal. However, he had read on more than one occasion that this was how a ghost manifested itself to the living.

The light began to expand and contract, ever so slightly at first, but more intensely as the moments passed. Jon had no idea what to expect next, but he was sure that this variation in its appearance definitely must have some significance.

The light slowly took on a human form. It wasn't solid or as well defined as Jon had expected it to be, but it was definitely the form of a human all the same.

Then the light suddenly changed again. This time it remained stationary, while a soft, gossamer form moved forward and slightly away from it.

The translucent form slowly became a shape, which appeared to be that of a young woman. She was wearing a long, flowing dress with six lapel buttons, a tight waist, a delicately embroidered bodice and choker, and puffy, wide-shouldered sleeves. Her face was soft and angelic, and Jon got the impression that she had dark red hair. Parted down the center, her hair was pulled back severely against the side of her head, just above her ears, and feeding into a twisted bun on the back of her head.

He had seen a similar hairdo in a magazine once. It was a story about Queen Elizabeth I, who had worn her hair in this fashion, only the queen had worn a jeweled net—this young girl didn't.

He wondered if this was the same woman he had seen earlier in the second-floor window. His impression was that that woman was much older, but this hairdo and her clothes would give anyone a false impression of age. As he pondered this question, he found himself unconsciously reaching for her inside the light.

In a brilliant flash, the girl was gone, throwing the room into total darkness. The clock on the nightstand showed that it was now 3:05. Carlie stirred softly next to him.

As Jon slid back under the covers, he noticed the room had warmed appreciably. He was dying to wake Carlie and tell her what he had seen, but he had no proof that anything had even happened.

He laid his head on the pillow, and before he knew it, he was waking up again. The sun was shining brightly through the eastern windows, and he could hear the shower running in the bathroom. Carlie's side of the bed was rumpled, still warm, and fragrant from where she had slept.

The encounter with the spirit of the young girl was no longer as vivid as the night before. Jon could still see her face, but its specifics were beginning to become fuzzy and ill-defined. He worried that by afternoon he would have very little memory of the encounter at all.

He only had a late class that day, so he took his time taking a shower and getting dressed.

～

In the kitchen, he poured himself a cup of coffee and sat down at the kitchen table. As he held the warm cup in his hands, he pondered the events of the night before and the images of the young girl.

Suddenly he knew exactly what he needed to do—exactly whom he needed to talk with.

# 15

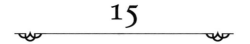

The tiny bell above the café door chimed as Jon entered. Breakfast was over and the early-morning crowd had left at least an hour earlier, but the aroma of pancakes, sausage, and cigarette smoke still lingered in the air. The only people in the room were Loretta Heinz and her husband, Cecil. When she stood to greet Jon, the scraping of her chair across the linoleum floor echoed off the walls.

"Well, well, bless my soul. How are you doing, stranger?" Loretta said.

"I'm doing pretty well, Loretta. How about you?"

"Not bad at all. Where is that good-looking wife of yours?"

"Ah, Carlie. … She's at work. I'm glad you're working this morning; I need to talk to you. Are you busy? Would you have a few minutes?"

"For you, I have all the time in the world. What's on your mind?"

"You were born and raised in Lakeview, weren't you?"

"Sure was. I'm fourth-generation, born and raised right here."

"Then you *are* the person I need to talk to."

"You go ahead and grab a seat, hon. I'll pour us a cup of coffee."

As Loretta poured two cups of what looked to be very old coffee, Jon walked to the booth that he and Carlie usually shared, and slid in. Loretta brought the coffee to the table and sat down.

As she slid into the booth across from Jon, she cocked her head slightly and gave him a curious look. "What seems to be your problem, sweetie? Don't remember ever seeing you quite so distracted."

"I'd like for you to tell me what you know about the old Baxter house."

"Wow, are you serious?

"Yeah, I'm afraid I am. I asked Dexter, but he pulled the lawyer card. If it isn't a verifiable fact, he just refuses to go into any detail, or he won't discuss it at all and changes the subject."

"Why, that old stick in the mud—when he was young, nobody in town loved a good rumor or a juicy piece of gossip more than Dexter Simmons. Over the years, that old house has been a lightning rod for gossip.

"Okay, Jon, where do you want me to start?"

"Carlie believes the spirit of her Aunt Grace is still there. I guess you could say the old woman is haunting it. Dexter did tell me that a number of people wanted to buy the property, yet no one did. He even mentioned that one couple left a deposit but abandoned the house and the money after spending the day out there. Can we start there?...I don't know how to ask this, so I'll just come right out and ask: Is the house haunted?"

"Of course it's haunted, honey. Christ sakes, I thought you two knew."

Normally, Jon would have been shocked, but not today. Today, he fully expected to hear that the house was indeed haunted. As much as he expected her confirmation, it still left a sinking feeling in the pit of his stomach.

"I wish I had known from the onset. Maybe I could have talked Carlie out of moving all the way out here to the middle of nowhere. Dexter should have told us."

"Jon, don't blame Dexter—and you surely can't blame Carlie. My grandfather used to tell anyone who would listen that for the last hundred and so many years, the house—or whatever haunts the house—selects who it allows to live in it.

"When I was a young girl—I guess I was maybe six or seven—my best friend Katie and her little brother Evan lived in your house; back then it was the McPherson place. Both Katie and her mom used to see the ghosts in the house all the time. She told me about them when she would spend the night at my house. I watched both her and her mom talk to the ghosts when I would spend nights over there.

"Jon, it was the damnedest thing to watch: Katie would hold full-blown conversations with this ghost, or ghosts, like they were old friends. I never saw them, but I could feel there was someone or something in the room with us."

"What did your grandfather mean, 'The house picked who lived in it'?"

"Over the years, only a certain type of family would move in. Of course, the man of the house worked the land, and they always had children. There was something about children. They seemed to be a kind of prerequisite for the house to allow these families to settle in and live there. The wife was usually expecting when they moved in. If she wasn't pregnant when they moved in, she was shortly after."

"That doesn't make any sense. William and Grace Baxter didn't have any children when they lived there. In fact, they never had children."

"Of course they did. They had Carlie. Sure, she wasn't their child, but she spent most holidays and every summer with them. She even lived with them for a few years."

"Wow, I didn't know that. . . . That brings me back to the subject of Carlie. She's starting to act possessed. I'm afraid that the way she's acting has something to do with the house, or whatever is in it."

Jon mulled over what Loretta had just said—but something didn't fit into her grandfather's theory. Then it dawned on him exactly what it was. "Loretta, we don't have any children. Unless we adopt, which is highly unlikely, we never will. Carlie can't have children.

"I guess there is always that one exception, and we're it."

"Well, sweetie, I don't know what to tell you. You know how rumors go; you take a small fact, spread it around, and before you know it, it's blown completely out of proportion."

"I'm sorry, I didn't mean to sound accusatory. I'm grasping at straws here, Loretta, trying to find an explanation for something that, more than likely, has no reasonable explanation.

"What happened to your friend Katie and her family? Why did they move?"

"Katie's dad was killed in a hunting accident. Then one day they were gone. I never heard from Katie or her mother again."

"Damn, that wasn't what I wanted to hear. I guess I expected you to tell me that the children grew up, got married, and moved away in search of greener pastures."

"I wish I could tell you that, but that isn't what happened. In fact, from the stories my grandfather used to tell, it never happened that way. Something tragic always happened just before whoever was living in the house disappeared.

"I could go on for hours. Like I said, that old house has been a lightning rod for gossip in this town my whole life."

Once back outside, Jon took a deep breath and stood by his car for a minute debating if he should go to class or go back to the house. He really had no idea what he would do at the house alone. He wondered how he—or anyone—could confront what he couldn't see. He slid in behind the steering wheel and headed out of town.

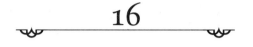

# 16

Jon was a little more than a mile from the house when a feeling of panic started to come over him; his stomach began to burn. In a few moments it tightened into a knot, sweat beads popped out on his forehead, and it was getting hard to breathe. He had never been subjected to panic attacks before in his life, but just the thought of spending another night in that house brought one on with a vengeance. His breathing was coming in short, rapid bursts—his stomach roiled and his mouth filled with saliva. He knew he was about to throw up. Swerving the car to the side of the road, he slammed it into park, threw open the door, and ran to the passenger's side. Dropping to his knees in the soft, cool grass, he retched and then retched again—but nothing came up.

The violence of the retching began to relax the burning knot in his stomach. Sticking his finger down his throat, he forced himself to retch again. The more he did, the better his stomach began to feel. After a few minutes, he quit sweating and his breathing leveled out; he stopped panting and started taking slower, deeper breaths.

Standing on unresponsive legs, he steadied himself on the hot metal of the car's fender until he regained some semblance of composure. He waited. Soon, he was feeling almost normal again.

Carlie was curled up on the couch and reading when Jon walked through the kitchen door. Looking at the clock, she realized it was 4:30 in the afternoon. She hadn't even heard her husband drive up.

"I'm in the living room, Jon!" Carlie yelled.

Without answering, Jon walked to the refrigerator and poured himself a glass of milk. *This is all I need,* he thought. *On top of everything else, I'm getting a friggin' ulcer.*

He was interrupted mid-thought when Carlie walked into the kitchen. She was smiling as she walked through the door, but that quickly faded when she looked at her husband.

"God, Jon, you look like crap." Carlie said. "Can I get you something?"

"Like?"

"I don't know. When was the last time you ate?"

"Geez … I don't even remember, to be honest with you."

"Why don't you go take a shower? I'll fix you a bowl of soup."

Jon nodded, took the last swallow of the milk, and headed up the stairs.

After showering and slipping into clean clothes, he dropped down on the edge of the bed. He was shocked by his own reflection in the bathroom mirror. Carlie was right; he looked exactly like he felt—like crap.

Exhausted, he lay back on the bed and closed his eyes. Within seconds, he was sound asleep.

Carlie walked into the room a few moments later carrying a tray with soup and a large glass of milk. Seeing that Jon was already asleep, she quietly set it down on the nightstand and left the room.

The door had just clicked shut when the side of the bed that Jon was lying on compressed ever so slightly. A soft, gentle hand brushed Jon's hair from over his eye and followed the contours down his left cheek. He stirred slightly from the unfamiliar touch.

In a matter of seconds, the wispy apparition of a young girl began to materialize and take form.

Jon opened his eyes to find the angelic young woman sitting patiently on the edge of his bed. Reaching out, she gently touched his cheek again.

Jon stared at the young woman in wonder. He could feel the coolness of her hand when she tenderly caressed him. He took special note of exactly how she looked. She was so petite, her feet didn't even reach the floor. By all appearances, she was merely a child in grown-up clothes.

Jon was positive that this young girl was the same translucent form he had seen the night before.

Anyone looking at this girl would believe that she couldn't be older than nine or ten, except for the minute worry lines at the corners of her eyes. But looking into her dark blue eyes, Jon could see that this girl was not as young as she appeared; this was actually a woman who had experienced a lifetime that most could never imagine, a lifetime peppered with joy and awe, but also steeped in sorrow and misery. Jon's heart went out to her.

Reaching out, she touched Jon's face one more time. The sorrow in her half-hearted smile touched the corners of her mouth, lifting the ends just slightly but never reaching her eyes. Then she was gone.

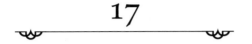

## 17

Sitting Jon down at the table, Carlie reheated the soup. His complexion looked better, but he still had the appearance of being slightly distant.

"Is everything all right?"

"Well, I guess that depends on your definition of *all right*."

Pulling out the chair across from him, she sat down and began again. "Okay, let me rephrase that. Is there something wrong?"

"I think I'm having a nervous breakdown."

Carlie stared at him in disbelief. For Jon to say something this out of the ordinary and not be joking was more than a little disturbing.

"What do you mean, you're having a nervous breakdown? What could possibly give you that idea?"

"I'm starting to see things. I'm seeing things that can't possibly be there, because they don't exist."

Carlie sat silently waiting for him to continue. Seconds and then minutes passed, but Jon just sat there staring into space.

"Okay, don't keep me in suspense. What do you mean?"

"Ghosts—I'm seeing ghosts. Let me rephrase that. I think I saw *a* ghost. It started last night."

Carlie's eyes lit up and she started to respond, but Jon held up his hand and silenced her.

"I know this will sound ridiculous, especially coming from me, but I know what I saw."

It took a little over a half hour for Jon to recount the events of the night before and what had just happened to him less than an hour earlier.

Carlie was at a loss for words. She couldn't think of a single thing to say in response. She watched Jon's expression; he seemed to grow more agitated as he related his story.

Finally looking up and making eye contact with his wife, Jon said what he was hoping to avoid. "Carlie, I'm afraid this house is haunted."

Carlie stared at Jon in disbelief. Shaking her head, she broke into a muffled, choking snicker that escalated quickly into a fit of uncontrollable laughter.

During a brief pause in her laughing fit, she caught her breath long enough to ask, "What the hell gave you an idea like that?"

More than shocked by Carlie's reaction, Jon was hurt. Carlie's offhand dismissal of what had happened to him was almost more than he could handle. Again, Carlie had reacted in a way that was completely out of character for her.

Jon slid his chair back and stood up. "Thanks for all your support and understanding. Nice talk. Let's do it again sometime real soon." Turning away from his still-snickering wife, he walked out of the kitchen and up the stairs.

Once in the bedroom, Jon had to suppress an overpowering urge to pack a suitcase and leave. In eight hours he could be back in Chicago, and he could leave this living nightmare behind him. What would happen to Carlie if he left? Could he possibly leave her in this house alone? Whoever or whatever was haunting this miserable place also possessed Carlie, not all of the time, but enough to scare the hell out of him.

～

The shower was running when Carlie walked into the bedroom. It had taken a few minutes for her to realize how much she had hurt Jon with her reaction. Jon had been serious; he had honestly believed what he had told her. Maybe, just maybe, he would forgive her.

Quickly undressing, she hoped she would be able to catch Jon before he got out of the shower. As she opened the bathroom door, the steam coming from the shower overpowered her. Jon had forgotten to turn on the switch to the two exhaust fans. Flipping the switch, she waited a minute for the fans to clear out most of the steam from the room.

In the shower, she could see Jon sitting on the seat in the far corner. He was just sitting there with his head down and the hot water pouring down on him.

"I'm so sorry, Jon. I shouldn't have dismissed you. There really is no excuse for my actions."

At this moment, being sorry was not the solution. She needed to be willing to listen to him. She needed to accept, at least in part, whatever he told her as being probable.

As the hot water pounded down on the two of them, it came to him. Jon knew exactly what he needed to do to convince her. If this house was indeed haunted, there had to be accounts of it. There would surely be tales of ghosts and things that go bump in the night scattered throughout the journals in the living room.

Standing, he lifted Carlie to her feet. "I'm not positive that I actually saw what I thought I did. As Ebenezer Scrooge said, what I saw may have been nothing more than an undigested bit of cheese. I'm paraphrasing of course."

"A nervous breakdown is serious, Jon, so please don't act like it's nothing."

A screeching sound caught their attention. Directly in front of them, a clear spot began to form through the condensation on the bathroom mirror.

Slowly at first, their eyes followed the droplets of water as they raced to the countertop just ahead of the disappearing haze.

There was a brief pause, and then the screeching began again. This time a ragged half-circle formed. The water droplets trailed their way to the countertop along the ridge of the first line.

The screeching and the tempo of straight lines, swirls, and half-circles escalated as the pair looked on in amazement.

In less than a minute, a complete series of lines and jagged patterns had materialized on the mirror. They had Carlie's rapt attention. Jon, on the other hand, watched the scene unfold before his eyes in dazed disbelief.

Carlie was the first to speak. "My God, Jon, look what it says!"

Jon stared at the markings on the mirror. His mind had gone numb. At first he couldn't make out a pattern, let alone words, but then it came to him.

He watched Carlie as she tentatively traced each letter with the tip of her finger. Backing away, Jon could see the letters scrawled on the fifteen-foot mirror with greater clarity.

PLEASEHELPUS

As quickly as the letters had formed, they began to disappear. The exhaust fans were rapidly sucking the moisture from the air. Carlie raced across the bathroom as fast as she could run without losing her footing. She reached out and shut off the fans before the words disappeared forever. As valiant an attempt as it was, when she turned around, her heart sank. The words were gone.

Jon was still staring at the mirror, his lips moving silently, repeating the words that were no longer there. His complexion had turned pallid, and he was beginning to shake uncontrollably.

Carlie waited for a response from Jon. When it didn't come, she turned to see what he was doing. She could clearly see he wasn't doing very well at all. Cinching her robe around her waist, she hurried across the floor, afraid that Jon would pass out before she could reach him.

Holding on to his arm, Carlie followed Jon as he sank to the floor. His face contorted in pain as his stomach balled into a tight, burning knot. He let out a gasp. His stomach roiled. Jumping up, he ran toward the toilet. Before he could reach it, he threw up the soup he had eaten for dinner.

Humiliated, he turned to Carlie. The look on his face was a mixture of both fear and helplessness.

"Jon? ... *Jon!* Look at me."

It took a few seconds before Jon's eyes focused on Carlie's face. When they finally did, she continued. "You're not having a nervous breakdown. If you are, then we both are, because we both just saw the same thing."

Tenderly, she placed her hand on the back of his head and pushed down until his face was resting on her shoulder.

"Shhhhh, I want you to tell me everything. This time, start from the very beginning—and don't leave anything out. Do you understand me, Jon?"

His voice was muffled in the heavy fabric of her robe. "Yeah, I understand. Carlie, did it say what I think it did? Did it really ask us for help?"

"Yes, I believe it did."

Jon retold everything he had told her earlier, but this time in explicit detail, leaving out nothing. When he eventually described the conversation he had had with Loretta, Carlie was on the edge of her seat. She had a million questions, but she knew Jon didn't have the answers.

Walking across the living room, Jon picked up the heavy leather-bound journal that Carlie had been reading. Flipping through it, he scanned the impeccable handwriting of Edith McPherson. Turning, he handed it to Carlie. "Catch me up!"

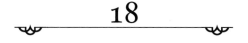

## 18

"The beginning of this book is pretty mundane, mostly the ramblings of a young girl in love. She talks about Ian's comings and goings. He evidently worked at the same boatyard that her father did. She wrote five whole pages about a day they spent at the shore. I guess it was the first time she had ever seen him, or any man for that matter, without a shirt. Girls!"

Jon smiled. He was sure that Carlie was correct. Fourteen-year-old girls do have a penchant for expounding on the mundane.

"It gets better—honest. It seems that Ian planned to come to America."

"Edith was in agreement with this?"

"Oh yeah. I think she would have walked to the gates of hell if that was what Ian wanted."

"What about her parents?"

"From what I read, it seemed like they were both okay with Ian's plan. Edith and Ian's romance started, from what I can gather, somewhere around the beginning of 1840. They had been a couple for about three years when Ian asked her father for her hand in marriage. That would make it around 1843 or 1844.

"*Damn her* for not dating any of this. I've had to pick a historical event in American and Irish history and backtrack from there to put a timeline to any of this."

Opening the book to the middle, Carlie scanned the page. Turning a few more, she found what she was looking for. "Here, this is what I was referring to."

When Jon returned to his chair, she began reading.

*Ian came by the house tonight. He told me that he feared **an Gorta Mór** was getting worse. He told me that he had been saving his money for years, and once we were married, he would be able to purchase two tickets in steerage to a place called New York. He says that New York is the biggest city in America.*

Jon gave Carlie a curious look.

"*An Gorta Mór* loosely translates to 'the Great Hunger.' This was what we in America called the Irish Potato Famine. It seems that at the time the kids were planning to get married, the famine was in its infancy. During the years 1845 to 1852, approximately one million people died and another million emigrated from Ireland. Many ended up here in America."

Jon found this interesting, but it wasn't what he was hoping to find, and the expression on his face gave away that disappointment.

"Jon, I know exactly what you're hoping to find hidden in these journals. Maybe in time we will. There are a lot of books to go through. If we don't do it systematically, we might miss exactly what we're looking for. Please be patient."

For the first time, Jon could actually see it in Carlie's eyes and hear it in her voice: she was working with Jon and not against him. Together, they finally had a common goal.

"I'm sorry, Carlie. It has been one hell of a day. I need to go to bed. Maybe when the sun comes up, things will start to look better."

"You go. I'll be up in a little while."

Jon stood up and dragged his sore, aching body up the stairs. Kicking off his slippers, he lay down on the bed. He pulled the comforter up to his chin and closed his eyes. Images of the young woman flashed through his mind, as did the letters as they mysteriously formed on the bathroom mirror. Just before he fell asleep, he wondered if she was by chance the tortured soul that had written them or if there were other spirits inhabiting the house.

~

The digital clock on the nightstand showed that it was 3:00 AM. When the clock clicked to 3:01, somewhere in the furthest recesses of Jon's mind he began to hear the buzzing sound of voices whispering.

The buzzing was relentless. It moved from the recesses to the fore-front of Jon's consciousness. He tossed and turned until he was fully awake. Carlie was still asleep in the bed next to him, with her arm draped over his side. Wide awake now, he opened his eyes and stared at the light coming through the window. This was the last full moon before fall.

Lying perfectly still, he waited for the reason he had awakened, and it didn't take long. There was a short reprieve in the whispering, but it started up again as he lay there listening.

Taking Carlie's hand, he gently moved her arm off his side and back onto her own hip. As gently as he could, he slid to the edge of the bed until his feet were on the floor.

He waited.

It sounded as if the whispers were moving up and down the hall. One moment he could hear voices right outside his door, and the next they were distant and muffled.

As he waited, the voices grew in intensity. They were loud enough now that he could almost make out the words.

He stood by the edge of the bed and waited. He expected the voices to quit the moment he moved, but they didn't. He walked slowly to the door. When he turned the handle, the voices remained right outside the door. Pulling the door silently inward, he held his breath in anticipation.

The hall was empty.

Stepping out of the bedroom into the dark and now silent hallway, Jon turned toward the stairs. He noticed that the air was brutally cold; he could see his breath when he exhaled. Standing in the empty hallway shivering, he debated whether to go back to bed.

Then a movement caught his eye. At the end of the hall, there seemed to be someone watching him from the head of the stairs. As he walked closer to the hazy human shape, he could hear the voices again—this time coming from behind him. Spinning, he was face to face with a huge dark-haired man. The man wasn't as tall as Jon, but he was at least twice—maybe three times—as broad at the shoulders, and his hands were massive.

Jon couldn't move; he could barely breathe. He couldn't stop staring at the man's eyes. They were pale gray with black irises, and they were literally alive with hatred, intense and all-consuming; it was as if they had taken on a life of their own.

As the two men stood transfixed, staring at each other, Jon felt a warm sensation coursing down the inside of his right thigh. The faint scent of hot urine wafted up from the floor where Jon had just evacuated his bladder.

When Carlie stepped out of the bedroom into the hall, the giant of a man turned slowly in her direction. The instant the two made eye contact, Carlie fainted. Jon watched as she fell. He remembered how graceful women fainted in the movies. This wasn't anything like that; Carlie dropped with all the grace of a rag doll, face-first onto the floor. Jon could hear her nose crunch as it broke.

Jon rushed to Carlie's side; he gently held the side of her face and slowly turned her over onto her back.

There was a single drop of blood at the tip of Carlie's right nostril. There were dark circles forming under her eyes, and her nose was already starting to swell.

When she opened her eyes, she smiled up at her husband. "This *has* been one hell of a day."

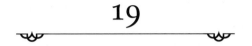

## 19

The sun had been up for hours by the time Jon and Carlie returned home from the emergency room. Carlie looked more like a demented raccoon than the beautiful woman she was. She had huge black and purple circles under both eyes. Thin strips of bright white surgical tape secured a metal brace across the bridge of her nose, and nasal tampons protruded from each nostril.

Resetting her broken bones had caused moderate swelling around both eyes and in her cheeks. The most distinguishing feature of her new face, however, was the blue-black bruise on the tip of her nose.

Jon had fed the cardinal its breakfast and was fixing a pot of tea when the telephone rang. Carlie sat at the kitchen table wondering if she should even attempt to answer it. Jon, almost as if it were second nature, picked up the receiver and stretched the phone cord back to the stove, where the kettle had just started whistling.

"Hello? ... Yeah, she's here, Dexter, but I don't think she'll be able to talk. ... Huh? Oh yeah, she's all right, but she had a small accident last night. She fell down and broke her nose. ... Of course I didn't hit her! Don't be ridiculous." Jon looked over at Carlie, rolled his eyes, and shook his head slowly. Carlie tried to smile but winced, and tears filled her eyes from the effort.

"Jon," Dexter said, "I think the best way to approach this would be for Carlie to meet with this man in person. He wants to buy the house, and this is a very lucrative offer. I feel you should consider it—we may never get another offer as good as this. If you're interested, I'll set up a meeting."

"How about next weekend? Right now she looks like a raccoon....
That'll be fine then. You have a nice weekend too. I'll touch base with
you next week.... Okay, thank you. Goodbye."

Carlie's eyes were alive with curiosity. Jon wordlessly fixed another
cup of tea and sat down at the table before he began. "Dexter has an
interesting proposal. It seems someone has made him a very substantial offer on the house. He wants to discuss selling it with you."

Carlie was the first to notice the appreciable change in the temperature in the kitchen. She shuddered as a blast of frigid air blew
across the room. Jon watched as the gentle plume of steam rising from
Carlie's cup began to swirl and blow sideways across the table.

The cabinet door next to the sink suddenly flung open, and the
dishes inside began flying across the kitchen. Some seemed directed at
Carlie, and others at Jon, while still others slammed aimlessly into the
walls of the room.

Diving to the floor, Jon scrambled around the table on his knees to
his wife's side. Standing, he wrapped his arms and body around her,
blocking the onslaught of flying china with his back and shoulders.
Carlie remained huddled inside the safety of Jon's embrace until the
last dish had flown across the room and smashed against the far wall.

When the maelstrom finally subsided, Jon slowly moved away
from Carlie. Standing in the center of the room, he surveyed the mess
on the kitchen floor.

Carlie scrunched her eyes shut. She appeared to be saying a silent
prayer.

Taking her arm, Jon gently raised her to her feet and guided her
carefully across the floor, avoiding the shards of broken china.

Once out of the kitchen and safely on the carpeted runner going
up the stairs, Carlie shook her arm loose and ran to the bedroom. Jon
couldn't catch her, but he followed close on her heels. Once they were
both inside the bedroom, Carlie slammed the door shut and locked
it. The two of them sat perfectly still on the edge of the bed for what
seemed like hours.

Standing, Jon moved in front of his wife. "Are you all right? You
didn't get hurt, did you?"

Carlie didn't answer; she only shook her head. Jon's biggest fear was that Carlie was going into shock. Standing in front of her, he examined her carefully, looking for any sign that she had been hurt and didn't realize it.

Earlier, the doctor had given Carlie a prescription for painkillers and one for the swelling. Jon placed one of each of the pills in her hand. She put them in her mouth, and he handed her a cup of water. When she was finished, she rolled over, pulled the comforter up to her chin, and shifted herself into a fetal position.

Jon waited by the side of the bed until she fell asleep.

It took Jon close to an hour to clean up the mess on the kitchen floor. He was pleased to find that nowhere as many dishes were actually broken as he had first imagined. After picking up the ones that were still intact, he swept and then vacuumed up the shards.

Jon washed and dried the survivors by hand, then put them back into the cupboard. He was putting the last coffee cup back on the hook when he thought he heard a rustling sound coming from the living room. He draped the hand towel over the handle of the oven door, then turned and walked toward the sound.

At first glance, the living room was empty. Jon walked into the room and looked around to see if anything had been disturbed. That was when he saw what looked to be a body lying covered up on the couch.

Jon's pulse began to race as he watched the inanimate form. When it didn't move, he slowly approached it. Tentatively he reached down and touched the edge of the blanket. Pulling it back one inch at a time, he watched and waited anxiously for his biggest fear to come to life. Would this—could this—be the young girl or, God forbid, the man he had seen in the hallway the night before?

As he moved the blanket to uncover the unidentified shape, the first thing he noticed was the head full of auburn hair. Pulling it back a little further, he could clearly see the white tape across the bridge of Carlie's nose. Relief washed over him. He hated the idea of being spooked at every shadow or shape. He felt like such a wimp.

While tucking the blanket under her chin, Jon's toe touched the stack of journals in front of the couch. Intrigued, he picked the second one in the pile and opened it. He read the first couple lines, then carried the book across the room and sat down in his chair.

He had been reading most of the day when Carlie finally stirred.

Throwing back the blanket, she sat up and blinked at Jon. "What are you doing?"

"I'm reading one of Edith's journals."

"Did you discover anything exciting?"

"Not really. She and her mother are busy planning her wedding."

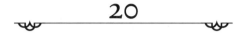

## 20

Jon and Carlie spent the next five hours reading Edith's entries. Jon stopped long enough to heat a can of soup for Carlie. After the two had eaten, Jon started jotting something down on a yellow legal pad. As he turned the pages of the journal, he quickly wrote what appeared to be notes.

After watching him for almost an hour, Carlie finally asked, "Are you finding something interesting?"

Standing, he picked up his pad and walked across the room.

Handing it to Carlie, he casually said, "I'm not really sure. Why don't you take a look at this and tell me what you think?"

Carlie took the pad and began reading.

*We're being watched. We both know we're not alone, so I think it's important that we be very careful what we say out loud. Whoever or whatever it was made it pretty clear that it does not want you selling this house.*

When she finished reading, she looked up at him and nodded in agreement. She lowered her head for a moment, then looked up at him again. "Jon, I've wanted to say something about what happened last night, but I couldn't find the right words. First off, I honestly don't have any idea who that man in the hallway was, but I have seen flashes of him before in my dreams.

"Consciously, I didn't recognize his face—but I did recognize his eyes. Subconsciously, though, when I looked into his eyes, I knew everything about him and I knew deep in my soul exactly what unspeakable horrors he was capable of. Does that make any sense?"

"Actually, it makes perfect sense. I can't remember ever seeing so much hatred in anyone's eyes.

"So it wasn't merely the fact that we had a ghost standing in our hallway last night that caused you to faint?"

"After watching the words 'please help us' materialize on our bathroom mirror? I don't think so. Even though the whole experience was brief, I felt like I had just come face to face with *someone's worst nightmare.*"

Jon could see that their conversation and the pain were wearing Carlie out. Taking her by the hand, he lifted her to her feet, pulled her close, and gave her a gentle squeeze. She laid her head on his shoulder as they walked upstairs to the bedroom.

Wrapping her arm around Jon's waist, Carlie pulled herself tight up against him in the bed and dropped off to sleep.

~

The snow was up to her calves. However, it wasn't the chill of the snow nor the icy wind sweeping across the open land that was making her shake. She had been crying.

Sitting alone with her knees pulled up tight against her chest and her chin resting on folded arms, she watched as the older boys played games in the front yard of the farmhouse below.

She would hike across the road to this remote spot on the hill every time they allowed her to go outside to play. She was never included in the games the other kids played, at least not in the real sense of being their equal. On occasion they would include her, but it always turned out to be a cruel joke at her expense. She always ended up hurt, crying, and feeling rejected.

She could hear the peals of high-pitched laughter as the boys chased each other across the yard. They were extremely handsome boys; she envied how they looked, so strong and masculine, completely unlike her. They were boys any mother would love and any father would brag about. She wondered why she had even been born.

As she watched the boys, she heard a twig snap somewhere behind her. She sat perfectly still, waiting. On rare occasions, a deer would walk past her. If she was still enough and the wind was blowing in the right direction, it might walk up and sniff her.

As she daydreamed, a powerful hand grabbed her neck from behind. Its massive fingers and long, ragged nails bit deep into the side of her neck. Her mind's eye flashed instantly to a bear; she could imagine its massive jaw as it wrapped itself around the base of her skull. Any second now she expected it to clamp its jaws shut, snapping her neck like a twig.

As she waited to die, something awkwardly yanked her from the ground. The vise-like grip around her neck released and spun her around by the shoulder. There he was, standing in front of her. Worse than any bear, it was her tormenter.

Yanking her completely off her feet by the front of her jacket, he pulled her up against his massive chest. As she stared into his pale gray eyes, she could see the loathing he felt for her. As he spat his venomous words directly into her face, she could smell the hatred that oozed from every pore in his body and the foulness of his breath.

"You miserable little fuck, we've been looking for you everywhere. What in the hell are you doing up here? Are you spying again? You little piece of shit, I should have drowned you like a fucking barn cat the day you were born."

It wasn't the words that terrified her; she had heard those before, and worse. It was something else, something in his eyes. This could be the day—the day he actually killed her.

Before she realized it, she was flying backward through the air. When she hit the ground, a cloud of soft, white ice crystals plumed into the air from the impact of her small body. She felt the soft snow as it rained down on her face.

Her head snapped back hard against the frozen ground, and the world went black.

Carlie's eyes popped open, and she sat straight up in bed. It took a few minutes for her eyes to adjust to the darkness. When they did, she looked around the room and then over at Jon, who was stirring slightly in bed next to her. Turning onto her side, she shook his shoulder.

"Jon? ... *Jon!* Wake up."

Jon was instantly awake and sitting straight up in bed. In the back of his mind, he expected to find the young woman or the huge man hovering over him. He was relieved to find that they weren't. He was surprised, though, to see that the clock showed it was exactly midnight and Carlie was sitting up in bed next to him.

"Are you all right?" he asked. "What's wrong?"

"Jon, I think I've figured it out."

"Figured what out?"

"The ghost of the young girl—even the ghost of the man in the hallway—I think I know the answer to all of it, everything that's going on in this house."

Jon ran his hand through his hair. "How? What happened?"

"I had another dream. I truly believe that the nightmares I've been suffering from are in reality me, reliving this poor, abused girl's life while I'm asleep."

Jon sat in bed watching Carlie as she slipped on her robe. When she was finished, she turned and looked at him.

"Well, are you coming?"

"Give me a couple minutes. I'll be right down."

~

When Jon walked into the kitchen, he smelled freshly brewed coffee. Carlie and two cups of the aromatic brew were already at the kitchen table waiting for him.

Jon sat silently as Carlie told him her nightmare.

When she got to the end of the story, she stopped for a moment and looked at her husband. "I'm not positive, but he may have killed her that day. I remember everything going black, and then I woke up in bed."

Jon sat staring into his cup as he listened. When Carlie finished, he looked across the table at her and asked, "What do you think it all means?"

"This is purely speculation—I don't have all of the facts yet—but I believe that whoever the ghost is that we saw in the hallway, he and the young girl are what these hauntings are all about. I really believe that she was one of his children."

"If she was—and I'm saying *if*—what on earth could she have done to make this man hate her so badly that he would want to kill her?"

"God only knows, Jon. All I know right now is that he does, and she is trying to tell me the only way she knows how. If I'm not mistaken, she's the one that led me to the journals. I think the answers are somewhere in those books, and she knows it."

"Well, this should keep us busy for a while."

Carlie smiled at his insight. After pouring each of them another cup of coffee, she pointed toward the living room. "There's no time like the present to get started."

Jon felt that what Carlie had dreamed was important; however, it was still only the tip of the iceberg. It was hard for him to imagine that everything he had seen was merely two feuding spirits. Then, of course, there was still the writing on the bathroom mirror: "Please help *us*." Jon knew without a doubt that the man from the night before did not want their help. So that still left the nagging question—who was the *us?*

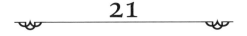

# 21

Carlie pulled out another half-dozen journals, emptying the first crate.

Jon finished scanning the journal he had picked up earlier. Looking over at Carlie, he caught her up on the journal's contents. "As I said before, this is more about Edith's upcoming marriage than anything else. I'm hoping the book you're reading will give us a little more insight."

Carlie set down the completed journal and started scanning the pages of the next when something caught her eye. "Well, they finally made it to America. After almost three weeks at sea, they, and fifty or so other couples, landed in New York. She mentions that as soon as they are settled, she plans on asking Ian if she could send for her sister Emily."

Jon looked over at Carlie. "I don't think we need to cover every single day in the life of Ian and Edith. We need to pick up from where they built this house."

"You're right. None of this means anything. I just can't believe how young this girl was. At fourteen, getting married and moving halfway around the world would never have crossed my mind."

"I can't say marriage was much of a consideration when I was fourteen either."

Carlie started scanning more quickly, as did Jon. Within an hour or so, they had finished the stack next to Jon. Carlie started putting the journals back into the crate, while Jon went to the kitchen to refill their coffee cups.

Carlie was emptying another crate onto the floor when Jon walked back into the room.

A hazy black shadow passed in front of him as he crossed the living room threshold. As it did, the air density changed immediately. A heavy rancid smell was the first thing he noticed. Carlie was on her knees replacing the journals they had just read. She never even looked up.

The air seemed thick, almost liquid. Jon tried to take a deep breath, but it felt like only half his lungs were working; he wasn't getting any air at all. He started panting in quick, short gasps for what little air he could find. His first thought was to not panic. Not panicking, however, was impossible, as intense panic brought on by his impending suffocation had already set in.

Looking up from the floor, Carlie could see that Jon was having serious problems breathing.

Jumping to her feet, she grabbed the coffee cups from his hand before he dropped them.

Jon bent over and placed both hands on his knees. He stood motionless and stretched his back from the bottom to the top in a slow rolling motion, hoping to fill his rapidly depleting lungs. He mentally tried to slow down his breathing—even just a little—to avoid passing out. As he tried counting backward from one hundred, sweat washed down his forehead and dripped to the floor. His hair took on a soggy, greasy film, and his complexion turned a sickly gray. His lips and fingernails were already turning a pale blue, and bright red lines were forming at the corners of his eyes.

As hard as it was to concentrate on anything other than getting a breath of air, he managed to wiggle the fingers on both hands. He rotated his jaw and scrunched his face, looking for any sign of paralysis. Fortunately, he didn't find any. Unfortunately, that ruled out a cause as simple as a stroke or a heart attack—which left something he didn't even want to begin to consider.

As quickly as the attack had started, it began to dissipate. Jon's breathing slowly returned to normal. The episode lasted nearly fifteen minutes before it was over. When it was, he stood up and looked at his wife. The earlier fear was back in her eyes.

"My God, Jon, are you all right?"

"I don't know. You didn't notice the air in here? I felt like I was breathing underwater."

"No, the air was fine. I didn't notice a thing."

Jon sat back down in his chair, his breathing still labored. Leaning forward seemed to take some of the pressure off his lungs, allowing the air to flow a little more freely.

Carlie sat down on the arm of the chair and gently ran the palm of her hand up and down the center of his back. "You scared the hell out of me, Jon Summers. I thought you were having a heart attack or something."

"To be honest, I did too." What he didn't say was that his first thought was about what had happened to Dexter. Jon had not hallucinated, but all the same, he believed that he had just received a taste of the same warning Dexter had been given.

Jon seemed to be doing better when he returned from taking a shower. His complexion was still a little pale, but he seemed to be breathing normally again. Running her hand over his forehead, Carlie found that he was no longer clammy to the touch, so she returned to her place on the couch.

"Are you ready for this? If not, I understand. We can just go to bed and start fresh in the morning."

"I'm feeling better now. You read. I'll just listen, if that's all right."

"That's fine. You just relax." Picking up her journal, she opened it to the place she had bookmarked. "They just left New York. There were apparently rumors of a government land giveaway sometime in the near future out west. Ian heard about it and saved all his money so they could go.

"Ian bought a wagon and a pair of horses for two hundred dollars. After loading everything they owned, they headed west."

"Good for Ian," Jon mused. "He evidently had never taken a road trip with a woman in a moving vehicle. If he had, he never would have left New York. Imagine stopping at every bush and tree from New York to Iowa so Edith could pee."

The laughter in Carlie's eyes spoke volumes—but she still gave him the finger.

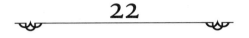

# 22

After a long day of reading, neither Carlie nor Jon had found the journal entries they were looking for. The contents of the cases were stacked in smaller piles around the living room. It was becoming a tiring, thankless job as they dug through and read excerpts from each journal to find the set of books that followed Edith's life story in sequence.

Jon's eyes were burning from reading Edith's tiny script for so many hours. He finally stood up and stretched his aching back. "Carlie, I've had it. I can't do this one more minute. You know, if we stop right now, all of this will still be here in the morning." To emphasize his point, Jon swept his arm across the living room.

Carlie looked around the room. There were stacks of journals everywhere. Each stack represented a period of time or a specific event. She had managed to find journals that were from the house era, but some were Edith's and some belonged to other families that had lived in the house after them. Without knowing what had happened from the time the two kids arrived in Iowa, none of Edith's journals made any sense at all. Exhausted, Carlie agreed with her husband. They had been at this for nearly twenty hours straight.

Lifting Carlie to her feet, Jon escorted her into the kitchen. "Give me an idea of what sounds good, and I'll fix us some dinner."

"Spaghetti sounds good."

Once their dinner was simmering, Jon sat down at the table with Carlie. "What do you think?" he asked.

"I'm at a loss. It's not about the journals. I know we'll find what we're looking for eventually. It may or may not be exactly what we hope to hear, though. What's bothering me now is the increasing severity of my nightmares, not to mention what happened to you this afternoon. Do you have any idea how bad you scared me? I thought I had lost you."

Jon knew without even looking at Carlie that this was not the time for levity. Besides, he didn't feel very funny at the moment. "I know. I thought for a second that you had lost me too. I don't think it was another panic attack. This was something entirely different, and to be honest, it scared the living hell out of me."

During their meal, they looked at each other frequently, but neither could think of anything to say.

After dinner, Jon cleaned up and headed up the stairs to catch up with Carlie.

~

The clock on the nightstand clicked silently from 11:59 to 12:00. Jon turned in his sleep—possibly due to the invisible weight that compressed his side of the bed, or perhaps because of Carlie's relentless jerks and twitches.

A hollow voice whispered into his ear, "*Please help us.*"

Jon's eyes flicked open. He sensed more than he felt that someone was sitting on the bed next to him. Reaching his arm out from under the covers, he waved it through the darkness, but no one was there.

He felt a slight breeze as whatever or whoever it was moved in the dark.

An invisible finger gently moved his hair away from in front of his eye.

Jon held his breath.

He felt someone exhale a breath of cool air against his right cheek. The sensation gave him the chills, sending goose bumps down his arms.

Again, a feminine voice whispered into his ear, "*Please—please help us!*"

"Who do you mean? Who are *us*?" he whispered.

"*Aaaallll offff uuussss,*" exhaled the voice, as it faded into the night.

Jon lay perfectly still, his heart pounding as he waited to hear more.

Carlie placed her hand over his right shoulder, causing him to jump. Nuzzling up to his side, she whispered into his ear, "I heard. How are we supposed to find out who she is referring to when she says *us*?"

Jon stared up at the ceiling in the darkness. He could visualize Carlie watching him—waiting—expecting an answer where there was none.

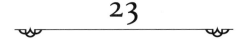

# 23

Hours before the sun rose, the rain pelted the bedroom window in torrents. Jon awoke to the sound, rolled over, and watched as the florescent rivulets streamed down the windows in waves of diffuse colored lights.

A sudden flash of lightning illuminated the night sky; a bone-jarring clap of thunder immediately followed, rattling the house's rafters.

In the corner of the room, a young girl stood silently watching him. As the light began to fade, she dissolved into the shadows.

A second flash of blinding white light lit the bedroom. Instantly a crash shook the entire house, rattling the window glass inside the frames and leaving the scent of fresh ozone in the air.

There she was again. This time she was holding an infant in her arms.

As the light transformed into a soft amber glow, she again melted away into the darkness.

He could hear her voice as clear as a bell through the roaring din of the storm. He couldn't be sure if she had actually spoken or if he had just heard the words in his head. Either way, they were unmistakable: "*Hhheeellllppp uuusssss!*"

The rain seemed to pick up in intensity during the early morning hours.

When Jon walked into the kitchen, he found Carlie sitting at the table watching the torrent of rain as it washed in sheets down the window. Lying on the table next to her was one of the leather-bound journals.

"How long have you been up?" he asked.

"I've been up and down all night. I got up for good after the lightning hit the house. I can't believe you slept through it."

Jon wondered if Carlie was right. Had he really slept through the whole thing? Had the girl and the baby just been a dream? It had sure felt real.

Could everything he had experienced that night have been a dream brought on by the lightning and thunder? Or had the images been planted into his subconscious by someone else?

After pouring himself a cup of coffee, he sat down next to her. Patting the journal, he asked, "Find anything interesting?"

"Believe it or not, I actually did."

"Well, are you going to leave me hanging?"

"Before I tell you, you need to go look in the living room."

Puzzled by Carlie's abruptness and intrigued at the same time by her request, he stood and walked to the living room.

Flipping on the light switch, he was amazed to find the journals stacked in nice, neat piles. This was not how they had been when he went to bed the night before.

"Wow, you've been busy!"

"I didn't do it! They were like that when I got up."

"Oh!"

Shutting off the light, he returned to Carlie at the kitchen table and picked up his cup of coffee. "I'm not sure if this is good or bad. What do you think?"

"What do I think? I'll tell you what I think. I think that whoever did this is getting impatient. He or she is getting tired of waiting for us to find the answer on our own. As far as good or bad goes, I'm like you—I don't have a clue."

Opening the journal, Carlie turned to the sixth page and began reading.

*Ian and I have been on our new land now for nearly six months, and Ian cleared a beautiful section of the property, big enough to erect a grand house. This morning, he loaded the wagon with logs and headed*

*for town. If all goes well, he will be home day after tomorrow with enough
cut lumber to finish the first section of the house.*

*I don't mind at all living in the back of the barn as long as I am with
Ian. It's as Ian says: the animals must always come first; they are, after
all, our food and our livelihood, and we can't very well survive without
them.*

*Tomorrow, I will check the garden again. We have been so blessed; the
bounty of this land seems immeasurable.*

Jon listened intently as Carlie read Edith's entry. When she finished, he asked, "Is this the first reference to the house?"

"No, she writes about how they arrived in Iowa. How they were
planning on going on to Oklahoma. However, a land auction in Iowa
interested Ian, so he decided to stay in town for the week to attend it.

"There was a piece of property that interested him a great deal. It
had a very small house, a barn, and a few outbuildings, all sitting on
approximately 2,400 acres."

"Wow, huge piece of property," Jon replied.

"Yeah, it was. Anyway, after looking at the land, Ian decided to bid
on it. He won the bid. Unbelievably, he paid only two hundred dollars for it and a twenty-five-dollar transfer fee. According to Edith,
the only other bid was from an Amish farmer who owned most of the
surrounding land."

"What about the house?"

"I'm getting there. Hang on. . . . As I said, the property had a small
house already on it. They lived in there until Ian cleared the trees from
a whole section of the property surrounding it. He had the lumber
milled into boards somewhere near Des Moines. He fixed what needed
to be repaired on the barn first and then started building their new
house. When the new section of house was about halfway finished, he
tore down what he didn't like of the old house and attached the new
house to the remaining structure."

"So that's where we're at now?"

"Yep!"

"Very interesting. How old did you say Ian was?"

"He was nineteen."

Looking around the kitchen at the workmanship, Jon could barely suppress his admiration.

"I know. I'm mildly impressed myself."

Carlie was now reading Edith's journal page by page. It was slow-going because Edith was switching languages between Gaelic and English. Carlie wasn't positive, but this may have been some sort of safety precaution.

"Jon?"

"Yeah?"

"This journal is from the first year they lived in the house. It covers the time from when they arrived in Iowa and bought the property through the construction and completion of the house.

"She and Ian had some interesting conversations. I really can't believe how grown-up these two were. Ian was a worker; that's evident by the amount of skill he needed to build this house. Edith, on the other hand, knew how to read and write exceptionally well, which was rare in those days. Even rarer was the fact that she understood and could do very complicated advanced math."

"Wow, that is impressive!" Jon knew this was leading up to something, something Carlie felt was important, so he waited patiently until she continued.

"She calculated how many cows they could raise for food and how many for dairy on the piece of land Ian had reserved for cattle. She also calculated how many acres of alfalfa and corn they would need to carry the animals through the winter.

"What's really sad is that Ian was basically an idiot savant. He couldn't grasp how to read or write, but he could make exact measurements and calculate complicated angles."

Jon could see that something was running through Carlie's mind. It had to be something she had read. "What?"

"Maybe it's nothing. I have a nagging feeling that I'm missing something, but I don't have any idea what it could be."

The lights flickered once—then flickered again, an instant before they went out for good.

The pressure from the lightning strike made Jon's ears pop. The air inside the enclosed room was instantly alive with electricity and the smell of ozone.

The flash of blue-white light left both Jon and Carlie temporarily blinded.

The electrical charge in the room left Carlie's beautiful auburn hair standing straight out at odd angles, resembling a kinetic energy experiment gone horribly wrong.

Jon and Carlie blinked more or less in unison, and it was almost a minute before the brilliant dancing lights behind their retinas had dissipated enough for either of them to make out the shadowy images standing in the middle of the living room floor.

The second flash was even more brilliant than the first.

An ear-splitting crash followed instantly, leaving Jon and Carlie yawning to clear the hollow roar and the exaggerated hiss that had replaced their normal hearing.

They were still reeling from the blinding flash when the subsequent thunder hurled them into a silence as oppressive as it was dark.

Neither of them could hear or see the living room window as it exploded. They didn't notice a thing until a lethal shower of glass shrapnel rained down on them.

With flailing hands and arms, Jon and Carlie fell to their knees on the floor. They covered their faces, crouched in front of the couch, and, in a duck walk, waddled as fast as they could to the safety of the stairwell closet. Slamming the door against the rage of the storm unleashing its fury outside and the one brewing inside, they huddled against each other in blinded silence.

While the wind howled through the hole that was once their front window, heavy, unidentifiable projectiles careened off the closet door.

The barrage lasted for close to an hour, leaving Carlie shaking, muttering incoherently, and on the verge of insanity. Her eyes were the size of saucers, wildly flitting back and forth in her head.

Jon was beyond scared—he was petrified. Clutching Carlie protectively around her shoulders, he pulled her tight against his chest.

During the worst of the storm, he blocked the space between her and the closed door with his own body.

Once the violent storm was over, the only remaining sound was made by the waterlogged curtains, as the wind coming through the shattered glass whipped them like bat wings against the walls.

Jon held his breath until he couldn't hold it any longer. He didn't even realize he was doing it until his burning lungs felt like they were going to explode. Exhaling in one huge gush, he caught himself replacing it with another massive intake of the stagnant closet air and holding it again.

Carlie was whimpering softly into the hollow of Jon's neck and rocking slowly in his arms.

Jon stroked her hair and whispered assurances in her ear. "Shhhh, it's over. We're okay. Shhhh, Carlie, you're all right, just breathe. Take deep breaths." As he repeated this mantra, he found that he was doing it as much for himself as for her.

# 24

The storm's gale force winds left Jon and Carlie's living room a soggy mess, covered in leaves, debris, and mud. Downed tree branches, barn shingles, and even the odd piece of frog-green lawn furniture littered the front yard.

It was well past lunchtime when Jon and Carlie finally ventured from the security of the stairwell closet.

The first thing that caught Jon's attention was the organized chaos of the living room. There was, of course, the destruction caused by the storm itself, but there was also the mess that wasn't due to the wrath of Mother Nature. The pounding on the closet door didn't seem to be due to anything storm related. The journals—not all of them, just specific ones—were scattered on the floor in front of the closet door. The rest had been hurtled against the far wall.

The carpet was drenched from the deluge of rainwater. Glass shards and soggy leaves were scattered on the rug between the window and the couch. However, that was where the brunt of the actual storm damage seemed to end.

With his arm wrapped firmly around Carlie's shoulder, Jon pulled her protectively against his side. He walked her carefully through the mess on the front room floor as if he were guiding a blinded soldier through a live mine field.

Head down and eyes diverted, Carlie allowed Jon to maneuver her to the base of the staircase before she managed to wriggle out of his grip and run up the stairs. Slamming the bedroom door behind her, she turned the lock and sat down on the edge of the bed.

Amazed by her reaction to what she had just experienced, everything inside of Carlie screamed for her to have a nervous breakdown. She felt that she should at the very least cry, but she couldn't.

Jon understood the fight-or-flight instinct that Carlie was struggling with; he felt it too. He had two choices: give in to it, and retreat back into the stairwell closet, roll himself into the fetal position, and give up, or buck up and mindlessly go about the job at hand, cleaning up the living room and fixing the window.

Miraculously, he chose the latter.

~

Jon was, admittedly, a neophyte when it came to any kind of construction work. Standing in the barn, his father's voice still echoed that all-too-familiar code of carpentry: "Measure twice, cut once."

Some twenty 4' x 8' sheets of ¾-inch plywood had been left behind when the construction was finished, and boarding up the window seemed pretty cut and dried. However, after three failed attempts, he was grateful they had left so much plywood behind.

He really had no idea what he did right the third time; the wood just happened to fit perfectly into the hole. It was almost as if someone else had done the work for him. A couple nails to hold it in place, and he was well on his way to being finished.

After cleaning up the mess he had made with the window patch, he ventured back into the house to assess the rest of the damage.

Carlie hadn't come downstairs yet, so before he started working again, he needed to make sure she was all right; he didn't want to alarm her with the noise he was about to make.

Finding the bedroom door closed didn't surprise him, but finding it locked did. He could understand the fear she was feeling when she retreated to the security behind a locked door, but what Carlie didn't seem to understand was that a locked door was no defense against Mother Nature—or the things that go bump in the night.

Knocking on the door, he got no response. He waited a minute and then knocked again. This time he could hear Carlie—*or someone*—stirring around in the bedroom. He heard the bed squeak, and then he heard footsteps. He waited, but Carlie still didn't answer. In a panic, he was just about to throw his shoulder against the door when he heard the faint click of the lock as it turned.

Reaching for the door handle, he watched as someone turned it from the inside. The door whispered softly across the carpet as it swung inward. Jon expected to see Carlie standing in front of him. However, she wasn't—in fact, no one was.

Stepping into the room, he saw Carlie—or what appeared to be Carlie—lying on the bed with the comforter pulled up tight around her neck.

He could see her mane of auburn hair sticking out at all angles from the end of the down bedspread, but he couldn't see any movement.

Stepping to the edge of the bed, he reached down and gently touched her shoulder. She moved restlessly for a few seconds, inhaled deeply, and then exhaled softly, settling back into a deep, peaceful sleep.

Jon checked the bathroom and the closet, but he didn't find anyone there either. He really didn't expect to—and he was glad that he hadn't. After checking on Carlie again, he left the bedroom and softly pulled the door closed behind him.

As he started down the hallway, he heard the soft click of the bedroom lock as it snapped into place.

～

It had to have been well after midnight when Carlie awoke from a restless sleep. She was freezing. Her hands and face were numb from the cold. She could actually see her breath billow in the pale flickering light of the candle on the table next to her bed. The fire in the wood-burning stove had burned itself out again.

One thin cotton blanket would never stave off the cold of an Iowa winter, nor could one single log heat the room for an entire night.

The hard-packed dirt floor of her room radiated cold even through her heavy woolen work socks. As she made her way through the dimly lit room to the door, she held her breath, praying *he* had not locked it tonight.

With apprehension, she touched the handle. Slowly turning it, she held her breath and waited.

Pulling the door open just a few inches, she peered around the edge. No one was standing in the hallway waiting for her. Pulling the door open the rest of the way, she was overwhelmed by the glorious heat that radiated from the living room fireplace.

She strained her ears to hear any sound that would send her scrambling back to her room, safe again behind the closed door. But there was none.

In stocking feet, she crept silently down the hall. A quick peek showed her that the living room was empty, lit only by the glow of the roaring fire. Wrapped in her thin little blanket, she padded across the floor and sat down cross-legged in front of the warmth of the fireplace.

Finally warm and comfortable, she nodded off to sleep.

At first Carlie heard the baby crying in her subconscious. When she finally realized what she was hearing, she jumped up to run back to her room, but it was too late. She could hear footsteps coming down the hall. The only path back to her room was blocked.

The stairwell closet was only a few feet away, so she slid across the wooden floor, turned the handle, opened it a few inches—just enough to pass through—then pulled it silently closed behind her.

From the oppressive darkness of the musty closet, Carlie held her breath and waited.

The coats and boots in the closet reeked of cow manure and sweat. Carlie could barely breathe in the enclosed space. Afraid she would pass out, she lowered herself to the floor and wrapped the blanket around her tiny shoulders and face.

Outside, she could hear the sound of the giant maple rocker as it ground against the wooden floor, the same rocker that *he* had made for her mother years earlier. She listened intently to the baby as it nursed. The soft, gentle sounds of the infant sucking accompanied the soothing voice of its mother as she sang an old religious song.

Carlie sat patiently in the dark. She was sure that eventually both mother and child would fall asleep, or they would go back to their own room. All she had to do was wait.

Falling asleep, Carlie's head slipped off her hand, snapping her neck forward. Wide awake now, she had no idea how long she had been sleeping. She listened for the sounds of the mother or the infant and waited until she felt that it wasn't safe to wait any longer. Standing, she opened the door just enough to see the rocking chair. The woman and the infant were both there and appeared to be sound asleep. Still wrapped in her cotton blanket, Carlie tiptoed across the living room floor toward the hallway.

When she was next to the rocker, the baby made a soft snorting sound that caught Carlie's attention. Pausing, she caught a whiff of lavender soap and chamomile-scented powder. Carlie stopped and watched as the baby sucked gently on his mother's exposed breast.

Carlie knew she needed to go back to her room. However, for some reason, the sight of the mother and her child fascinated her.

The mother opened her eyes to find Carlie standing in front of her. Carlie's eyes widened, knowing the woman was about to scream at the top of her lungs, waking everyone in the house.

Except she didn't; she just stared at Carlie with a questioning look on her face.

Carlie was thankful for the reprieve, so she made a mad dash down the hallway to her own room and closed the door.

Carlie wasn't sure if her room had actually warmed up or if she was just scared, but it didn't matter anymore. She jumped back into bed, covered up, and, in a matter of a few minutes, was sleeping soundly.

Carlie awoke to an accented voice whispering softly in her ear. "Wake up, you little motherfucker. It's time to die."

She opened her eyes just in time to see the massive fist as it crashed into her face.

There is a state of consciousness that lies somewhere between fully alert and complete unconsciousness. This peculiar state was exactly where Carlie found herself. She instinctively knew that being dragged backward by the hair hurt. She also knew that she could feel the pain of having her head and shoulders slammed into every wall they passed. However, she knew instinctively that she didn't feel it anywhere as bad now as she would later—if she survived to have a later, that is.

Carlie heard him cussing at her, cursing the day she was born. She recognized the voice. It wasn't the voice of her normal tormentor—it was the voice of her eldest brother. His wife must have told him about last night, watching her and the baby as they slept. That's what this beating had to be about.

Carlie couldn't talk, or she would have told him that it wasn't what he thought. She'd only wondered what it would have been like to have a mother who loved her—what it would have been like to have a mother hold *her* and sing to *her*.

The last thing Carlie remembered was how it felt when he kicked her on the side of the head.

# 25

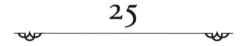

Jon had just finished cleaning up the front porch when the electricity came back on. His main concern now was to get the house cleaned before Carlie woke up and came downstairs.

"Quite a mess you got here, mister."

Jon turned toward the voice. Standing not four feet away was a young man with flame-red hair, freckles, and a radiant smile. Jon was more surprised than alarmed by the boy's sudden appearance.

The young man read the bewildered look on Jon's face, so he continued. "Nothing to be concerned about here, sir. My name's Smitty. I live down the road." Lifting up his arm, he swept it across the open field in the general direction of the farm on the other side. "I figured you might need some help cleaning up, so I hurried on over."

For the first time, Jon took a minute to survey the damage the storm had caused. There were downed tree branches everywhere. There were some huge branches in the front yard that he was sure would require a chainsaw to cut up and a truck to haul away.

With an ambling gait, Smitty walked slowly toward Jon with his right hand extended. Without a second thought, Jon took the young man's hand and shook it. He was amazed at how hard and calloused Smitty's hand felt in his. The boy's hand was also nearly twice the size of his own.

Jon finally looked the young man up and down. The boy had a pleasant face, with a deep white scar starting above his left eyebrow and disappearing into the hairline above his temple. He resembled someone else he knew, but he couldn't quite put a name to the face.

He was a gangly youngster almost as tall as Jon and twice as broad at the shoulders.

"I don't have a truck to haul everything away, so when you get to that point, give me a holler and I'll make arrangements."

With that, Smitty burst into laughter. "Boy, Mister Summers, you sure have a lot to learn about country living. All that wood out there in the yard you'll need this winter. The shingles will go back on the barn, and everything else will become compost.

"You're going to need a roll of forty-pound felt for the barn roof and a new double-pane front window. Just give Jake's Farm Supply a call, and tell them it's for the McPherson—I mean, the Baxter place. They'll send it out on their next delivery run."

Looking up at the bedroom window, Smitty continued. "You probably need to be getting back to Missus Summers. I imagine she's a little freaked out by the storm and all.

"I'll get busy here. You go, Mister Summers. I have everything under control."

When Jon turned around, the young man was already walking toward the barn. Jon couldn't help but notice the boy's slight limp.

Within a half hour, Jon had the leaves, the glass, and the majority of the water in the carpet sucked up. He found the carpet cleaner under the sink, so he got down on his hands and knees and scrubbed at the dirt until the stains were barely noticeable. One more pass with the roaring Shop-Vac, and the carpet was almost dry and the dirt completely gone.

Jon could hear a chainsaw chewing through the downed branches in the front yard as he worked in the living room. Maybe he could find a way to keep Smitty around to help him and teach him how to do some of this on his own.

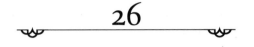

# 26

When Carlie came to, she found herself lying in the mud behind the barn. She could barely take a breath due to the pain from her freshly broken ribs, and her face was beaten almost beyond recognition. She had received beatings before this that had left her broken and bleeding, but this had been the mother of all beatings. She could almost crawl, but she couldn't stand. The best she could manage to do was sit up, but even that was rather lopsided. If she had known anything about concussions, she would have realized that she was sporting a bad one.

Her right iris was three times the size of her left one. The slightest light penetrated clear to her brain, causing excruciating pain, the likes of which she had never experienced before. She was dizzy and nauseated, and if she had had anything in her stomach, she would have thrown it up.

As Carlie sat in the mud and filth, she hung her head, resting it on her knees. She was about to doze off when a shadow blocked the morning sun. Covering her right eye, she looked up to see if she needed to run—if she even could run. Recognizing the housedress, she knew she was safe, at least for the moment.

"Up with you now, child. Let's be taking a look at ya."

Carlie found that she couldn't focus on the woman's face. With her right eye swollen completely shut, the cut above her left eyebrow oozed droplets of blood, distorting the vision in her one good eye. The side of her face was already turning black from the savage kick, and her jaw no longer opened and closed completely. Two, maybe three fingers on her right hand also seemed to be broken or at the very least dislocated.

"My God, look at what they've gone and done to ya now. Can ya stand, child?"

The woman lifted Carlie carefully from the ground and helped her into the barn. Setting her on a bale of hay, the woman left Carlie sitting there while she busied herself finding antiseptic and bandages that her husband and sons used to treat the animals. After throwing one of the horse blankets across two bales of hay, she laid Carlie down on it and began tending to her wounds.

As the woman silently worked on Carlie's damaged body, never once did she acknowledge the actions of her eldest son.

When she was finally finished, she covered Carlie with another horse blanket and walked toward the door. Stopping, she turned back and said, "Now don't ya be falling asleep. I'll fetch you something warm to eat. When I can, I'll come back out and sit with you for a while."

After the woman was gone, Carlie began to sob. Again, she was not crying out of sadness or pain—at least not the physical pain anyway—but out of anger. Actually, the emotion ran so much deeper than anger; Carlie seethed with a rage so potent, there were no words in her limited vocabulary to describe it.

When she felt a hand gently shaking her shoulder, she realized she had fallen asleep even after Edith had expressly told her to not to. Opening her eyes, she didn't know exactly what to expect. Would Edith punish her for not staying awake? Or would she open her one good eye to welcome a new, more brutal beating?

"Carlie! *Carlie!* Are you all right?"

Carlie recognized the voice, but it took a few moments to register who it was. As she rose to the surface from her deep sleep, the fresh, moist aroma of mown hay and horse manure no longer enveloped her. All she could smell now was the warm, seductive scent of Jon's aftershave.

Before she was willing to open her damaged right eye, she tentatively touched the area around it to see if everything that had happened to her had been a dream—or if it had been real. When there was no immediate pain, she took a few moments and mentally inspected the rest of her body. Her fingers and jaw were working normally again, and her body was virtually painless. She could breathe again without wheezing, and the grating pain in her chest cavity was completely gone. When she was satisfied that it had just been another nightmare, she reached out and pulled Jon down on top of her. With her arms wrapped around him as tight as she could, she squeezed.

"CAR-LIE! I can't breathe!"

"God, it was horrible, Jon. They damn near beat this poor kid to death—again."

Carlie relaxed her stranglehold on Jon and began sobbing into his shoulder. She eventually got her sobbing under control. Pushing Jon away, just enough to get a better look at him, she shook her head and said, "It's never going to be all right, Jon. Maybe for you and for me it will be—we're more or less on the outside of this looking in—but for that poor, tortured little soul, it will *never* be all right. You can't possibly imagine what those people subjected that child to on a daily basis. She's stuck in time, reliving those horrors for all eternity."

Looking out the window, Jon realized how much of the day had slipped away. The sun had gone down, and the stars were already out. Staring at the ceiling, he let out an audible sigh. This whole situation was so far out of his knowledge base that he found it almost impossible to begin focusing on any kind of a solution. Above all else, he was not a psychic or even a believer in the paranormal. What concerned him wasn't Carlie's insisting that he refocus all of his scholarly attention on finding a solution for the intangible, but rather the undisputable fact that someone or something needed their help. He found the whole situation more than a little unsettling.

~

When Jon opened his eyes again, the sun was breaking over the eastern horizon. There wasn't a cloud in the sky, and a gentle breeze was blowing the bedroom curtains. Carlie was still lying on his arm, exactly where she had fallen asleep. He'd actually had a peaceful night's sleep—no visions, no visitations. He felt refreshed and ready to face whatever the day might bring.

Carlie rolled off his arm and sat up in bed. When she turned to him, Jon could see that her eyes were clear and bright. She looked better than she had in weeks.

"Jon, my appointment is at 9:00 AM."

Jon had to think about that for a few seconds. Then it dawned on him that it had been over a week since Carlie had fallen and broken her nose. The packing was coming out today, and the brace was finally coming off. The bruises under her eyes had cleared up days earlier, and the swelling in her cheeks was completely gone.

It was going to be a good day—Jon could feel it.

Shortly after 8:00, Jake's Farm Supply delivered the roofing felt, a new window, and a box of whatever was required to install all of it. After signing the bill, Jon and Carlie left for town. He was comfortable in the belief that Smitty would find everything he had requested sitting next to the barn, and could get started on his own.

When Carlie was finished seeing the doctor, she walked into the waiting room with her head held high, showing off her new nose. Jon was pleasantly surprised at what he saw. Her nose was again perfectly straight. The slight upturn of the tip of her nose was even more pronounced now. This slight change was breathtaking; it made her face look angelic.

"Boy, you look great," Jon said with a smile. "I have an idea. Why don't you and I go out for breakfast? We can go over and say hi to Loretta and show off your new nose."

"That's a great idea. I'll be able to taste food again."

Jon signed the paperwork, and the two stepped out into the clean, fresh air.

~

Jon sat in stunned silence as he stared at the "Closed" sign on the door of Loretta's café. He couldn't remember ever seeing the café closed during the day.

The look of concern on Jon's face prompted Carlie to ask, "Do you think something's wrong?"

Remembering their conversation about the house, he envisioned Paul's accident and Dexter's stroke. Just the thought of Loretta being hurt because of their conversation left him with an empty feeling.

Backing out of the parking space, he pointed the car toward the end of town. The woman who worked behind the counter at the Pantry Mart would know what had happened to Loretta; he was sure of it.

"Good morning, Pauline," Jon said. "I was wondering if you might know why the café is closed. Is everything all right with Loretta?"

Before she could answer, a booming voice from the back of the store spoke up. "Retta's fine—it's that idiot husband of hers that got hurt."

In a whisper, Pauline introduced the big man at the back of the store as Loretta's brother Kenneth. "Loretta should be opening up any minute now."

Jon thanked her and returned to the car. As he was opening the door, he spotted Loretta's pickup going the opposite direction. Settled behind the steering wheel, he put the car in reverse and backed out into the street.

After creeping across town again, he found the café open and two pickups already in the parking lot. The sign now told him that it was open and to come on in.

"Are you still in the mood for breakfast? I never thought to ask, I'm sorry."

"I'm ravenous."

With that said, they went inside.

When the bell over the door tinkled, announcing their arrival, Loretta's voice rang out from the back. "Well I'll be damned. You two are a sight for sore eyes. Come on in and sit down. I'll right over."

Sliding into the seat next to Jon, Loretta stretched her arms across the table and took Carlie's hands in her own. "It's been so long. How have you been, sweetie?"

"Well, okay, I guess. Things could be better, but I imagine they could be a lot worse, too. Enough about me, though. We heard about Cecil. Is he all right?"

"He'll be fine. His pride was hurt more than his body."

Jon looked to Carlie to initiate the conversation. He had no idea what, if anything, she would be willing to talk about. Carlie's first order of business, however, was to order breakfast.

Once their order was in the kitchen, Loretta returned to the table and gave Carlie her undivided attention. Not saying a word, the waitress just sat and waited; Carlie would tell her what was on her mind when she was good and ready.

She didn't have to wait long.

"Loretta, I need to talk to you about our house. It's haunted!"

"I know, Carlie. I know."

Over the next three hours, between eating and Loretta waiting on the occasional customer, Carlie told her everything that had happened at the house since she had last seen her. Then she went on to tell her about the disturbing nightmares she had been having. Carlie went into such detail that it actually surprised Jon. A great deal of what she was telling Loretta was information he had never heard before. He was amazed that Carlie could remember every detail of her dreams with such rich, vivid clarity. It really was, just as she had said, as if she were actually reliving these events of the past.

When Carlie was finished, she sat waiting for Loretta to respond.

Loretta's voice was calm when she began. "I think I can help you figure this out—that is, if you'll let me. We have a lot of records and even more photographs from back then. I had family that worked at the county recorder's office. The records building burned, destroying most of the records. Hundreds of the old records that they thought had been destroyed in the fire actually weren't. They were part of this town's history, and my family members went out of their way to save them."

"What about Cecil? It sounds like he needs your help right now, probably even more than we do."

"Don't you go giving Cecil another thought. He's just fine. Doctor says he'll be in a walking cast for about a month. Besides, his crops still have until the end of November or maybe even the end of December before they'll be dry enough to harvest.

"I work the morning shift here, and Pauline and Shirley work the lunch and dinner shifts. I can spend a couple hours in the afternoon with y'all."

The look of excited determination on Loretta's face made it virtually impossible for either Jon or Carlie to say no, so they both agreed to let her help.

While they drove home, Carlie worked hard to justify their decision to involve Loretta. The only reason they could both agree upon was that three sets of eyes were better than two.

# 27

During the long drive home, Jon made a special point to look at the houses on the highway for any apparent wind damage. He was surprised to find that none of the houses had suffered anywhere near the severity of damage that theirs had. He had the feeling that the barrage outside the house had been an extension of what had happened inside. He didn't mention it to Carlie—he had no earthly idea how he could explain his feelings, or how she would react if he did.

It was late afternoon when Jon pulled into the driveway. He didn't see Smitty anywhere. He hoped that the boy hadn't flaked out on them.

It was impossible not to notice the front yard. It was completely clean. The ugly patio furniture was even gone. Slowing to almost a crawl, Jon inspected the yard for anything out of place—a branch, a shingle, even a twig lying in the grass—but there wasn't a single piece of debris left anywhere. Looking up at the roof of the barn, he could see that every shingle was back in place.

As he idled by the front porch, he saw that the plywood board was no longer covering up half the house. He couldn't believe his eyes; the boy had even replaced the front window.

After he parked the car, he and Carlie were walking up the back porch when he noticed that there was a stack of freshly cut lumber sitting next to the side of the house. Stopping, they both went back down the stairs to inspect it. There had to be at least a cord of wood neatly stacked under the kitchen window. A wooden crib piled high with kindling sat against the side of the house next to the logs. Neither Jon nor Carlie could remember ever seeing the wooden box before.

Turning to Carlie, Jon said, "I have to go over and thank Smitty for all the work he did. I was also thinking about asking him to do a little extra work—you know, some of the projects I've been meaning to get around to but haven't yet. Do you mind?"

Biting her lip to keep from nailing Jon on his "projects," she smiled and settled for a nod of her head.

After getting Carlie settled in the house, Jon turned around and drove back down the driveway. He stopped for a moment to get his bearings. He remembered the general direction in which the boy had pointed toward his home, so he took a left onto the main road. The nearest intersection was almost a mile away. He had driven down this road before, but it had been months. He remembered only ever seeing one Amish farmhouse on it.

The house was pretty much the way he remembered it; it was a well-kept farm—in fact, it was immaculate.

Pulling into the drive, Jon noticed movement inside the barn. Rather than knock on the door and bother whoever was in the house, he walked back to the barn. In the corner, he saw an elderly man with a neatly trimmed beard, wearing a straw hat, a blue work shirt, and a pair of blue jeans held up by a pair of black suspenders.

"Excuse me," Jon said. When the man acknowledged his presence, he continued. "I don't mean to bother you, but I believe I'm looking for your son."

Picking up a rag, the man wiped his hands, and in a voice only loud enough to be heard inside the barn, said, "Jacob, there's an English-man here to see you."

Walking across the barn, the man extended his right hand, which Jon gladly accepted. A movement in the corner caught Jon's attention. A young man—possibly in his early teens—walked out from behind the buggy he was working on. Wiping his hands, he walked across the barn toward Jon, only he showed no intention of shaking Jon's hand.

"Come, boy. This man says he's here to see you."

Jon hadn't even had a chance to introduce himself, so he immediately rectified his rudeness. "I'm sorry, I'm Jon—Jon Summers. My wife and I moved into the old Baxter house."

"I'm Ezekiel Yoder, and this here is my son, Jacob."

Shifting his attention to the boy, Jon saw that he was dressed exactly like his father. He also noted that this boy didn't look anything like Smitty.

"You don't have another son, by chance? I believe they call him Smitty." As quickly as he asked it, Jon realized how stupid the question was.

"I'm really sorry to have bothered you, Mr. Yoder," Jon said. "I can clearly see that the boy I'm looking for isn't your son. Maybe you do know who I'm looking for, though. He's rather tall and has bright red hair and freckles. He's maybe nineteen or twenty years old. He told me that he lives out in this general direction, and this is the only farm that I'm familiar with on this road."

Ezekiel's eyes narrowed in concentration. After a few moments of deliberation, he answered. "Can't say as I do—sorry."

After shaking the man's hand again, Jon left and drove back to the house.

All the way home, he tried to remember exactly which direction Smitty had pointed. Even at the time, Jon remembered thinking that the boy was being rather vague about where he lived. *There are only a few farms out here—he has to live on one of them,* Jon thought. *Maybe Loretta knows where he lives.*

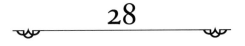

# 28

When Jon walked in the back door, Carlie greeted him with a winning smile and a big hug.

"I called Dexter a little while ago and made arrangements to stop by the office every morning. I'm going to bring what work he might have for me home, so I can do it here. Loretta also called and said she would be here tomorrow afternoon around 2:00 or 2:30 to get started.

"By the way, that boy did one hell of a nice job on the front window; you can't even tell it's a replacement. How much did he charge us for all that work anyway?"

"Not a dime. He actually was offended when I offered him money. Go figure!"

"Well? What did he say? Is he going to help you out around here?"

"I don't know. I couldn't find him."

Carlie gave him a curious look, but it lasted for only a second before she was off onto something else.

"What about you?"

"What about me?"

"What time do you expect to be home tomorrow?"

"I really hadn't given it much thought. Around 3:30, I imagine."

"That will work. I want you here for at least a little while when Loretta is here."

"Not a problem."

Once she was satisfied that all her plans were falling into place, she ushered Jon to the table and sat him down. She busied herself with small talk about anything she could think of while she finished getting dinner ready. She purposely avoided talking about the one subject that she really wanted to discuss.

After they finished eating, Carlie followed Jon into the living room. When Jon flipped on the light, he got the surprise of his life. Everything was back in place exactly as it had been before the storm. He had cleaned the rug, the couch, and the curtains, but he hadn't put all the journals back in order, nor had he picked up the papers and the other small items that the wind had scattered around the room.

Carlie was purposely avoiding picking up the journals. She wasn't quite ready to delve back into the life and times of Edith and Ian McPherson, at least not until she was completely sure that Jon fully understood the ramifications of what they might find.

"Jon, I want to ask you a question, but I don't want you to answer until you've thought it over. All right?"

"Of course. Ask away."

"Are you sure you want to do this? I mean, rooting through the dirty little secrets of the McPherson family. I'm afraid we're going to find that this family was full of monsters, and their lives are best forgotten."

"I *have* given it a lot of thought. I sincerely believe that we need to find out who these people really were and what they did.

"It just may be the only way to end your nightmares. If what you believe is true, then it may be the only chance for the girl I'm seeing to be at peace.

"Christ, I can't believe I just said that."

Carlie couldn't help but admire his attitude.

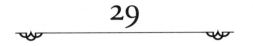

## 29

Loretta knocked on the front door again, this time as hard as she could. Carlie had assured her that she would be home when she got there. Walking around to the back of the house, Loretta hammered on the back door with her fist and jiggled the handle. When the handle turned, she tentatively opened the door and stuck her head inside.

"Carlie? *Carlie! Are you home?*"

When she didn't get a response, she let herself into the kitchen. Standing in the middle of the room, she hollered again. "*CARLIE? JON? IS ANYBODY HERE?*"

Possibly it was the fleeting glint of light that caught Loretta's attention, but more than likely it was the bright purple color. Out of the kitchen window, she saw Carlie in a purple housedress walking across the far corner of the back yard. She appeared to be carrying something reflective in her right hand. The sun glinted off it again, like a mirror against the kitchen window.

Carlie walked slowly and deliberately, with a definite purpose, as she moved through the weed-choked garden. Loretta left the house in a rush, keeping an eye on Carlie as she did. She could see Carlie walking across the yard but only for an instant or two before she disappeared behind the barn.

Cutting between the buildings and up the stone steps, Loretta intercepted Carlie just as she entered the back entrance to the barn. Carlie walked through the empty building completely unaware that Loretta was standing in the doorway watching her. In her right hand, Carlie was still holding the chrome garden spade that Loretta had seen the reflection from earlier. The distant look on Carlie's face was the first indication that something was not quite right. Her expressionless eyes were fixed on a spot light years away from the table in front of her. Her hands moved automatically, collecting, separating, and placing in a large cardboard box three small sacks of colored stones and multicolored flowers in ceramic pots.

Curious, Loretta walked up behind Carlie to see exactly what she was doing. After a few minutes of watching, she cleared her throat to get Carlie's attention. When she got no response, she reached out and touched Carlie's shoulder. Carlie turned robotically toward the older woman; her eyes narrowed, showing absolutely no recognition of Loretta.

Carlie gripped the handle of the spade tight enough to cut off the blood to her fingertips. When Loretta made no overt attempt to engage Carlie in conversation or to stop her from what she was doing, Carlie turned back to the table and picked up the box. Without giving Loretta a second look, she walked past her friend, out of the barn, and toward the garden.

At a distance safe enough not to disturb Carlie, Loretta followed her back to the corner of the yard.

Loretta watched as Carlie knelt down in the freshly excavated dirt. Sometime in the recent past, Carlie had repositioned the polished granite stone prominently in the center of the 3' x 3' area of raised dirt.

Digging small holes with the spade, Carlie systematically buried the flowerpots around the edge of the small grave. When she finished arranging the flowers by size and color, she carefully laid out the colored stones in a starburst pattern around the center.

When she was finished, she stood and wiped the dirt from her hands onto her dress.

Loretta watched her intently. When Carlie finally released her death grip on the spade, it dropped to the ground next to her.

Her eyes slowly transformed from a stormy shade of gray-green to the exquisite emerald Loretta had come to recognize from the lovely woman standing before her. Carlie's shoulders hung limp and her head slumped forward in shame when she finally realized that Loretta had been watching her the whole time. Before Carlie could make an excuse for her behavior, Loretta pulled her close against her chest and rocked her gently, as one might a small child.

"Shhhh, it's all right," Loretta whispered. "Everything will be all right."

"I've heard that before, Loretta. Jon says it all the time. The problem is, nothing ever gets any better—it only gets worse. I think I'm losing my mind . . . and Jon in the process. I'm scared to death."

"Maybe it's time you told him the truth. He'll never understand the connection you have to this house until you do. Right now he sees everything going on around him as separate and individual random acts. But you and I both know that they aren't."

Carlie began to sob and nodded her head. Loretta held her tight, rubbing her back until Carlie regained her composure. When her tears finally subsided, Loretta pushed Carlie upright and said, "I think it's time we get started. Jon will be home soon."

Again, Carlie only nodded and allowed Loretta to guide her back to the house.

When Jon walked in the kitchen door, the aroma of coffee and warm pastry filled the air like a fragrant cloud. There was a rustling sound and voices coming from the living room. After filling the empty cup next to the coffee pot, he took it and the plate of danish out to join Carlie and Loretta, who were already busy reading Edith's journals.

"Good afternoon, ladies. I see we're already hard at it."

Carlie gave him an imperceptible smile, but Loretta beamed. "Hi, Jon. Glad to see you could join us," she said.

Setting his coffee cup down, he placed the plate of danish in the center of the coffee table. "Have we found anything interesting yet?" he asked.

Carlie was so engrossed in what she was reading that she barely acknowledged Jon's question. After she finished, she laid the open book in her lap. Without looking up, she said, "The McPhersons had two sons. Patrick was the first. He must have been born in the mid-1800s, around 1850 or so.

"They were married for almost ten years before Patrick was born."

Looking up, she saw that Jon was listening to her intently. Glad to see that she had his attention, Carlie continued her story.

"Their second son's name was Daniel. Edith named him after her father. Patrick was five when Daniel was born. The boys were a mirror image of their father. Both boys had coal black hair and pale gray eyes." Carlie stopped her narrative, picked up the journal, and resumed her reading.

After a few minutes of silence, she turned to face Jon and waited for him to get comfortable.

Jon took a sip from his cup of coffee, sat back in his chair, and put his feet up on the ottoman.

Carlie began again. "It seems they had three sons. Actually, Ian and Edith had two sons together, and Edith had a third. Patrick and Daniel were ten and five, respectively, when the farmhand who was helping Ian with the summer crops raped Edith."

Carlie paused for a moment, partially for dramatic effect and partially because she was picturing in her mind what Edith had gone through.

Loretta moved from the floor to the couch next to Carlie. Once she settled in, she marked her page with a piece of paper from the table and closed her journal. When all eyes were on her, Carlie began again. "Edith was so ashamed. She didn't tell Ian about the rape, but when she found out she was pregnant, she had to."

She stopped reading and looked up at her husband. She hoped that what she was about to say would in no way defend the actions that were to follow, but rather would give Jon some insight into the internal turmoil Edith must have felt. "You see, Jon, in those days, short of throwing one's self down a flight of stairs, there was no such thing as an abortion."

When Jon nodded his head in both agreement and understanding, Carlie continued. "Ian stipulated that only under one condition would he raise Edith's bastard child. When the child turned eighteen, he would have to leave.

"She had very little choice, so Edith reluctantly agreed.

"This brings us back to the house—that's when Ian built the third addition, the one Paul warned me about. He built that room for the new baby. It had basic amenities, a heavily bolted door, a dirt floor, no windows, and a very small heater. He designed and built it to be nothing more than a rudimentary shelter. That was all Ian promised Edith.

"From the very beginning, Ian refused to claim the child, and he treated him with indifference and contempt, so Edith put the name Andrew Smith on the baby's birth certificate."

Carlie picked up a piece of yellowed paper that was lying next to her on the couch and handed it to Jon.

Jon looked up from the document with the words "Certificate of Live Birth" across the top and started to speak, but she immediately silenced him. "Please," Carlie insisted, "wait until I'm finished."

Carlie started again. "The other boys were the spitting image of their father, but Andrew was like his mother, with red hair and freckles. By all appearances, he would eventually be taller than the other boys, but he would be nowhere as big across the chest and shoulders.

"During Andrew's first few months, he was basically ignored. Ian didn't allow Edith to give the boy even the most basic maternal comforts. As an infant, Ian never allowed him to sleep in any other room—especially their room. Andrew spent every night of his life in the addition Ian built for him. Edith fed him, changed him, and kept him quiet. The whole family, including Edith, treated this little boy as if he were a stray dog.

"Jon, wild animals tend to their young better than Ian and Edith cared for Andrew. He didn't even eat at the same table as the rest of the family; Ian confined him to the kitchen, like the hired help, for his meals—even on holidays."

Before Carlie could continue, Loretta stood and carried her coffee cup out to the kitchen. Carlie sat in silence, waiting for the older woman to return. When Loretta finally did return, she smiled at both Carlie and Jon and said, "I believe you two are on the right track now." Tapping a heavy wooden crate with the tip of her toe, she continued. "Every record that was ever filed on this house is in this box. I also saw a copy of a notice that the county condemned the house at one point in time. You'll find that records of live births and death certificates are in this box as well. I'll come back tomorrow afternoon. Right now, though, I imagine you two have a lot to talk about." In the palm of her hand, Loretta held a small picture. As she passed Jon, she stopped and laid it face-up on the arm of his chair.

Once she saw the recognition flash in Jon's eyes, she continued walking toward the door.

Carlie stood and, taking the woman's arm, walked Loretta out.

Standing on the front porch, the two women hugged as Carlie thanked her.

Jon joined Carlie on the front porch when he heard Loretta's truck door shut. Together they stood and watched in silence as she drove away.

When Loretta was out of sight, Jon turned to Carlie. For the first time, he began to understand the significance of the haunting and of Carlie's nightmares. They had both been wrong—so very wrong.

# 30

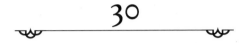

Jon hadn't moved since Carlie had insisted that he sit down next to her on the couch. He held her hands in his and gave her his undivided attention.

All through dinner something was bothering her—something unrelated to what she had discovered in Edith's journals. He was about to ask her what was wrong when Carlie began talking first. "Jon, there's something I need to tell you. I should have told you a long time ago, but I guess I was afraid of what you would think of me—that you wouldn't love me anymore."

Jon didn't have a response, so he waited quietly for Carlie to continue.

"I was fifteen when it happened," Carlie began. "There had been a pep rally after school, and it lasted a little longer than they had originally planned. By the time it was over, the sun had set and it was getting dark. My friend Julie and her stepfather offered me a ride home. I didn't think anything of it; they had given me a ride home from school dozens of times over the years, so I accepted. I also didn't think anything of it when Julie suggested that he drop her off at home first. He told us that he had to go back to his office, and my home was on the way. I could have called my dad and had him come pick me up from their house, but it all sounded so rational. It all seemed so normal at the time; I can't believe how naïve I was.

"You know, I can still see him staring at my legs on the ride to their house, but I never gave it a second thought. The boys in class stared at our legs all the time. That's why we rolled up our skirts—it was a game. The girls would dare each other to see who would roll up their skirt the shortest—who would be daring enough, or foolish enough, to give a glimpse of panty and not get caught by the nuns."

Taking a breath, Carlie let out a long sigh. "To make a long story short, he took me to a remote area and parked the car. I know this will make you uncomfortable. I wasn't scared at all by what he did. Actually, I was even a little excited and flattered. He was much younger than Julie's real father and extremely good-looking."

She could tell by the look of confusion on Jon's face that he was about to ask her what on earth she possibly could have been thinking.

"Don't judge me, Jon; just try to understand. I didn't know anything about sex back then. A lifetime of Catholic school had ingrained in me that even kissing out of wedlock was a mortal sin. We did a lot of kissing back then—kissing was Catholic girls' sex.

"I considered the possibility that Julie's dad would try to kiss me, and I even considered what it would be like to have him kiss me. I didn't have any idea what he really wanted.

"Believe me, when I did find out, I did everything in my power to stop him. The whole thing lasted less than a minute. I truly believed at the time that he had quit because I wanted him to and not because he had actually finished. He drove me home afterward and begged me not to mention to anyone what *we* had done.

"He made it sound as if it were my idea too. It made me feel guilty and dirty. He convinced me that I had actually asked for it.

"I never told anyone—until I found out that I was pregnant. The first person I told was Julie. I told her everything that had happened, everything her stepfather had done. She already knew. I found out that she and her stepdad had been having sex for years.

"When I finally told my parents I was pregnant, I told them that it was by a boy who had moved overseas. I couldn't have Julie's dad sitting on the couch across from my parents telling them how much I had asked him for it. So I lied to them.

"You have to understand, Jon, that I had a very strict Catholic upbringing. Abortion was completely out of the question, under any circumstances. In all of my parents' discussions of what they should do with their wayward daughter, having an abortion never came up.

"My parents went through the normal stages of grief at what they had lost. After their grieving period was over, they packed me up and moved me out here to live with Aunt Grace and Uncle William.

"Don't get me wrong—I loved being out here on the farm. I really loved Aunt Grace; she was a very special woman. She was the one who arranged the adoption of my baby through Catholic Charities. My parents literally dropped me in her lap with all my belongings and told her to deal with the situation."

The look of disgust on Jon's face told Carlie that by the way she had phrased what she had said, he was getting the wrong impression.

"It wasn't like that, Jon. It was all Grace's idea—that I come live with them, that I have the baby here, and that Catholic Charities handle the adoption. She was a rock; my parents were worthless. Please don't think less of them; it really wasn't their fault. They just had no preparation in life for handling something of this magnitude. It was so much different back then than it is now."

Carlie waited and watched Jon's reaction. When he finally nodded in acceptance, she continued.

"I had a wonderful life out here. I really did.

"I was in my ninth month when something horrible happened. I tripped on the rug at the top of the stairs and fell all the way to the bottom landing. Other than a huge knot on the back of my head, I didn't believe anything was wrong, but Aunt Grace insisted that I go to the hospital so I could get checked anyway.

"I started spotting on the way to the hospital. By the time we got there, I was hemorrhaging. They rushed me into emergency surgery and delivered the baby by Caesarian section.

"My baby lived just eighteen hours. I never found out why she died, but I grieved her passing. Even though I knew I wasn't going to keep her, a mother automatically bonds with a child that is growing inside her body.

"We had refrained from picking out names for her or him. We never even considered what sex the baby might be until after she was born. However, once I did know, it made it that much worse. I really grieved hard over my loss.

"When the baby died, they called Uncle William to come and pick her up. I was still recuperating, and Aunt Grace stayed by my bedside day and night.

"Uncle William was a gentle soul but not the sharpest knife in the drawer. He had no idea what to do with the baby when they gave her to him. We had never even considered what to do if she didn't survive, so there were never any arrangements made for a funeral. Uncle William was afraid to ask Grace what to do, so he handled her burial himself. He built her a tiny coffin and buried her in the most beautiful part of their garden. He bought a small plain granite stone, had it polished, and marked her grave with it. He didn't know what to have written on it, so he just left it as it was.

"I was in the hospital for a week. On the day they discharged me, the doctor came into my room and told the three of us that the fall had caused an irreparable rupture in my uterus and I'd never be able to have children. I think that was when Uncle William decided never to mention what he had done with the baby. Aunt Grace finally told me on the day of his funeral. It's funny how you just never think of things like that. I just assumed that the baby's burial had happened by the grace of God.

"I stayed with Grace and William for well over another year. After the baby died, I didn't have anywhere to go, so I stayed with them until I received acceptance into a university. They paid for my tuition, room and board, even my books. I didn't talk to my parents again until the day I received my letter of acceptance into law school. That was their plan for me before I got pregnant. They chose that life for me, and they believed they had lost it forever. I felt I owed them that.

"I know you won't understand this, and I can't really explain it in a way so you will, but I somehow managed to block the memory of the baby from my mind for over twenty years—that is, until I finally returned to this house. I'm positive that my baby was the reason I was so adamant about moving back here. She will always be a part of this house, and because of her, this house will always be a part of me.

"Jon, this is the only home my baby has ever known!"

# 31

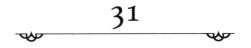

It had been a painfully emotional evening for Carlie. She had revealed secrets to Jon that she had not spoken about for two decades. In many ways, she was begging for Jon's acceptance and forgiveness for what she believed to be the unforgivable. More importantly, by bringing her sins into the light of day, she was finally seeking forgiveness for what had happened—both for her and for the baby she never knew.

Carlie had lived with the ingrained belief that God had taken her baby away as punishment for what she and Julie's stepfather had done.

Jon knew better, though. He believed that if there were a God, it was not a vengeful creature. God would never take an innocent life as retribution for a simple transgression.

Moreover, he couldn't fathom how anyone, even God, would consider what had happened to Carlie a transgression.

As he held her, he knew that nothing he could say would provide her soul with the peace and serenity that finding forgiveness within herself would.

That night, as Jon lay staring at the ceiling, he couldn't help but wonder if Carlie had actually fallen down the stairs as she remembered—or if she had been pushed. It was not a question he wanted to ponder; however, it was not a possibility he was ready to completely dismiss either.

The question of the morality of having a child out of wedlock, or even the legalities of having sex with a minor, never once entered his mind. For hours, he replayed the conversation he and Loretta had had at the café. There was one common factor that he couldn't manage to dispute, no matter how hard he tried. Loretta's grandfather had been right—everything in this house seemed to revolve around the children. He remembered how adamant he had been about him and Carlie not having children. Loretta must have thought he was a naïve idiot to carry on like that.

Carlie's dreams involved her reliving the horrific abuses one child had suffered at the hands of his parents and siblings. This was an indisputable fact. It was beyond him how this child's life had any bearing on the violence that seemed to be increasing in intensity and regularity, and why the visions of the young woman were coming more frequently and with such clarity.

Loretta was bound to tell him who this girl was; after all, she had given him the picture of her.

～

As the sun began to break the horizon, the last image that ran through Jon's mind before he fell asleep was of the young woman holding the infant in her arms. Could these two possibly be the *us*?

～

Carlie spent most of the next day reading Edith's journals. Edith's cavalier attitude toward the physical and psychological abuse of her own child absolutely appalled her. Edith had made notes in her journals describing, in part, many of the same experiences that Carlie had relived in their entirety during her nightmares. But it was beyond her how this woman could dismiss everything that had happened to her child as being either justifiable punishment by her husband or—how had she put it?—"a little overzealous but simply mischievous play by her other sons."

How the fuck could anyone—especially a mother—consider the barbaric and unconscionable beating of her own child *justifiable* or even *overzealous*? Carlie was positively livid when Loretta arrived that afternoon.

Stepping out of her car, Loretta stopped for a second and focused her attention on the farthest corner of the property. There was no movement in the garden, so she reached in across the car and retrieved a large brown paper bag from the passenger seat.

Loretta scanned the property for Carlie. It took a moment before she could make her out sitting in the shadows on the front porch. When Carlie looked up from what she was doing, she waved at Loretta. Loretta waved back and headed across the driveway to meet her.

When Loretta reached the top of the steps, Carlie stood and opened the screen door. She allowed Loretta to go in first and then followed her into the living room.

Tossing the journal on the couch, Carlie stood in the middle of the room with her hands on her hips. Looking at her friend, she said, "I can't believe that woman. She pisses me off to no end."

Loretta didn't seem to be following Carlie's one-sided conversation. With a quizzical look, she asked, "Who pisses you off, sweetie?"

"Edith—Edith McPherson pisses me off—like no one ever has before."

Smiling, Loretta took Carlie's arm and ushered her toward the kitchen. "Come on, cutie, you tell me all about it while I put these sandwiches together."

Carlie pulled out a chair at the table and sat down while Loretta busied herself at the stove.

"Do you remember my telling you about the dream I had about Edith's youngest son being beat almost to death by her eldest son, Patrick?"

Loretta stopped for a second and thought back to a couple days earlier at the café. "Of course I do. Poor little guy. I can't believe his mama let that happen to him."

"Well, I woke up; I don't know what happened to the boy after that. The last thing I remember was Edith telling me/him to not fall asleep and that she would be back with some food and check in on him. Evidently, that never happened. In her journal, she wrote that Andrew had been badly hurt; however, she went into no detail as to what had happened to him. I don't know for sure that she knew any more than it had been Patrick who had done the beating.

*Only known photo of Patrick McPherson.*

"She wrote that the incident had started at breakfast. Ian, Patrick, and Patrick's wife, Becky, were at the table talking when Patrick jumped up and left the room. A few minutes later, Patrick dragged Andrew through the kitchen and out the back door.

"About ten minutes later, Patrick returned without Andrew. When Edith tried to find out what had happened to the boy, Ian told her to shut up and cook breakfast, and that it was none of her concern.

"When Andrew didn't come back in an hour, she went looking for him. That's when she found him sitting in the mud by the barn. She did tend to him exactly as I remembered, but that's when she actually forgot about him. She completely forgot to feed him, and she left him lying in the freezing barn.

"Can you fucking believe that?"

Loretta just stared at Carlie, disbelief and disgust turning her face into a mask of contempt. Unable to find any words, Loretta simply shook her head.

"It was well after Ian and the other boys had gone to town the next morning that she remembered Andrew was still out in the barn. She never once mentioned that she was worried about him. She left him in the barn with a concussion, dehydration, and freezing temperatures for the greater part of one day and an entire night.

"She managed to get the boy back into his own room, build a fire in the stove, and bring his body temperature back up.

"You have to admit, Loretta—that was one tough little boy. After reading Edith's accounts and reliving this kid's life in my dreams, I can't find a single reason why he would have *wanted* to survive. Personally, I would have lain down and died. I would have relished death; it would have been so much better than what I was living through."

Loretta was so captivated by Carlie's recounting of Andrew's story—and Carlie in its telling—that neither of them heard Jon when he walked through the back door into the kitchen.

Having missed the crux of the conversation, Jon had no idea at all what would prompt Carlie to tell Loretta that she would relish the idea of dying. Curious and a little disturbed by what he had just heard, he set his briefcase on the counter loud enough to draw the women's attention.

Carlie jerked her head up and after a moment gave Jon a radiant smile. "Hi, babe, I didn't hear you come in. So, how was your day?"

"Good, good. How was yours? Did something happen that I should know about? Something that might make you welcome death?"

Both Loretta and Carlie sat silently looking at Jon as if he had two heads.

Loretta was the first to realize what had happened—what he had overheard. "Oh God, sweetie. Carlie was just telling me what happened to that poor little boy Andrew. She couldn't understand why this kid had such a will to live. Anyone else—including Carlie and me—would have given up. That's what you heard."

Relieved, Jon broke down and started laughing at his foolishness. His laughing jag was actually relief that Carlie hadn't gone into another fit of depression.

Edith's journal portrayed an entirely different picture of the woman than the one Jon had mentally painted.

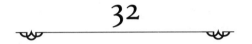

# 32

As the three of them ate dinner, Loretta had a million questions for Carlie. She wanted to know exactly what had happened in each of Carlie's dreams. For the next hour, Carlie relayed her experiences, thoughts, and impressions of what Andrew had endured in his short life to that point.

When Carlie finally finished, Loretta had Jon relive his experiences with the young woman. When he got to the night of the storm, he told her about seeing the girl standing in the corner holding an infant in her arms.

This bit of information caught Carlie completely off-guard. This was the first time she had heard anything about a baby. She looked at Jon in confusion, but Loretta offered up a possible explanation.

"Listen, you two, I wouldn't place too much importance on the presence of a newborn child in Jon's manifestation. Over the years, there have been dozens of miscarriages, premature births, and babies who died of natural causes in this house. There was a woman who lived here in the early 1900s named Abigail Newsome. She and her husband, Robert, had thirteen children, but only one survived past its first birthday. Of course her only living son, Theodore, lived to the ripe old age of ninety-one. He finally passed away in a nursing home up near Ottumwa. The point being, *that child* could be anyone's child; it was the nature of the times.

"I imagine, from what you and Jon have told me, that it might be this woman's purpose to protect them from the spirit of the man who tormented poor Andrew—the spirit that seems to still be here and is still tormenting the other inhabitants."

*Edith, circa 1848. Ireland.*

Jon could see by the expression on Carlie's face that although Loretta's explanation was reasonable, it couldn't completely dissuade her from believing that the infant could have been her child.

Reaching into his shirt pocket, Jon pulled out the small picture Loretta had left with him the day before. Flipping it as he would a playing card, it hit and slid across the table, coming to a stop directly in front of Loretta's coffee cup.

"Who is she?" Jon asked.

"I assumed you would have figured it out by now. It's Edith McPherson. I believe this picture was taken the year before she and Ian left Ireland."

Before Loretta could say anything else, Carlie's arm flashed across the table as fast as a python strike and snatched the picture from where Jon had pitched it.

Carlie examined the picture long enough to burn the image of Edith's face to memory before she set it on the table and looked up at Jon.

*Ian and Edith's wedding picture, circa 1849. Ireland.*

Jon only nodded his head at Carlie before he directed his attention back to Loretta.

Loretta had taken that moment to retrieve from her purse a small manila envelope, which she laid on the table next to her. Reaching inside, she pulled out another small picture, which she pushed to the center of the table so both Jon and Carlie could see it.

"This is Edith and Ian's wedding picture."

Carlie stood and pulled her chair beside Jon's so she could see the picture too. Jon was already examining the two young faces. He recognized the girl's face as being that of Edith, but he wasn't sure about the young man. He had assumed the ghost in the hall was the ghost of Ian, but maybe he was mistaken. There was no doubt, though, that the eyes were the same eyes he had seen that night. By the terrified look on Carlie's face, she also recognized the eyes as being those of the huge apparition from the night she had passed out in the hall.

Loretta could see by the look on Jon and Carlie's faces that there was more than a slight recognition of the images in the photograph. "You do realize that this picture was taken when Ian was nineteen and Edith was fourteen. There are no more pictures of Edith, but there are a couple more of Ian."

Sliding the photograph in her hand across the table, she started again.

*Ian McPherson standing with horse, circa 1900. Iowa.*

"This photograph was taken almost thirty years later."

Carlie missed what Loretta was saying as she stared at the tiny image. As Loretta gave her opinion on the origin of the picture, Jon and Carlie's attention locked onto the image in the next picture. This was definitely the same person who was currently haunting their house and Carlie's nightmares.

*Ian McPherson, circa 1880. Iowa.*

"This is a picture of Ian McPherson," Loretta said. "I don't have any idea how old he was when it was taken, but I'd say he was in his mid- to late forties.

Jon was the first to speak. "My God, Loretta, where did you find these pictures?"

"When they emptied the contents of what was left of the house after Ian and Edith passed away, the photos were taken out of the frames and put in the file. There are a few more, but no one can put a name to them. Maybe we'll be able to identify them after we finish reading Edith's journals. I'll leave them here," she said, pushing the envelope across the table.

Loretta stayed until after the sun had gone down. None of them were able to work up the courage to pick up Edith's journals and delve into the next chapter of the woman's life, so they spent the rest of the evening speculating about what had happened to Andrew.

As Loretta was packing up to leave, Jon remembered what he wanted to ask her. "Loretta, after the storm, a really nice young man helped me do some clean-up and repairs that we needed around the house. He said his name was Smitty. Do you by chance know how I could find him?"

Loretta thought about Jon's question for quite some time before she finally answered. "I do remember Grace telling me about a young man she and William had working for them. *His* name was Smitty, too. That boy would have to be pushing forty or so by now, though. He may have a son; I just don't know. Their Smitty was a drifter, I think. He lived here on the farm until Grace passed away. I never heard where he went; he just left. I can't say that anyone ever saw or heard from him again. I wish I could help; I just don't know him."

Leaning down to eye level, Jon crossed his arms on the window frame of her car door and said, "I can't tell you how much we appreciate your help, Loretta. I don't think Carlie could do this without you. I know I couldn't. She's been pretty good the last few days—no new nightmares. She seems to be able to talk to you. I assume it was your idea that she tell me about the baby, and for that I thank you. She seemed to find an inner peace after it was finally out in the open."

"Sweetie, you don't have anything to thank me for. I really haven't done anything that she wouldn't have done on her own when the time was right. This is a confusing time for both of you. I'm afraid that it'll only get worse before it gets any better."

Jon's look of confusion demanded that Loretta explain.

"Jon, you are also a large part of this quest she has undertaken. Whether or not you like it, or even believe in it, she is trying to get answers to questions and hopefully bring an end to a situation that no one else in all these years has been able to resolve. I'm not saying she can't do it, because honestly I just don't know. However, what I do know is, she is compelled to do it and she's scared to death that she will lose you in the process. Please don't let that happen!"

"I promise you, Loretta, I will not let that happen. I worry about her, though. I don't want to lose her—or, for that matter, for her to lose herself in all of this."

"Then the best advice I can give you is, just be patient with her."

"Tomorrow is my day off from the café, and Cecil is planning on going to Des Moines for an implement sale, so I'll be out here in the morning. Carlie said she wanted to get an early start on it, so I guess I'll see you then."

Jon rested his hand tenderly on her shoulder and thanked her one more time as she put the truck in gear.

Carlie stood on the porch and waved goodbye as Loretta drove away.

When Carlie finished her shower, she found Jon lying with his back to her and already snoring softly. She considered waking him; she desperately wanted to talk about what she had told him the night before. She wasn't sure what she could possibly say that would help him understand, or what he could say in return to alleviate even the smallest part of the guilt she still felt.

As she stood watching him sleep, she decided that possibly she didn't need to discuss it any further after all. She had taken Loretta's advice and told him everything there was to tell, and here he was sleeping as if she hadn't told him anything that he didn't already know. Maybe Loretta was right, and there really was nothing for him to forgive. All he needed to do was listen and, hopefully, understand—it was she who needed to forgive herself.

~

The old maple rocking chair was starting to make a barely discernible squeak when she rocked forward. She attributed the sound at least in part to the chair's age and normal wear and tear.

Combined with the warmth of the fire and the slight groaning the floorboards made as they compressed under the weight of the chair and its occupant, she found herself fighting to stay awake. Carlie loved everything about this room: its warmth, its sounds, and its security. To her, this was the most relaxing place on earth.

As she rocked, the baby in her arms jerked itself awake and began suckling on her exposed breast again. Pulling the baby's radiating warmth tighter to her, she stroked its silken hair and inhaled the scent of the soft, tiny object of her affection. The baby's aroma hinted of sleep and warmth, of comfort and newness. All of this intermingled with the faintest scent of lilac soap.

As the baby nursed, its tiny pink hand reached out from under the cover of its rainbow-colored blanket and explored the texture and lines of Carlie's face.

Laying her head back, Carlie readjusted her position in the rocker and closed her eyes to the incredible sensation of something so small—and so dependent on her for its every need—sucking quietly on her nipple.

Lulled into a shallow sleep, she could feel the tiny fingers as they scratched, caressed, and explored the tender flesh of her breast. Touching and kneading, the baby used it as a handhold to pull itself even tighter against her chest.

Carlie awoke from her sleep when the gentle sucking became obscenely sexual. Where she had felt the warmth of her child radiating against her chilled skin and its soft lips as it nursed, she now felt hot breath and a flicking tongue as it rotated in ever-tightening circles around her exposed nipple. Violently, sharp teeth bit down on the tiny protuberance before it began sucking again. This time, like no other in her life, the sensation felt dirty; this time, something—or someone— was demanding that she respond sexually to its advances.

Desperately she tried to open her eyes, but she couldn't. Tears coursed down her cheeks as she tried to push the source of the pain away. She could do nothing to protect her tender skin and aching breasts from the savage attack.

Weakened from the intense pain and exhausted from her efforts, she made one more attempt; she pushed the clinging hands away from her with all her might, jumping out of the rocker and to her feet at the same time.

Her eyes snapped open as the intruder dislodged itself from her breast, and she found herself standing alone in the middle of the darkened living room.

Dazed and confused, she stood in the silence of the empty room as she worked to get her bearings. She couldn't remember for the life of her coming downstairs. The last thing she did remember was kissing Jon goodnight.

The chilled air in the front room amplified the burning sensation in her left breast, and goose bumps crawled over the exposed flesh of her arms. She couldn't understand why she was naked from the waist up; the top half of her cotton nightgown cascaded loosely around her hips. She didn't remember dressing in a nightgown. She had given up wearing nightgowns some twenty years earlier.

A cursory examination revealed that the burning was from a spot about two inches in circumference at the tip of her breast. Tucking her arms back inside the straps of her nightgown, she hurried upstairs to the bathroom to find a possible cause and get a better look at the rest of her body.

Under the glaring bathroom light, Carlie slowly lowered the top of her nightgown. It was impossible to miss the dark purple bruise on the inside of her right breast. On closer examination, she saw what appeared to be teeth marks in the center of the circle. Amazed, she pulled her top completely down. Her left nipple, still burning intensely, looked as if a serrated knife blade had nearly severed it. She slid onto the counter and closely examined the damaged area in the mirror. After wiping the oozing blood from her breast, she couldn't believe what she was looking at; there was no mistaking the two perfect semicircles—they were large bite marks. Two teeth on the top and three on the bottom appeared to have broken through the skin where it was now bleeding freely.

Just looking at the damage caused the intense burning pain to return. Almost instantly, a wave of nausea overcame her.

In the medicine cabinet, she found the prescription for the pain medication the doctor had prescribed when she broke her nose. Dumping out two into the palm of her hand, she popped them into her mouth and dry-swallowed them. On the top shelf, she located an antiseptic spray and a large sterile gauze pad. After spraying and scrubbing the wound, she rubbed on an antibiotic cream. The pain was excruciating—almost knee-buckling; she wished the Vicodin would hurry up and kick in. She placed the gauze pad over the treated area and taped it to her breast.

The sun was coming up when Carlie finally finished doctoring herself and dressing. She chose an oversize hooded maroon sweatshirt and slinky black jeans. She figured that if she wore a sweatshirt two sizes too large, Jon wouldn't immediately notice that she wasn't wearing a bra, and the tight jeans would help keep his eyes where she wanted them—down below her waist—at least until she was ready to share what had happened to her.

As badly as her breast hurt—even under the numbing influence of the pain medication—she seriously doubted that she would be covering her damaged breast with a bra any time in the near future.

Carlie had already set out three cups of coffee and enough breakfast to choke a horse when Jon came into the kitchen.

"Sit down and eat. Have I got a nightmare to tell you about."

There was a slight knocking on the kitchen door, and without looking up, Carlie motioned for Loretta to come in.

"Good morning, y'all," Loretta said as she dropped her purse and jacket on the counter. "Boy, something smells good." Dropping down into the chair between Carlie and Jon, she commented, "I really like what you two have done to the front of the house."

Jon was the first to respond. "What do you mean? We haven't done anything new to the house."

"The new trellis—you didn't just put up a row of trellises against the front of the house?"

"Uh, no."

"Well someone did."

Jon stood and excused himself; curiosity got the best of him.

Carlie just shrugged her shoulders and smiled at Loretta as Jon barreled out the back door and around the house.

Loretta picked up her cup of coffee and took a sip, giving Carlie a long, thoughtful gaze, then said, "So, do you want to tell me about it?"

"Yes, I do, but later. I'm not sure I'm willing to share all of it with Jon quite yet. Don't get me wrong—I will tell him, but not until I can explain it to myself a little better than I can right now."

"It's that bad?"

"Yes, I think it is."

The door to the kitchen slammed shut behind him as Jon rushed into the kitchen. "Damn, you need to see this, Carlie."

Jon was standing with his hands on his hips staring at the new row of trellises when Carlie and Loretta rounded the corner of the house. "It's such a beautiful thing, isn't it?" Jon asked. "It had to have been that boy Smitty. I don't remember mentioning to him what I had planned for the trellises, but he must have taken it upon himself to put them to use. These have to be some of the rose of Sharon growing wild out by the fence—you know, the ones out by the garden.

"What baffles me is that, being uprooted like they were, the flowers would surely have wilted a little or showed some signs of stress, but these guys seem to be thriving. You have to hand it to the boy—he definitely has a green thumb. I thought the rose trellis Paul put up was beautiful; these blend the colors perfectly around the front half of the house."

Carlie thought back to her conversation with Paul. She remembered him being emphatic that neither he nor his men had had a hand in the small, delicate work of restoring the grounds or the outbuildings. Maybe Jon's Smitty was the son of Grace and William's Smitty. Maybe it was a form of obligation from one family to another, or maybe it was just a country thing.

Edith's journal was still lying on the couch where Carlie had pitched it a few days earlier.

Carlie reached down to pick it up, but recoiled as soon as she felt its cool, smooth surface against her fingertips. It no longer held her fascination; she had only contempt for its author and her family.

Loretta saw Carlie hesitate, so she took the book from where it was lying. Opening it to the bookmark, she pointed to the couch and told Carlie to sit down; she would take over and read for a while.

Jon plopped down in his chair, swung his leg over the arm, and waited for Loretta to begin.

Thumbing through the next twenty to thirty pages, she picked a page and began reading and paraphrasing aloud.

"It's been a month since Patrick's brutal beating of Andrew. According to Edith, the boys have managed to keep their distance from each other since that day. If you can believe what you read here, even Ian has seemed to lay off the boy. Andrew is still having residual effects from the kick in the head. He's suffering severe headaches. Edith describes them as blinding-light pains. He sleeps most of the day but roams the farm at night, probably because it's dark, quiet, and easy on his senses."

While Loretta relayed the story from Edith's journal, she couldn't help but notice how agitated Carlie was becoming. Laying the book down in her lap, she looked over at Carlie and said, "What is it, sweetie? What exactly is it that's bothering you?"

"I'm not sure; I'm getting these fragmented impressions. It's almost as if I know where this story is going and how it's going to end before I hear it. Edith lived in a world of denial. The worst possible abuse could be going on right in front of her, and if that jackass of a husband of hers told her that everything was perfectly normal, she would shut everything bad out and go on with her little life as if nothing were happening.

"I'm not positive how this relates to the nightmare I had last night, but I'm sure it does. It seems like my nightmares are one step ahead of what we're reading in Edith's journals. This little boy wants the truth to be known—not his mother's version of it."

Sitting up in his chair, Jon asked, "What happened in your nightmare? You mentioned you had one."

"I was attacked."

"Attacked? By whom? Were you Andrew in this dream?"

"No, I think I relived one of the memories of Becky Jacobson, Patrick's wife. Or it was possibly something Andrew had personally witnessed. " For the next half hour, Carlie relayed her dream to Jon and Loretta. When she finished, she waited for a response, but neither said a word. Afraid that they didn't believe her story, Carlie lifted the front of her sweatshirt, exposing her damaged and bandaged breast.

Loretta jumped to her feet, took Carlie by the hand, and directed her down the hallway to the bathroom. Once inside, she closed the door and gently lifted the bulky sweatshirt over Carlie's head.

Delicately, Loretta peeled back the taped bandage, exposing the red and swollen flesh circling the distinctively eerie teeth impressions. "My God, what in the hell is going on? I don't understand any of this at all. It sure looks like a bite, but you said the attack was sexual in nature. This doesn't make a bit of sense. And the violence seems so out of place—so needless."

"In a way it makes perfect sense, Loretta. Think about it for a minute. These are not your normal family dynamics at work here. Andrew knows the truth about this family—its violent nature and its secrets. He is trying to let me know the only way he knows how."

"What do Becky Jacobson and her baby have to do with Andrew, other than that her little boy was loved and Andrew wasn't?"

"That's exactly what I thought at first. Then it hit me like a sack of bricks: Becky's son was a replacement for the third son Edith and Ian would never have. After the farmhand raped Edith, Ian wouldn't have anything to do with her again, romantically or sexually. She was nothing more than a housekeeper for him and the boys. I think Ian was forcing himself on Becky.

"I may be way off base here, but last night I think I was shown a much darker side to Ian and Becky's relationship."

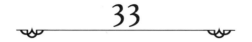

# 33

Jon was reading the journal Loretta had laid down when the two women returned to the room. Not privy to Loretta and Carlie's conversation and concerned about why they had left the room so quickly, he asked, "Is everything all right?"

Loretta didn't know exactly how to answer—but Carlie did. "Jon, personally I'm going to be just fine, maybe a little sore for a while. I might even have a few small scars, but I don't think that this mess we're involved in is ever going to be all right."

He continued. "Well, speaking of a mess, it seems the life and times of the McPherson family just took a turn for the worse."

The three boys and the old man had left the house well before dawn to start tilling the fields.

"It's after midnight now, and only Ian and Daniel have returned home. Patrick was tilling with Andrew on the double disc, and neither has returned.

"Ian and Daniel took off with kerosene lanterns and searched most of the night, but couldn't locate them in the dark.

"Daniel left again just after dawn to see if he could retrace the direction Patrick and Andrew were supposed to follow. He finally returned to the house just after noon. Edith was the first person to hear Daniel yelling as he galloped up to the house. She shooed Ian out the door to find out what was wrong. After almost two days, Edith was positive that something horrible had happened to one or both of the boys.

"Up to this point, Edith was taking quick notes as to what they were thinking and doing. She is writing a little more directly now.

She's sitting at the kitchen table waiting for Daniel and Ian to return with the other boys."

*Ian and Daniel have been gone for nearly three hours now. Becky is holding on to Noel so tight, I fear she will squeeze the life right out of the poor little guy. I'm trying to keep faith that Patrick will return to us alive and well. But the more time passes, the less I believe that will be the case. I am not sure how Becky or Ian will react to the worst happening to Patrick —especially if Andrew managed to survive. God help us all in that event.*

Loretta gave Carlie a pointed glance. Carlie could only shrug her shoulders; she understood the ramifications for Andrew and possibly Edith if the worst-case scenario should happen and Patrick didn't return alive.

"Edith sort of skips a lot of immediate detail here, but picks up with the explanation of what apparently happened to the boys.

"She goes on to say that it *seems* as though something must have spooked the horses. When one of the horses reared, it kicked Andrew in the face. A second kick caught him in the chest. Lastly, the horse and tiller ran over the top of him, nearly severing his right leg.

"Patrick fell backward into the blades when the horse reared. As the horse trampled Andrew, Patrick fell backward and got wedged between the blades, where he was twisted and turned against the sharp metal edges. That's how Daniel found him. Daniel didn't bother to look for Andrew until he returned with Ian.

"Edith doesn't mention Andrew anywhere in here again. I don't know for sure if the boy survived or not. Edith goes into pretty specific detail about the family grieving Patrick's death and his funeral, but there's nothing about Andrew at all."

The three sat in silence as they tried to absorb and make sense of all that they had just heard.

Jon stopped reading to point out what he considered to be an obvious contradiction. "You know, up to this point, Edith has been pretty mundane in her writings. They were not always complete and were usually devoid of facts and details. Each of her entries was the same until she started describing what happened to Patrick and Andrew during the accident. Admittedly, some of it was supposition; she claimed that it was. But that supposition quickly became fact. How would she know what was—and what was not—factual?

"I get the impression that the wrong son returned. Andrew was supposed to be the one who died that morning, not Patrick.

"Again, I'm just guessing here, but this accident seems like it was premeditated."

Carlie nodded her head in agreement; she also considered the incident as being something other than an accident.

Loretta needed a little more clarification. "So what you're saying here is, Edith was basically being spoon-fed the party line from Ian."

"I can't see it being any other way, Loretta. Edith had always been the weak link in Ian's mind, so when it went wrong, he needed to create an accident scenario that both she and Becky could accept—one that left none of the three men to blame."

Carlie was the first to notice the incredible drop in temperature in the living room. Pulling her sweater around her shoulders, she found herself retreating deeper into the corner of the couch.

Loretta started twitching and rubbing the end of her nose. Her eyelids were growing heavy from a buildup of frost on her lashes.

Because he was so wrapped up in his heated dissertation, Jon was the last to notice that the living room temperature had dropped to well below freezing. Looking over at Carlie and Loretta, he saw that they were visibly suffering. Carlie's teeth were chattering uncontrollably, and Loretta had a severe case of the shakes. Both women were showing the onset signs of hypothermia; their skin was white, and their lips were turning a pale blue.

Jon realized what was happening, but he didn't know why. Moving across the room, he pulled the curtains back. A heavy layer of frost completely covered the glass. He found the latch encased in a thick layer of ice, rendering it useless.

He tried the front door and found that the frozen handle wouldn't budge. Realizing they were trapped, he yanked his hand free from the handle, leaving pieces of skin attached to the frozen metal surface.

His breath came in quick billows of white haze. With each breath, the cold burned like fire deeper into his lungs. Carlie and Loretta were already starting to nod off; he needed to find a source of heat before they all froze to death.

Moving toward the kitchen, he wasn't surprised—but was only disappointed—when the door slammed shut in his face and sealed from the inside.

The room was as cold as a deep freeze. It was so cold, Jon could barely feel, let alone control, his extremities. On shaky legs, he hobbled to the stairwell closet. Turning the handle, he yanked on the door with all his strength. The door didn't budge. He tried it again, this time using his leg for leverage; he could feel a slight give in the frozen wood.

His mind was cloudy and numb from the intense cold, but he knew he had to keep trying.

The fireplace implements were on the hearth nearby. His only hope was to break a window or open a door, but his strength was beginning to wane. Grabbing the heavy iron coal shovel, he slammed the thin metal edge into the closet doorjamb and pried outward. The wood began to crack. He pushed once again and the door shattered, swinging out with such violent force that it threw him to the floor.

Lying on the floor not three feet away was a stack of heavy woolen blankets. Even closer were Jon and Carlie's winter coats hanging on the hooks just inside of what was left of the doorframe. Standing, Jon reached for the coats, but a heavy black shadow blocked his way. It was as if he were grabbing at air; he could see the coats, but his hand kept missing. Exhausted, Jon dropped to the floor. He needed to rest for just a few minutes, then he would try again—just a few minutes rest and he would be fine.

As Jon lay down on the hard wooden floor, the black shadow moved over the top of him. When it did, Jon's head snapped forward and then back hard against the surface of the polished oak floor. His back arched and his hands slapped the wood uncontrollably. Trying to move on his own was impossible—something was pinning him to the floor.

The voice sounded as if it were coming from the end of a tunnel. The intensity of the voice was as quiet as a whisper, but it reverberated inside Jon's skull like a sledgehammer against the porcelain walls of time and space: *"Leave what does not concern you alone."*

Opening his eyes, Jon's face was only inches from the face of Ian McPherson. He saw a loathing in the man's eyes that he had never seen before.

Once when he was very young, Jon had found a badger caught in a jaw trap. The look of terror and hatred reflected in that poor suffering animal's eye as it snapped and bit at everything—including itself—was one that Jon knew he would never forget as long as he lived. He had just seen the exact same look in Ian's eyes. The hatred that emanated from this man was so palpable, it was overpowering. Jon could not just see it and feel it, but he could actually smell it in the air. Ian's breath reeked of burning wood and decayed flesh.

Jon blinked once, and Ian was gone.

Standing, Jon reached inside the broken closet and retrieved the stack of woolen blankets. He didn't realize the room was no longer freezing—in fact, it wasn't even cold. Turning toward Carlie and Loretta, he found them standing in the middle of the room staring at him.

"Are you girls all right?" Jon asked.

Carlie moved her mouth around and shook her hands to get the blood flowing before she committed to an answer. "My lips are still a little numb and my fingertips tingle, but I'd say yes, I'm all right."

Loretta wanted to say something; Jon could see it in her eyes. "How about you, Loretta? Are you all right too?"

"My God, does this happen to you two all the time?"

"Well, not all the time, but a lot more often than we had planned on. Welcome to our world, Loretta."

"Carlie, you're a much braver soul than I am. Just the thought of a one-on-one encounter with Ian McPherson would be all it would take for me to put this place in my rearview mirror—forever."

Jon watched the two women climb the stairs to the bedroom. He and Carlie had more or less asked for whatever might happen simply by living in the house. But Loretta was a different story. She only wanted to help; she didn't deserve any of this.

The living room was so quiet that Jon could actually hear his heart beating. The temperature was exactly as it should have been. The thermostat on the wall showed that it was seventy-two degrees. No one would ever believe that less than fifteen minutes earlier, three perfectly healthy people had been moments away from freezing to death. The only thing out of place now was the broken closet door. In fact, it was the only tangible piece of evidence that anything had happened in the house at all.

~

Jon picked up the telephone receiver and tentatively placed it to his ear. He wasn't exactly sure what he expected to hear—quite possibly Ian's threatening voice. Fortunately, all he heard was the droning sound of the dial tone. Punching in a set of numbers, he waited again.

A voice on the other end answered on the third ring. "Jake's Farm Supply. Dick speaking."

"Hi, this is Jon Summers."

"Hey Jon, what can I do for you today?" said the friendly voice of the counterman at Jake's Farm Supply.

"I need a door."

"Exterior or interior?"

"Um, interior, a closet door."

"Do you need the casing or just the door?"

In hopes of not sounding as stupid as he felt, he told Dick to send out everything.

"Sure thing, Mister Summers. I'll have it on the first truck in the morning. Is there anything else I can get for you?"

"No, that should do it. Thank you."

"Sure thing, Mister Summers. Thank you."

Jon hung up and walked to the broken door. He picked up the shovel and hung it back in the utensil holder on the fireplace hearth. He couldn't believe that the door had broken completely in half. Inspecting the damage, he wondered just how cold it actually needed to be to freeze a solid wooden door. As he touched the shattered edge, he heard Carlie and Loretta's voices coming down the stairs.

When they reached the bottom step, Jon saw that the repercussions of this day were far from over. Carlie had that look in her eyes again, the look that told Jon she was only one more bizarre incident away from running off screaming into the night. She had had the same look in the bathroom when the letters had appeared on the mirror and in the kitchen when flying china had attacked them. Even Loretta was showing signs of distress. Although her voice was animated and coherent, her face was slack and her eyes glassy. Jon knew he needed to do something, but exactly what, he had no idea.

Once the three settled themselves at the table, Jon decided to broach the subject of where to spend the night, but he knew he needed to tread lightly after what they had just been through.

"Listen," Jon said, "I was thinking that maybe we should spend the night someplace else. The living room is kind of a mess, and I'm afraid staying here will be a little distracting."

Carlie thought about Jon's suggestion for at least a minute before she said anything. "Loretta and I discussed this when we were upstairs. She has agreed to spend the night here with us. I don't believe that anything else will happen tonight. They need to be shown that they don't have the power to drive us out of our home."

"I'm worried about you two. I'm not positive that spending tonight here is the best idea. I do understand your determination and I commend you in light of what just happened. I'd feel better if we all stayed together in the same room—a safety in numbers kind of thing."

"Hopefully it will be a quiet night," Loretta said.

"One thing is for sure," Carlie remarked. "We hit a nerve. I think Jon's assumptions were right on the money. Something happened that day—something that Ian intended to keep a secret, especially from Edith and Becky. He felt so strongly about it that he is still keeping it a secret.

"Maybe if we discover exactly what that secret is and get it out in the open, it will end the reign of terror he has waged on us. My God, it's been over a hundred years. What could possibly have happened that he is so scared someone might discover?"

Jon gave Carlie's question serious thought before he answered. "Quite possibly we have tunnel vision on a single event. Let's consider the possibility that Edith and Ian's life was like most people's, layered in many events. Let's look at their life like an onion. If we keep peeling back the layers, eventually we will get to the center, and I believe we're going to find something very disturbing."

Looking across the table, Jon could see that the old Carlie was returning. Her eyes were bright and inquisitive again. Even Loretta was beginning to show signs of life. Jon was getting excited again about the possibility of solving the mystery surrounding Grace's house until he flashed on the image of Ian's face and the hatred in his eyes. The thought reined in his enthusiasm as fast as a glass of ice water in the face.

"Listen," Jon said, "let's call it a night. We'll start again tomorrow."

Carlie and Loretta both fell asleep as soon as their heads hit the pillow. Jon decided that he was going to stay awake for safety's sake, but he quickly found that he couldn't keep his eyes open.

A rustling sound disturbed him. Opening his eyes in a sleepy haze, he saw three small children sitting on the steps watching him. As hard as he tried, he couldn't keep his eyes open, and in seconds, he was in a deep, dreamless sleep.

# 34

The early morning temperature was well below freezing, and the light coat Carlie was wearing was hardly warm enough to ward off the cold. Her feet were so numb that she kept losing her balance; she couldn't even tell if her fingers were still on the handholds of the tiller.

Her lips were beyond the point of functioning; she couldn't have formed the words to tell her brother to stop long enough for her to warm up if her life depended on it. Not that it would have done any good—Patrick couldn't have cared less if she fell off. He more than likely wished that she would. Patrick's lack of concern was Carlie's motivation to hang on at any cost.

In the distance, Carlie could see the stand of trees marking the western boundary of their farm. It was miles away from where they were supposed to be tilling. Carlie knew instinctively that Patrick was up to something, but only time would show her what.

She was shaking uncontrollably from the bitter cold, but the sun was beginning to come up and she prayed that it would warm up before she froze to death.

Stopping the horses at the edge of the tree line, Patrick turned to Carlie and told her to get off. She had no idea why, but before she could ask, he pointed to the ground ahead of them.

"We're going to be needing that rock. The ground is just too hard to cut without the extra weight."

The rock he was pointing at was huge; it had to weigh at least three hundred pounds.

Carlie stepped off the plow and walked over to it. Her first test of its weight found it frozen solid to the ground. She rather hoped that

Patrick would climb down and offer to help, but she knew that would never happen.

Squatting down, she grabbed the front edge and lifted with all her strength. It rocked backward and partially stood up, but she had no way of lifting it from that position. Dropping it, she looked to Patrick for help, but he was staring off into the stand of trees.

Wrapping her arms as far around the rock as they would go, she squatted down again and lifted with all her might. As the rock began to move, she adjusted her stance to compensate. As hard as she tried, she couldn't lift it past her knees.

"Maybe you might be needing some help with that," Patrick said.

When she looked up at him, he was smiling at her.

"You might ask your da—he's right over there. I'm sure he would be happy to help you."

Carlie had no idea what he was talking about and was scared to death to ask. She dropped the rock and followed his eyes. He was looking at something deep within the shadows.

"Go on, boy, he's right over there," Patrick said, pointing to where he was staring.

Carlie knew he wasn't going to let it go until she complied, so she started walking toward where he was pointing. Any minute she expected him to snap the reins and leave her stranded in the middle of nowhere—at least a day's walk from home. But he didn't. Instead, he waited patiently on the runner of the tiller.

Carlie could see something hanging from the branch of the oak, but she couldn't make it out. The deeper into the stand she went, the more the shadows played with the sunlight. She was practically on top of it before she realized that she was looking at a dead body. Some-one had killed this person and left the body hanging on the tree. The stench of death and decay was overwhelming; every breath left a ran-cid, greasy taste on the roof of her mouth.

She couldn't believe her eyes. It was a man—or what was left of him. His face was no longer recognizable; someone had crushed it, and the crows had done the rest.

His clothes appeared to have been ripped from his body, hanging in shreds and gently flapping in the early morning breeze, exposing a gaping wound and an empty hole where his stomach had been.

When she turned back to where she had left Patrick, something struck her hard in the chest, knocking her to the ground.

"We figured you would want to be with your old man when you died. He's been hanging around waiting for you for quite some time. I'm sure by now, though, he had almost given up on you."

Carlie knew in an instant why he had brought her out here. He was going to kill her.

"You're fucking nuts, Patrick," Carlie said as she tried to jump to her feet.

Falling directly underneath the body, she landed in something wet, slippery, and horrible-smelling. She couldn't manage to get her footing. As Patrick rushed at her, she pushed her hand through the soft and squishy intestines and rolled herself onto her side.

Finally, she was slightly away from Patrick and out of the abomination she had been lying in. Standing, Carlie ran toward the horses. She had gone only a few feet when Patrick grabbed her by the collar. She twisted to her left and broke free from his grip, but she knew she would never reach the horses before he got hold of her again.

Frantically she swung her arms out in hopes of connecting hard enough to stun him, giving her the edge she needed to escape. However, she connected with nothing but air. Her fear was now panic, and she was running toward the light harder and faster than she had ever run before in her life.

Clearing the last tree, she broke into the light to find Patrick standing in front of her holding the massive rock in his powerful arms. "Here, you little pissant, hold this," he said as he heaved the rock at her.

Carlie felt the force of the enormous rock against her chest. Balancing herself, she pushed against its tremendous weight and shifted to her right, falling to the ground and slightly away from where it landed.

Carlie knew she couldn't stand up and run; the rock had done serious damage to something inside her chest. She was seeing pinpricks of colored light in the oncoming black shroud that threatened to envelop her.

In a frantic attempt to get away, she tried desperately to ignore the pain as she crabwalked as fast as she could from where she had last seen the horses.

Exhausted and finding it impossible to breathe, she rolled onto her back and closed her eyes. She knew she was going to die; running would only speed up the process.

Panting, she could not take a full breath; the rock must have broken her breastbone, puncturing her lung. She had suffered broken ribs before, but this was different.

A few years earlier, a steer had kicked Ian in the chest. The broken rib punctured his lung. She remembered how painful it must have been when the doctor jammed a piece of broken glass tube between his ribs to reinflate the lung.

Carlie opened her eyes to the sound and feel of something pounding on the ground. She lifted her head, and what she saw almost stopped her heart: the horses were heading right for her. In seconds, the horses would trample her—just before the blades of the tiller cut her in half.

Covering her face, she held her breath, waiting for the pain and the quick death that the thousand-pound horse would bring.

Then, for no apparent reason, the world went silent. The next sound she heard was the whinny of the horses. Opening her eyes between her fingers, she saw the horses standing quietly in front of her and Patrick smiling down at her.

Patrick did something then that she never expected him to do: he grabbed the reins in one hand and held on to the front of the tiller with the other. With every ounce of strength in his body, he pulled on the reins until the horses were standing straight up on their back legs.

Carlie couldn't believe it; he was going to have the horses stomp and kick her to death.

In an instant, she was sitting and pushing herself backward in the dirt.

The horse's hoof came down on the edge of her right leg, snapping the bone and slicing through most of the flesh and muscle just below her knee. Doubling her effort, she ignored the incredible pain and pushed herself with her one good leg faster and farther away from the lethal hooves of the massive horses.

Patrick pulled the horses up again, yanking even harder on the reins. The horses screamed in pain and kicked out in protest, this time landing a glancing blow just above Carlie's left eyebrow and around the side of her head.

Pain seared through her head and down her back and arms. Every inch of her body hurt beyond comprehension. She knew she had to move, or die for real.

She had to do something, and she had to do it right now. She somehow rolled her stiff and damaged legs backward over her head and pushed up with her hands. Standing, she held herself up on her one good leg. She watched the horses as they began to rear up on their back legs again.

She had no idea what was wrong with her, but brain damage popped into her mind. Her right arm was so much heavier than the other. Looking down, she saw a rock the size of a cantaloupe in her hand. She barely had enough strength left to lift it; she wondered what good it could possibly do her.

The scream of the horses brought her back to the moment. Looking up, she saw the sun glint off the bridle of the horse directly in front of her. As the horse kicked out, she threw the rock with all her strength.

The rock missed the horse completely and hit Patrick below his right eye, opening a deep gash directly on his cheekbone. There was enough force combined with the element of surprise to knock him off balance. With both arms flailing, he dropped the reins and slipped off the rail onto the ground.

As the horses lurched forward, the sharp metal-edged blades caught him in the back of his legs, knocking him to his knees.

Raising her arms, Carlie began waving and screaming. The horses veered away from her, twisting Patrick deeper into the first set of blades. As Patrick screamed out in pain, the horses reared again and ran even faster.

Carlie stood and watched as the horses, the tiller, and the rumpled body of her half-brother wedged deep within the blades galloped away.

Dragging her damaged leg, she staggered back to the security and shade of the tree line. A debilitating wave of nausea suddenly overcame her. As she bent over, the world went black.

Opening her eyes, Carlie saw Jon sound asleep in the chair across from her. The front room was quiet except for the gentle breathing of Jon and Loretta. The grandfather clock showed that it was a few minutes past 9:00 PM. She had been asleep for less than an hour. Picking up three of Edith's journals, she quietly moved into the kitchen. She turned on the light and closed the door behind her.

# 35

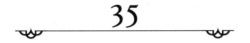

It was 4:00 AM when Carlie heard the door to the kitchen opening. Not knowing what to expect next, she held her breath and waited for the worst.

She was relieved to the point of being almost giddy when she heard Jon's voice asking her what she was doing up so early.

"Jesus, Jon, you scared me to death."

"I'm sorry—I didn't mean to. What are you doing?"

"I'm just reading."

"This couldn't wait until morning?"

"No, it really couldn't. Last night I relived Edith's story about the death of Patrick. I think Patrick finally succeeded in killing Andrew."

Jon finished loading the coffee maker and pressed the button for it to start. When Carlie didn't continue, he said, "Well, what happened to him?"

Over the next hour and two cups of coffee, Carlie recounted her nightmare of the dead body in the woods and Patrick and the horses trying to kill Andrew.

When Carlie was finished, Loretta, who had been listening from the doorway to the living room, gasped and said, "My good God, what the hell was wrong with those people?"

Walking into the kitchen, Loretta poured herself a cup of coffee and sat down at the kitchen table with Carlie and Jon.

Carlie took a moment and thumbed through the journal she had been reading when Jon interrupted her. "A lot happened over the next year. Becky and Noel moved back to her parents' house. Ian fell into a deep depression and became even more abusive toward Edith.

*Emily, Edith's younger sister. Ireland, circa 1848.*

He moved into Patrick and Becky's bedroom, completely away from Edith. The farm was going downhill pretty quickly. Considering Daniel was doing all the work alone, they barely planted enough crops to keep the cattle alive for the winter. Ian had taken to drinking and spent days at a time in town getting drunk.

"That was when Ian started beating Edith worse than he had before.

"Edith's sister Emily arrived in New York expecting to find Ian and Edith waiting for her. When they weren't there, she quickly found herself a job and an inexpensive place to live. After she settled in, she sent Edith a letter telling her how disappointed she was with her. Edith wrote her back telling her not to come, that living conditions with her and Ian had changed for the worse, and if they didn't get better soon, she would probably be joining her in New York.

"Andrew was still gone—and Edith never mentioned him. Then one day almost eight months after the accident, Andrew showed up at the door."

Opening the journal to where she had marked it, Carlie began reading.

*Andrew came home today. This is a day I have been dreading all year. I know Ian is going to go into a rage when he sees him again. The thought of him surviving and Patrick dying has driven Ian to the bottle and the brink of insanity.*

Carlie turned to the end of the journal. "Basically, all we skipped were the days Edith spent catching up with Andrew. Ian was on one of his binges and was gone when Andrew came back, so Andrew pitched in and started helping Daniel with the farm. He moved back into his room as if nothing had happened. He apparently never told Edith about the dead body in the stand or the truth about what Patrick had done to him. He let her believe what Ian had told her."

"This is where it gets interesting."

*Ian came back home today. He was still drunk and reeking of women's perfume. I haven't told him yet that Andrew is home. I will wait for him to sober up. If he is true to form, he will sleep it off for a couple days before waking up and demanding more money from our already depleted funds.*

*Ian finally woke up; he had been asleep for going on thirty-six hours. He got the shock of his life when he found Andrew sitting with Daniel and me at the dinner table.*

*I thought Ian was going to demand that Andrew leave, but he didn't. Instead, he told Andrew that he would honor his promise and allow him to remain on the farm until he reached the age of eighteen. But at that time, he would have to move on.*

*Andrew stood up to leave, but stopped and turned to Ian and told him that he accepted his terms, but if he ever laid another hand on him or his mother, he would kill him. Ian didn't say a word.*

"I find Ian not saying something after Andrew threatened him to be completely out of character for him," Carlie said. "I'm kind of proud of the boy for finally standing up for himself.

"Ian did do one thing that Edith found unusual. He sealed off Andrew's room from the inside of the house. Andrew now had to walk out of his room and around the house to the kitchen door.

"Andrew didn't seem to care at all; he was working hard on the farm and gaining his strength and size back pretty quickly. Daniel was impressed with how easy Andrew's being there made his life. Edith commented on the fact that they seemed to work very well together. She assumed there would be some animosity between them, but she never saw any outward sign that there was.

"Ian even started working again. She wasn't sure if it was to help save the farm or to keep an eye on Andrew. She didn't really care; she was just glad to see him doing anything other than getting drunk."

Picking up the third journal, Carlie started reading again.

*Today Andrew came to me and told me that one day soon, he would own the farm. He said that I'd be allowed to stay as long as I wished. I told him that Ian was determined to have him leave when he was eighteen—there wasn't any way Ian would share ownership of the property with anyone except Daniel, and then Patrick's son, Noel.*

*That was when he gave me a look that I had never seen before. He was furious; his face turned red, and there was clearly something menacing in his eyes. "You are a silly, naïve woman if you think for one second that Noel is that asshole Patrick's son. He's the spawn of that lying, cheating bastard of a husband of yours."*

*The hatred in his eyes never left, but he gave me a tight-lipped smile like he knew a secret that I didn't. "I never said I was going to share ownership with anyone. I said I was going to own the farm."*

*I quoted him exactly, just in case anything happens. I can honestly say that Andrew scares me. He is not the same sweet boy he was before the accident.*

Carlie looked up at Jon and Loretta, who were sitting quietly, enthralled by Edith's journal entries.

"That explains a lot," Carlie said. "I understand the attack now. I have to assume that Andrew had witnessed Ian's attack on Becky and relayed it to me the only way he knew how."

"It's like I said," Jon started. "This family's life is like an onion, only the more we peel it back, the more rotten the core gets."

Loretta looked up from her coffee and asked, "Do you think she believed Andrew's accusation about Ian and Becky?"

Carlie just shrugged her shoulders. "I'm not positive, but I believe that somewhere deep inside she did. Remember, she told her sister Emily not to come. She knew what Ian had planned for her."

"What did happen to Emily?" Loretta asked.

"Oh yeah…She married her boss. She was doing quite well for herself; she had a daughter and a wonderful husband. She eventually stopped answering Edith's letters."

Loretta took her cup to the sink and rinsed it out. Turning around, she stared at Edith's journal and shook her head. "I don't know what to say. Why don't you two come to the café? We'll have a little breakfast and forget about this for a while."

~

Stopping at the office, Carlie ran in and grabbed the brief Dexter had left on her desk. As she turned to leave, Dexter called out to her. "Hi, kiddo. You have a minute?"

"Crap! Dexter, you scared me to death. What are you doing here so early?"

"I'm just catching up on a little work. I was wondering if I could impose on you and Jon tonight for a little while."

"Of course. Why don't you come out for dinner?"

"You don't have to go to any trouble on my account."

"It's no problem at all, Dexter. We're going to eat anyway. Say seven?"

"Seven it is then."

With a quick wave over her shoulder, Carlie closed and locked the door to the office. On the short drive to the café, Carlie told Jon that they were going to have company for dinner and told him how vague Dexter had been about why he wanted to talk.

Jon was a little concerned; he prayed that Dexter didn't have plans to try to convince them to sell the house again. He wasn't sure that Carlie or Dexter could handle another run-in with Ian.

Carlie and Jon spent a relaxing morning with Loretta. She was in her element; it was like nothing had happened the day before.

After they were finished eating, Carlie thanked Loretta, gave her a big hug, and told her that she would see her the next day.

When Jon pulled into the turnaround, he found the barn door closed. He had to get out of the car to open it.

There was also a thin stream of smoke coming from behind the building, which was not that unusual; the farmer who owned the crops often burned weeds, sticks, and stocks after harvest.

Parking in the barn, Jon didn't see the box inside with the new closet door. Figuring he would come back out later and see if he could locate it, Jon followed Carlie inside the house.

Taking his and Carlie's coats, Jon went to the front room to hang them up. His mouth dropped when he saw that someone had already replaced the door. The new closet door matched the old one perfectly. It looked like nothing had ever happened.

Seeing that Carlie was busy in the kitchen, Jon slipped out the back door. As he rounded the backside of the barn, he saw Smitty leaning against the wall of the barn watching what was left of the old closet door turn from hot coals to ash in the burn pile.

Without even looking up, Smitty said, "Mister Summers, I was told that you've been looking for me. It's harvesting season and I've been very busy, but I figured I'd take a few minutes this morning to see if you needed my help. Jake's driver showed me the door you ordered, so I figured you needed some help installing it.

"Your front door was locked, but I found the kitchen door unlocked. I hope you don't mind, but I took the liberty and did the work. I cleaned up the old door, and that's it on the burn pile."

"Damn," Jon said, "I can't believe this. Are you just going to show up out of nowhere whenever I need your help?"

Smitty just laughed. "Mister Summers, I come by here all the time to take a look at the property. I can tell if you need my help." Looking up at the sky, he continued. "By the end of next month, we need to start preparing the old place for winter. We'll cut back the roses and some of the other plants that don't fare so well in the cold, then I'll get the storm doors and windows out, clean them up, and get them hung."

"Thanks, I appreciate that."

"It's not a problem, Mister Summers. You might as well go on back inside; this fire is almost to the point where I'm sure it won't spread even if the wind comes up. I'll be out of here in about ten minutes."

Jon nodded his head, turned around, and walked back to the house. As he walked into the kitchen, Carlie gave him a curious look.

"Just talking to Smitty."

Dinner was still a few minutes from being ready when the doorbell rang. Carlie looked at Jon and asked if he would get it while she finished setting the table.

Jon opened the door and invited Dexter to come in.

Dexter made polite conversation during dinner even though both Carlie and Jon could see that he was chomping at the bit to get to what he had come over to talk about.

Jon hoped to head him off before he broached the subject of selling the house. "You do realize, Dexter, that Carlie has no intention of selling the house."

"That's not why I'm here." Wiping his mouth with the cotton napkin Carlie had placed on his plate, Dexter pushed himself away from the table and stood up. "My sincere compliments to the chef. I haven't had anything this tasty since Doc Tremmel put me on an all baby food diet. The man is an absolute food nazi.

"Actually, I'm here to offer you a permanent position with the firm. How does senior partner sound to you?"

Carlie looked at him in disbelief. Before she could say anything, he raised his hands, stopping her.

"This is not premature or a spur-of-the-moment decision. I have given it a great deal of thought. I'm positive the decision I've made is the correct one. I'm planning to retire fully at the beginning of next year; I'd like to leave you in charge of the firm.

"Now, I have changed my will also. In the event of my untimely or timely demise—whichever may occur—I am leaving the law firm to you and Jon. It will be entirely up to you as to how you run it if you keep it, or you can sell it if you so choose."

Carlie was shocked into silence; she had no idea what to say.

"If you want to adjourn to the living room with me for a few minutes, I'll give you the paperwork to review. I'm not looking for an answer today or even tomorrow. You two read it over and let me know whenever you have made up your minds."

Dexter was sitting on the couch with his briefcase in his lap when Carlie and Jon entered the room. In his hand, he held a thick stack of papers with colored Post-it notes and yellow-arrow stickers scattered throughout. Closing his briefcase, he stood and handed the paperwork to Carlie.

"Take a look at it, and if you are in agreement, sign where your signature lines are marked. The last twenty-four pages are a copy of my will." Smiling, he looked at Jon. "The partnership is negotiable—the will isn't."

"I don't know what to say, Dexter," Carlie said.

"I don't expect you to say anything until you've reviewed all the paperwork."

Dexter walked to the door and opened it. Stopping, he turned and looked directly at Carlie. "Thank you again for dinner. You are an amazing cook. I almost forgot how good a cook you really are. I enjoyed it more than you will ever know."

Both Carlie and Jon stood in silence as Dexter walked to his car.

As the elderly lawyer drove away, they both waved goodbye. Long after Dexter's car was out of sight, they were still standing on the steps staring at the empty highway.

# 36

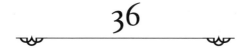

The clock on the nightstand quietly revolved from 11:59 to midnight when Jon's side of the bed compressed slightly. Turning over onto his side, he unconsciously slid his hand across the mattress to where he had felt the movement. His hand stopped against something soft yet surprisingly solid, bringing him fully awake. Opening his eyes, it took a few moments for his eyes to adjust to the darkness of the room.

The dark silhouette shifted slightly into the ambient light shining through the window, making recognition easier for him. Jon didn't have to see her face to know exactly who it was—it was Edith, or at least the woman he believed to be Edith McPherson.

It had been months since he had last seen her; he had almost forgotten how young and innocent she looked. Even after what he had read in her journals, his heart still went out to her. She was such a deeply troubled soul—he wished he could help her. But deep down inside, he knew that the traumas she had carried over from her life into death were at least in part of her own making.

He could hear Carlie breathing softly in the silent room. He knew she wouldn't wake up tonight.

Edith's mouth never moved, and her eyes never left his, but he could hear her voice as clearly as if she were speaking aloud. This was the first time he had actually heard her voice in its normal speaking range—no whispers and no false or echoed modulation, but just her sweet lilting voice wrapped in a heavy Irish brogue.

He could see, in the subtle changes in her body language, that she understood completely what he thought and when he thought it.

He was just about to ask her what she wanted when she reached out and touched his lips to silence him. He hadn't even realized he was about to speak aloud.

"Just listen," she said. "Not everything is as you understand it to be."

Jon merely thought a response. "I can only go by what I've seen with my own eyes and what you've written in your journals."

"Help us!!! You are the only one who can."

Again, the question entered his mind, "Whom are you referring to when say *us*?"

He had no sooner thought it than the room filled with fleeting shadows and brilliant blue lights; some were as large as softballs and others as small as pinpricks. He instinctively knew that each was a representation—actual or otherwise—of a soul trapped within the walls of Grace Baxter's home. There were hundreds of them—maybe more.

The sheer number of trapped souls was intimidating, but the thought that he was the only person who could set them free was mind-numbing. "I don't know what to do to help. I'm not even positive that I believe in you, at least not in the sense that you're requiring of me."

"You have let him into your life. You are the only one who can stop him. Shut him out. Allow him no access to your family or friends before it is too late for you and for all of us."

Carlie moaned softly as she stirred, rolled over, and laid her arm across Jon's waist. Carlie's movements broke his mental connection with Edith. When he looked back to where she had been, the room was empty. Only the fresh scent of wild honeysuckle lingered behind.

Jon lay staring at the ceiling. *How on earth am I expected to stop Ian?* he wondered.

# 37

Jon faintly remembered making a promise to Edith, but he wasn't completely sure if he had or not. As he racked his brain to remember, it suddenly came to him. *Holy crap. I'm the only one who can get rid of Ian.* Just the thought of Ian made him physically sick. The idea of confronting him on any level gave him a burning knot in the pit of his stomach.

Still wrapped up in the memory of his last encounter with Ian, he didn't even hear Carlie when she walked into the bedroom.

The mornings were turning decidedly cooler, and she wrapped herself in her heaviest robe. "Well, good morning. I thought you might sleep all day. Don't you have class this morning?"

"Yes, I do. My afternoon class, though, is a lecture by a superior court justice. I'll be home at lunchtime."

"I'm going to go into the office this morning. With a little luck, I'll be able to catch Dexter in. I want to talk to him about this partnership."

"Have you read his proposal yet?"

"It's all legal. It's a typical partnership agreement. I was surprised to find that he's offering a full and equitable partnership, not just a small percentage and voting rights. Two other partners hold ten-percent equity in the firm. Dexter has the eighty percent. He offered me half of his equity: forty percent. More surprising than that, he didn't require me to buy in. I've never heard of anyone doing that before."

"That's quite generous."

"It's too generous—that's what concerns me."

"Dexter including us in his will really bothers me. He doesn't know us from Adam, so why leave his practice to us?"

"That's what I'm hoping to find out this morning."

When Carlie pulled behind the Victorian house that served as their offices, she saw Dexter's Mercedes parked in the last parking space, directly in front of the employee entrance.

Using her key and the touchpad, she shut off the alarm but reentered the activation code once she was inside. The offices were deathly quiet.

Dexter's office door was open and his desk light was on. Carlie poked her head inside to see if he was sitting behind his massive mahogany desk. He was leaning back, eyes closed, with his hands behind his head.

"Good morning, Carlie," he said without even opening his eyes. "I've been expecting you. Come on in and have a seat."

Allowing his chair to rock back, Dexter folded his hands on the desk and stared at her. "I trust you, and that's enough for me. I hope it's enough for you."

"I have one question. Why now?"

"I'm not dying, at least not yet. I'm just retiring. I want to travel, see the world outside of this town. In order to do that, I will need an income commensurate with that lifestyle. I have no immediate family to leave the business to when I pass, and I can't see anyone else in this firm taking the reins. When I'm gone, this firm might as well go to the person who runs it."

"Well, is there anything else?"

"Nope, that pretty much covers it."

Opening his desk drawer, Dexter pulled out a large manila file folder and slid it across the desk to Carlie. "This is yours."

Across the front, Carlie saw the name "Baxter" in black marker.

With that, Carlie stood and excused herself. When she got to the door, she stopped and turned around. "I'll have the paperwork signed and returned to you in a day or two."

"Take your time. No rush."

Carlie walked to the parking lot with a lot more spring in her step than when she had walked in. She was now confident that this was the right choice. There wasn't a person on earth who could wipe the smile off her face.

Loretta was sitting at the table with Cecil when Carlie walked through the door. The smile on her face was still as big as when she had walked out of Dexter's office.

Smiling, Loretta said, "We both know that Dexter offered you a partnership. I assume that's what the ear-to-ear smile is all about."

Carlie looked at both of them in amazement. "How did you know? I just found out last night."

"Sweetie, not much goes on in this town without our knowing. Congratulations!"

"Thank you. I mean it."

After a celebratory breakfast of pancakes and eggs, Carlie left for home. Loretta planned to be there around 2:00, which left Carlie with almost four hours to read.

She felt invigorated, with a new sense of purpose. She was going to get to the bottom of this haunting—hopefully today.

Carlie had always found Jon's chair the most comfortable and the easiest place in the house to concentrate. After turning on the radio, she picked up a stack of Edith's journals and laid them beside Jon's chair. After brewing a pot of coffee, she returned to the living room, sat down, and picked up the first journal.

With a little stack of Post-it notes at hand, Carlie began to scan the pages, marking any entry that she found to be of significance.

Things were apparently going well. Maybe *well* is too strong a term, but things were definitely going better on the farm. Andrew had more or less taken charge. Every morning during breakfast, he would lay out the work schedule for Daniel and Ian. Originally, this didn't set very well with Ian, but Andrew showed incredible patience. He would sit quietly and wait for Ian to revise what he had proposed. Over the first week or so, Ian would change everything around out of spite, but they would always go back to Andrew's schedule sometime during the day. Ian would be mad, but he would finally concede that Andrew had been right. In time, he finally gave his seal of approval without question to Andrew's work schedules.

Over the next six months, with Andrew's help, they put the farm back in working order and finally had a cash crop ready for harvest. Ian's acceptance of Andrew's new role—and how easily Andrew performed it—amazed and impressed Edith. Andrew had turned into a first-rate manager.

Carlie had been reading for nearly three hours straight. Her eyes were beginning to dry out and burn. Laying the journal in her lap, Carlie folded her hands on top of it and closed her eyes. In a matter of minutes, she was sound asleep.

For the first time in her life, Carlie had a pair of work gloves of her very own. The bales of hay were heavy at the end of the rope, but the course hemp rope no longer caused oozing blisters and deep stinging burns in the palms of her hands.

Looking out over the hay load opening at the top of the barn, Carlie could see Daniel on the ground below, wrestling the bales off the wagon and onto the ground. Carlie was comfortable that she had distributed the workload evenly between her and Daniel, but you would never believe it by listening to him. He always made it sound as if he were stuck unloading the bales, carrying each heavy bale up the ladder, and restacking them all in the barn by himself, while Carlie simply watched.

Carlie had seen Ian discreetly watching them, silently hoping that Daniel's complaints had merit. Unfortunately, what he did see was Daniel stomp off, leaving Carlie to unload the rest of the wagon herself, carrying every bale into the barn and wrestling each one up the ladder into the loft.

Ian must have found Daniel and tore into him, because when Carlie was restacking the bales, Daniel's head appeared over the edge. Making sure Carlie wouldn't knock him off the ladder with a swinging bale of hay, he finished climbing up and grabbed a hay hook anchored into the beam above his head.

"Listen up, you," Daniel began. "I don't like you. I never have and I never will. I'll work next to you only because it's the right thing to do. Don't try to ingratiate yourself with Ian or me. Next year at this time,

*Baler with Daniel (at right), circa 1880s.*

you will be nothing more than a distant memory. This farm will never be yours, so you might want to quit that nonsensical talk before Ian shows you the bottom of his boot and the road out of town."

Carlie felt betrayed that her private conversation with Edith had become public; worse yet, she was being mocked and ridiculed over it. If Daniel knew, surely Ian knew too, and Carlie understood that he would never let her comments go without some kind of retaliation. All she could think was what a sniveling wimp Edith was. Carlie quickly rescinded her offer to allow Edith to stay on the farm. Edith could walk the pavement with her husband for all she cared.

Looking into Daniel's eyes, Carlie let out a deep guttural laugh. "Listen to me, you miserable asshole," she began. "I can't stand the sight of any of you. I don't need your or anyone's help to run this farm. So when the day comes I show you the bottom of *my* boot, don't say I didn't warn you."

Carlie was not a fighter, but she recognized the move when Daniel shifted all his weight to his left leg. He intended to swing at her.

Carlie, unfortunately, found herself backed up against the bales of hay.

The look in Daniel's eyes showed that he was completely aware of Carlie's awkward position. He smiled a Cheshire grin as he tightened his grip on the hay hook in his right hand.

The thought of Daniel skewering her with a hay hook had not occurred to Carlie. That was something Patrick would do. She had seriously underestimated the depths of Daniel's hatred.

Moving forward as fast as a snake strike, Daniel leveled the business end of the hook directly at the side of Carlie's head.

Carlie closed her eyes and countered Daniel's swing with the hook in her own right hand. She expected to feel excruciating pain—but she didn't. Her arm moved freely through the air until the hook buried itself to the hilt into something soft and pliable.

Opening her eyes, she saw the hook in Daniel's hand fly by her head and drop to the floor. It was less than three inches from her face when he released it.

Pulling her right arm back, Carlie was prepared to block Daniel's next attack, but her arm wouldn't budge. Instead, Daniel let out the scream of a wounded animal, a scream so loud it reverberated throughout the entire barn.

Daniel staggered backward. As he moved backward, Carlie pulled forward, causing Daniel to scream even louder. She was still completely unaware that she was the cause of Daniel's suffering.

Daniel reached down and grabbed hold of her hand. Pushing down, his bloody hand slid off, driving the hook deeper inside of him.

Holding Daniel at arm's length, Carlie stopped pulling to figure out why he was screaming and what was preventing her from retrieving her hook.

She looked down and saw her hand covered in blood. Daniel's dark blue-checkered shirt was now black down the entire left side—the same side where she had buried the hook up to the handle.

Daniel's eyes were starting to lose focus and he stopped screaming; his sounds were now more like wounded whimpers. He looked so pitiful standing in front of her, whimpering like a lost puppy.

The longer she stared at him, the madder she got. "How dare you, you miserable piece of shit. I expected this from Patrick or Ian, but never from you. You disgust me."

Taking one step forward, she loosened the biting grip the hook had between his ribs and unceremoniously yanked it out. In one swift move, Carlie kicked out, hitting Daniel in the center of the chest.

Daniel staggered backward along the edge of the loft.

Flailing his arms to catch his balance, he backed off the edge. There was a soft thud and then a moan. Carlie looked over the edge, expecting to find him lying on his back in the dirt. But he wasn't. He was sprawled over the top of the metal tines of the baler.

Climbing down the ladder, Carlie stopped to check on Daniel before she went to wash off her hands and the hay hook and go looking for help.

Daniel was breathing, but his breaths were shallow and he was making a gurgling sound. His eyes were alert again, and they followed Carlie as she walked around him, but he couldn't manage to speak.

Pumping the handle of the well that filled the horse trough, Carlie allowed the cool water to pour over her hand and arm, rinsing away every trace of Daniel's blood. She took the corner of her shirt out of her pants and dried off the hay hook. Walking to where Daniel was lying, she took his right hand and placed the hook inside it. She wrapped his fingers tight around the handle and patted the top of his hand.

"Someone should be out here before long to find you, at least by suppertime, so don't give up hope. I have a lot of work to do, so thank you for offering to finish stacking the hay. Sorry you fell off the edge of the loft. You should have been more careful."

Carlie's eyes never left those of Daniel's. She watched as he listened to her. The expression in his eyes changed from contempt, to recognition of his situation, to surrender.

Carlie's eyes snapped open; she was disoriented and breathing hard.

Someone was knocking loudly on the kitchen door.

Setting the journal on the chair, she walked slowly into the kitchen. Loretta was smiling and waving at her from outside the door. As Carlie unlocked it, Loretta burst in, all in a fluster. "Are you all right? I've been pounding on your door for almost half an hour. I was scared something had happened to you."

"I'm fine, Loretta. I just dozed off for a bit. I'm sorry."

"Don't be sorry. I'm just relieved to see that you're okay."

Jon walked in about an hour later, apologizing profusely for being so late. Someone had decided to have a staff meeting, and the dean of student services had cornered him.

When Jon walked in, Carlie and Loretta were already sitting at the table with a stack of journals in front of each of them. Carlie looked up at him and gave him a smile. "Well, I'm glad you made it, even if you are late."

"How did everything go with Dexter this morning?"

"Everything went fine. I'll tell you about it later."

Picking up a stack of journals from the floor, Carlie set them on the table, turned to Jon, and pointed at the books. "Sit down and get busy. We're looking for Edith's entry where Daniel got hurt."

"Is it important?"

"It's important."

Pulling out his chair, Jon sat down and opened the first book on his stack. "Anybody want to share why we're looking for this one incident?"

Over the next hour, Carlie related her dream.

Jon laid down his book and looked at her. "So you're telling me Andrew killed him?"

"I don't know what happened to him. I woke up before I found out. I will tell you this: Andrew couldn't have cared less if Daniel died or not. He did absolutely nothing to help him—in fact, he set it up to look like an accident and then just left him there."

"Damn," Jon said as he picked up his book and started scanning the pages again.

# 38

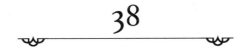

The trio had been reading for a couple hours before they happened on the first entry that mentioned Daniel having an accident. Loretta found it in her book, but they had to go back to one of Carlie's to find the beginning of the story.

"Here it is," Carlie said. "Edith starts off that she and Ian were sitting in the kitchen waiting for the boys to return from the field.

"Ian was the first to hear the wagon as it passed the house heading toward the barn. Putting on his jacket, Ian followed it. As it was nearly dark outside, he planned to put the horses up for the night and wait until morning to unload the wagon.

"Many minutes passed, Edith goes on to say, before Ian came rushing back into the house." Turning the page, Carlie began to read the journal entry.

*Ian was beside himself as he crashed through the door into the kitchen. He demanded that I make up the bed in his room with fresh, clean sheets. There had been an accident, and Daniel was hurt.*

*He saddled the mare, as she was the fastest of the horses. He was going to go into town to bring back the doctor as soon as we had Daniel settled into bed.*

*I grabbed his arm and demanded that he tell me what had happened and how badly the boy was hurt. Me poor heart almost stopped when he told me that Daniel might have broken his back—he couldn't move. But he was alive, and time was of the essence to make sure he remained that way.*

"It took all three of them to lift Daniel off the baler and onto a piece of barn siding. Edith ran back to the house and prepared the bedroom for Daniel while Andrew and Ian carried the boy from the barn.

"Ian left Edith and Andrew to make the boy comfortable while he went to town to bring back the doctor. This is the first time that Edith really examined Daniel."

*Daniel is so pale; his arms and legs are deathly cold. I fear that he has no blood circulating anymore. He does not appear to be in pain, which is both a good and a bad sign. At least if he had pain, I'd know that he still had feeling. At least he is not suffering.*

*Amongst the many cuts and bruises on him, I have discovered something quite out of the ordinary. He appears to have a pencil-size hole underneath a rib on his left side. There is also a great deal of bruising associated with it. Once Ian returns with the doctor, I will take my leave and inspect the baler. I don't remember seeing any part of the machine that would make such an unusual wound.*

"As close as I can gather from what she wrote, she didn't even ask what might have happened—or how it had happened."

Jon put his finger in his book to mark his place and turned to Carlie. "Edith is not always the sharpest knife in the drawer, but do you think she had some suspicions that Andrew might have been involved in Daniel's accident?"

"I'm not sure, but the wound on his side raised some questions in her mind."

Laying his book down on the table, Jon lowered his head and began to think about the conversation he had had with Edith's spirit the night before. "I don't think this is going to end very well."

Loretta looked up at Jon and asked him why.

"I saw Edith last night. She tried to warn me that all we see or understand is not as it appears."

Carlie smiled. "That's kind of cryptic."

"That's not the half of it. Evidently, I am the one who allowed Ian into our lives. I have to stop him before he destroys us."

Carlie was no longer smiling—neither was Loretta.

Carlie thought about what Jon had just said. "How the hell does she figure that all of this is your fault? You didn't invite that monster into our lives. If anyone did, it was me. I'm the one who started investigating this house, not you."

"Yeah, well, I don't know. She told me I had to stop him, turn him away. I'm not positive, but I think this next chapter in the perils of the McPhersons is just going to add more fuel to an already raging fire."

Opening her book, Carlie scanned the page and started reading again.

*It was well after midnight before Ian returned from town with the doctor. Nothing had changed during that time to give me any indication that Daniel was getting any better or worse. I am afraid to let him fall asleep—afraid that he won't wake up. There is a rattle deep in his chest that concerns me.*

*It took only a few minutes for the doctor to confirm my and Ian's worst fears: Daniel is paralyzed from the neck down. It is only a matter of time before his heart stops. The only thing we can do for him is to keep him as comfortable as humanly possible.*

*I have sat vigil over Daniel all night. On occasion, he opened his eyes and looked around the room. I know that he recognizes me; I believe it is good for him to know that I am by his side, but he seems to be looking for someone else. I assume that he is looking for his father. Ian has not been in Daniel's room since the doctor left. I am sure it is not because he does not care, but because he is helpless to do anything for him.*

*I heard Ian moving around alone in the living room last night. I believe that it was the first time I had ever heard the man cry. I wanted to comfort him, but I doubted that there would be anything I could say that would lessen the burden he is carrying.*

Carlie read a few more pages to herself before setting the book down on the table. Her eyes were burning from reading for so many hours. Excusing herself, she stood and went to the bathroom, leaving Loretta and Jon to absorb Edith's last entries.

Loretta was the first to speak. "This may have been the final straw, the one that drove Ian right over the edge."

"You may be right. First Patrick, then Noel, and now Daniel; Ian has lost everyone who mattered to him."

"What concerns me now is that he is left with only Edith and Andrew. How do you think he will react when this reality hits him?"

"God only knows."

After taking her seat, Carlie began to catch Jon and Loretta up on what she had read. "The next morning, Edith went out to the barn to examine the baler. She didn't find anything on the machine that could have caused the mysterious wound on Daniel's side. When she turned to leave, Andrew was standing beside her with his arms folded across his chest.

"He insisted on knowing what she was looking for, so she told him about the hole in Daniel's side that she couldn't explain. He pointed to the support beam above them, one of six that held up the loft. On each beam there were four large spikes. On the bottom spike hung a spare hay hook; the other three were empty and absolutely lethal-looking, sticking out at least eight inches from the massive wooden beam.

"Edith must have accepted this as being the only plausible cause for the damage to Daniel's side. I didn't find her mentioning Daniel's wound again."

Carlie took a sip of her coffee and began reading again.

*Yesterday we gave Daniel a proper burial next to his brother. Andrew helped Ian graveside and paid his respects to us both. I actually believe Ian was, in his own way, touched by Andrew's gesture.*

*Last night Ian returned to our marriage bed after all these many years. After we made love, we held each other and cried for our losses. The sun was just cresting the horizon when he finally told me what was on his mind. He had decided that this would be our last season on the farm. He couldn't do it anymore, especially without Daniel or Patrick to help him. The legacy he had worked all his life to hand down was over. It was time for us to return to Ireland.*

*I didn't know what to say. I just lay there as he explained how he would put the farm up for sale, hoping we could get at least part of our investment back so we would have enough money to give us a new start back home.*

Laying her journal on the floor, Carlie picked up a new one and placed it in front of her on the table. "This is the last of Edith's journals."

Jon looked up at her in disbelief. "Are you sure?"

"I'm positive. It stops close to the middle, and there is nothing but blank pages after that."

Loretta looked over at the book in front of Carlie. "Do you think the answers we're looking for will be in there?"

"Maybe some, but not all of them. I'm sure of it."

It had grown dark, and Loretta stood and stretched her aching muscles. "I better get going before Cecil sends out a search party for me. I'm in no mood to listen to him tonight."

Jon waved as Loretta's car made its way down the drive to the highway. Wrapping his arm around Carlie's waist, he pulled her close and walked her up the steps to the house.

As Jon pulled the door closed, he couldn't help but notice what looked like a dark silhouette watching them from the shadows of the barn.

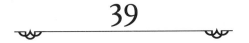

# 39

Jon could feel the presence of someone standing next to his bed long before he actually opened his eyes. When he did, he saw the same three children who had been watching him from the stairs a few weeks earlier. The one in the middle was a young girl. She appeared to be eight, maybe ten years old. She was wearing a white dress and had an enormous white bow in her hair. She was much too young to have a child of her own, but she was holding an infant in her arms.

Her face reflected a sense of desperation. Making herself known to him had to be a plea for help. The other two were young boys at least half her age. They appeared to be brothers, maybe even twins. They were dressed in dirty, ragged bib overalls. Dirt distorted their tiny young faces in the darkness.

As Jon sat up in bed, they became more translucent and distorted than they had appeared when he first awoke.

As the children began to fade, a taller, more solid presence took form directly behind them. Jon strained his eyes to make out the features of this new spirit. He was positive that it was not Edith; he had seen her enough to know her immediately.

This was an older woman, one he had never seen before. As she stood there before him, she wrapped her arms protectively around the children and gathered them closer.

As Jon lay there watching the small group, he was overcome by the scent of baking bread and cookies. These were the same odors that Carlie insisted she had smelled the first time they toured the house. Jon had never smelled them before, and he wasn't positive that he was actually smelling them now. If this was Carlie's aunt, it made sense that she would present herself to him with something comforting and familiar. Unfortunately, he had never met her or Carlie's Uncle William; there was no way he could be sure who was standing in front of him.

Minutes passed and the apparitions never wavered.

Jon was completely awestruck by the experience. He couldn't think of anything to say, even if he had wanted to. Their very presence spoke volumes. They were trapped here; it was exactly as Edith had told him.

A creaking sound started from the far end of the room, catching Jon's attention.

Once his eyes adjusted completely to the dark, he could see the bedroom door moving slightly. With the windows closed, there was no draft to move it, yet the door continued to rattle in its frame.

Looking up at the children and the old woman, Jon saw that the disturbance had drawn their attention as well.

The door shook more violently this time, and the handle began to rattle.

Looking over at Carlie, he couldn't believe that she was still asleep.

A moment later, the door exploded open. As the door slammed against the wall, the stench of death and decay was overpowering—nauseating; Jon gagged and retched.

A shadow rushed into the room, a shadow much darker and denser than the darkness of the room. It hovered silently, directly above the edge of Jon and Carlie's bed. The shadow began circling overhead, faster and faster; the wind it created whipped paper and small objects violently around the room. Knickknacks crashed against the walls, and Carlie's perfume bottles hit the floor, spilling their contents onto the rug.

Carlie was now sitting straight up in bed. She had a death grip on Jon's right arm; her fingernails bit deep into his soft flesh.

The small group of children protected by the old woman were staring at the apparition swirling in ever-increasing speed around the ceiling. As Jon and Carlie stared on in horror, the old woman began to scream. The sound was hollow at first, as if echoing from the far end of a tunnel. In seconds, it was deafening. Jon looked over and discovered that Carlie was the one screaming. He shifted his attention back to where Carlie was staring. He couldn't believe what he was seeing. The old woman was standing in flames to her waist. An instant later, the flames had completely engulfed her. As she struggled to escape, an invisible force held her in place.

As the old woman screamed in agony, Carlie and Jon watched helplessly. Her clothing quickly turned to smoldering clumps of sparks and ash dropping from her body and swirling into the air. The flames—now out of control—consumed her vulnerable and unprotected flesh. As she writhed and undulated under the control of the flames and their voracious need to feed, the skin on her face melted away, exposing white bone wrapped in pieces of blackened muscle and tissue.

The once comforting aroma of baking bread and cookies gave way to the sweet, pungent odor of burning flesh.

Jon's eyes watered and his lungs burned. Carlie was hanging over the side of the bed. As she tried to sit up, she inhaled another lungful of smoke, causing her to cough violently and throw up. Her eyes were watering and her nose was running in rivulets over the edge of her upper lip. She couldn't see a thing in the smoke-filled room.

In a last-ditch effort to survive, Jon pushed Carlie off the bed and onto the floor. Following closely behind her, he urged her forward to the door. When she couldn't do it on her own, he crawled over the top of her and dragged her by the arm through the doorway and into the hall. Slamming the bedroom door behind him, he lifted Carlie to her feet and half-carried her to the stairs, where they took two and three steps at a time until they reached the lower landing.

Racing out the front door, they both dropped to their hands and knees on the porch, gasping in mouthfuls of clean, fresh air. Hacking and coughing up lumps of phlegm dislodged by the smoke, they spit them out into slippery puddles between their hands.

Jon was the first on his feet. He moved to the yard and inspected the second floor of the house. Expecting to see flames and smoke pouring out their bedroom window, he was shocked to see that there weren't any. In fact, he couldn't see anything out of the ordinary.

Carlie, sitting on the bottom step with her head between her hands, was shaking violently; she was dressed only in her pajama top. Goose bumps covered both her arms and legs. Her teeth chattered as Jon lifted her to her feet. Wrapping his arm around her, he moved her back toward the house, where it would be warm.

Only after she was positive that there was no cloud of thick black smoke or flames devouring the ceiling above her head did Carlie cross the threshold into the living room.

Jon wrapped Carlie in a blanket and then ventured upstairs alone to their bedroom. Tentatively, he touched the door. It was cool to the touch. Then he placed his hand on the brass door handle. It was also cool. Turning the handle, he pushed the door open slowly. The floor was littered with paper and small objects, and the room reeked of perfume, but there were no flames or smoke, or even a telltale trace that there had been.

Jon knew that what he and Carlie had experienced was a warning. A warning of what, he had no idea, but it wasn't good—he was positive of that.

# 40

Carlie and Loretta were waiting on the front porch when Jon arrived home from work. After he parked his car outside the barn, Carlie's heart broke as she watched him walk toward her. Newly formed circles under his eyes gradually changed hue from a slight smudge of dark brown to smoky blue-black circles. With each tortured step, he resembled an inmate walking the last mile.

Jon hadn't slept at all the night before and Carlie knew it; however, these new signs of emotional stress were not due to a lack of sleep, but were in reality psychological. Everyone has a breaking point; she wondered if Jon had reached his.

Jon laid his briefcase down by the door and dropped his exhausted body into the confines of his overstuffed chair. Laying his head back against the soft leather, he closed his eyes and listened to the pleasant buzzing of Carlie and Loretta as they talked softly in the kitchen.

A gentle tug on his sleeve brought Jon straight up in the chair. Carlie stood next to him holding a plate and a glass of iced tea. She waited until he was fully awake before she handed them to him.

"This smells great. Thank you," he said.

Both women smiled at him. Loretta wanted to let him sleep, but Carlie figured that if he did, he wouldn't sleep that night.

After the three finished eating, Carlie asked Jon to tell Loretta about the night before. Jon was shocked; he had expected Carlie to have already filled Loretta in on their unearthly encounter.

Loretta looked over at Carlie, probably wondering why she had kept something so apparently significant from her. Turning back to Jon, she moved to the edge of her seat in anticipation.

Jon started from the beginning. Carlie had slept through much of what had happened the night before. Jon described the young girl and the two little boys, hoping that their descriptions might jog Loretta's memory; quite possibly, she might have known them or heard about them living in the house.

The look on Loretta's face told Jon that she had no idea who they might have been.

Over the next two hours, Jon relived every horrifying moment of their night. When he finally explained that, when it was over, there hadn't actually been a fire—that most of the experience had been a collective figment of their imagination or a memory planted in their conscious minds—Loretta responded.

"This house has been burned almost to the ground on at least four separate occasions. I believe that Ian McPherson caused the first fire. I remember my grandfather telling us stories of how Ian had set the house on fire in one of his drunken rages.

"Was this woman your aunt?"

Carlie remembered the woman vividly. It wasn't her Aunt Grace. As she thought about the woman's suffering, she couldn't help but wonder who she was.

"I don't know who the woman was last night, but she wasn't Aunt Grace."

Carlie's comment surprised Jon. "Are you positive? I was sure that she was. When I saw her, I'd have sworn it was your aunt."

"At first I thought it was too, but when I really saw her face, I knew it wasn't.

"I really only remember seeing Aunt Grace's spirit one time. I was in the bathroom. I had hurt myself somehow, and I remember her appearing behind me—she touched my shoulder. I saw her face as clear as I see yours right now."

Loretta sat on the edge of her chair listening to Jon and Carlie's conversation. "It makes you wonder how many ghosts are actually in this house."

Jon had a pretty good idea. "I wonder why they're here. What is holding them to this house?"

Carlie and Loretta spoke in unison. "Or who?"

"All right," Jon said, "I'll bite. Who?"

Carlie stood and excused herself. She was gone for a few moments and returned with Edith's journal.

"I read some of this the other night. Edith talks about how determined Ian was to return to Ireland. He and Andrew worked almost twenty-four hours a day to get the crops in before the first snow."

Opening the book, Carlie turned a few pages and read to herself. Turning a few more pages, she stopped and began to read aloud.

*I fear that Ian will not see his wish to return to Ireland come true. I am afraid that we are destined to remain right where we are. Ian is too proud a man to ever admit that he failed.*

Carlie thought about what she had just read before she spoke. "I figured that Ian's quest was over once Edith couldn't figure out a way to come up with enough money to make the move. However, old Ian had a different idea. She goes on to tell how he scheduled an auction of everything they owned for the following spring."

Loretta looked up at Carlie and asked the question that had just run through Jon's mind. "What about Andrew?"

"Well, if nothing else, Ian was a man of his word." Turning a few pages, she began reading again.

*Today is Andrew's eighteenth birthday. Ian waited until after supper before he asked Andrew to accompany him into the living room. I was hoping that Ian had recognized how hard Andrew had worked and that he had proven his worth. But Ian told him that he had until the end of the day to have his belongings off the property.*

*Andrew came to me and asked if I would speak to Ian for him. I felt obligated to tell the boy that it wouldn't do any good; Ian had arranged to auction off the farm in just a few weeks.*

*He didn't say a word. He simply left the room, emptied out his few belongings, and disappeared.*

Carlie stopped reading and laid the book down on the coffee table. Jon waited for her to continue. When she didn't, he finally asked, "Well, what happened?"

Carlie looked at him and hesitated for a few seconds before she answered. "I think he killed them!"

"*What?*"

"I think Andrew killed them."

Carlie picked up the journal again and turned to the middle of the book. "Edith said here that it had been almost a week since Andrew had left. She had seen him by the barn and the tack room, but he hadn't come to the house."

*My heart is breaking. I saw Andrew today; I don't think he saw me, though. I'm positive he was responsible for the deaths of Daniel and Patrick, but in hindsight, I can hardly blame him. I allowed Ian and the boys to torment him. I even allowed them to torture and hurt him. All Andrew ever wanted was to belong to the family, to be a part of our lives. I am as responsible as anyone for preventing that from happening.*

*Tonight I am going to ask Ian if there is something we might do for the boy. I don't feel right just throwing him out to the world as we did.*

*Ian promised to find the boy and see if there is anything we could do to make his transition easier.*

Carlie closed the book and laid it on the table. "That was her last entry."

## 41

It was early evening when Jon and Carlie walked Loretta to her car. The sky had turned overcast during the day, and the change in the weather had brought a bitter chill to the air. After Loretta's tail lights disappeared onto the main highway, Jon slipped on his pair of gloves and walked to the back of the house. To his astonishment, the woodpile was at least twice as high as it had been after Smitty cut and stacked the refuse from the storm.

Jon carried in enough wood for at least a couple nights. The weather reports predicted that the temperatures would drop into the lower teens.

After Jon built a fire in the fireplace, he sat down in his chair and began reading the last entries in Edith's journal.

Jon looked at Carlie. "It makes me very uncomfortable the way Edith's journal just ended. Have you checked the rest of the journals? Could there be another one?"

"Loretta and I double-checked. Edith didn't write another word."

"Do you think Loretta's grandfather was right? Could Ian have gone on a drinking binge and burned the house down?"

"I don't think so. They were weeks away from going home to Ireland. Ian hadn't had a drink in months. Whatever happened to them had something to do with Andrew."

"You're probably right. Andrew had every right to be pissed. But murder? I don't know."

Jon followed Carlie up the stairs to the bedroom. It still carried the heavy aroma of Carlie's perfume. They had aired out the room and used carpet shampoo, but eventually Jon was going to need to replace the carpeting. Jon cracked the window an inch or so, just enough to allow fresh air in the room to help dispel the oppressiveness of the perfume.

Carlie was sitting at the vanity brushing her hair when she noticed a slight movement in the mirror over her right shoulder. In the dimly lit room, it appeared to be no more than a flash of blue light, much like that of a flashbulb.

Setting down her brush, she waited and watched. In less than a minute, the light flashed again, but it took longer to dissipate this time. She wasn't sure, but it actually appeared to be a small woman or a child. Before she could figure it out, the blue light faded and disappeared.

"Jon, did you see that?"

"See what?"

Carlie was sure that if Jon had seen the light, he would have known what she was referring to.

"Nothing. It was probably just the light playing tricks."

~

Carlie rolled over and stared up at the stars in the sky. She had slept longer than she had planned; the fire had already burned down to glowing embers. Rolling up her blanket, she packed it away with the rest of her gear and hid it all in a hollowed-out spot under a fallen log.

Burying what was left of her fire, she took a few minutes to erase any trace of her presence. Taking one last look around to see if she might have missed anything, she was satisfied that she hadn't. She had a long day ahead of her. In one of her jacket pockets she had a small handful of dried meat, and in the other, an assortment of dried nuts and berries. She had to be careful though; she had to have enough left at the end of the day to provide her with the strength to do what she needed to do.

Setting off at an easy jogging pace, Carlie ran across the grain of the land. It was a more difficult run, requiring her to abandon the valley and run through the hills, but it kept her out of the line of sight of anyone who might be looking for her.

Midday, she stopped at an outcropping of rocks at the top of a hill. She had been running for over six hours and needed a break. Taking out the meat, she carefully divided it into two piles; one she ate, and the other she put back in her pocket. She then did the same with the nuts and berries. She didn't have any water, but there was a stream a little less than a mile away. She would wait there for the sun to set.

Climbing to the top of the rock, she could see the sun's rays reflecting off the top of the barn. She still had three to four hours left if she could keep up the same pace.

She needed to talk to Ian one last time. She had to convince him not to sell all of the property. Over the years, she had managed to save every cent she could lay her hands on. She had accumulated a fair amount—almost three hundred dollars. She was willing to give him all of it for the stand. There were plenty of trees to cut; she could build a cabin of her own.

As Carlie walked around the edge of the barn, she saw that there were lights burning in the kitchen. She watched as two shadows moved from one side of the room to the other. She didn't want to involve Edith in their conversation, so she stepped inside the tack room, where she could keep an eye on both the kitchen and their bedroom at the same time. Soon, Edith would go to bed; if Ian were true to form, he would come outside so he could sneak a cigarette while checking on the animals.

Carlie tapped her pocket for the hundredth time that day. Her money was still safe—wrapped inside a handkerchief.

She didn't have to wait very long. She had just gotten comfortable on a pile of horse blankets when she heard the screen door squeak and then slam shut. Ian slipped his arms into his jacket and pulled it tight against his massive shoulders. She saw the flash of the match in his cupped hands and the red glow from the tip of the cigarette as he pulled in his first lungful of smoke.

Carlie took a deep breath and stood up. At the doorway, she hesitated, almost changing her mind, when Ian spoke. "You might as well come on out here, boy. I know you're hiding in the shadows; I can feel your eyes on me."

Carlie pulled herself up straight, stuck her hands in the pockets of her jacket, and stepped out of the tack room into the moonlight. "Ian, I have a proposition for you."

"You do, do you?"

"Yes, sir. I do."

"I'm listening."

"I came here in hopes of talking you out of selling the farm." Before Ian could respond, Carlie held up her hand and continued. "But I've thought better of it. For you to keep the farm and allow me to work it would force me to be near you and your wife. The very thought of that repulses me. So I've come up with a better idea.

"You allow me to purchase the stand of trees at the western edge of the property and a small piece of land surrounding it."

Ian took a long drag from his cigarette and flicked it into the dirt. "Two questions. First, why the stand? Second, where in the hell would you get enough money to buy anything?"

"It seems to me that the stand would be a perfect place to live. There's plenty of wood and fresh water, and the land is rich and good for growing crops. It's also a great place to keep secrets buried.

"As far as the money goes, that's none of your business. If we come to an agreement, I will go with you to the bank and give you the money for the deed."

"Edith asked me to find you and see if there was something we could do to help you. At first I thought it was a horrible idea, but it matters to her.

"Come, boy, let's talk about it."

Carlie walked out of the shadows and up to Ian. Ian reached into his jacket pocket and pulled out two more cigarettes. He turned and offered one to Carlie, who just shook her head. Taking out another match, he lit the cigarette and inhaled. He tipped his head and exhaled a plume of white smoke into the night sky.

Putting his hand on Carlie's shoulder, he guided her toward the fields.

As they walked, Ian told Carlie of his and Edith's plans to go home to Ireland. It just seemed like the right thing to do now that both Patrick and Daniel were dead and Noel was no longer part of their lives.

Carlie had never shared a conversation this long or this personal with Ian before in her life. She had no idea how to respond, so she just quietly walked alongside of him, listening.

They had walked almost a mile when Ian stopped and lit another cigarette. "As I said, boy, I promised your mum that I'd do what I could to help make your transition as easy as possible." Reaching underneath his jacket, Ian pulled out a small caliber revolver.

Seeing what he had in his hand, Carlie stumbled backward away from it.

"You want the stand? Then you shall have the stand. It is, after all, a great place to keep secrets buried."

Fire leapt from the end of the barrel, and before she even heard the gun fire, Carlie found herself sitting on the ground. She touched her side—her shirt and jacket were wet to the touch.

Then fire erupted from the end of the barrel again. This time the bullet knocked her flat on her back; it felt as if someone had hit her in the chest with a board.

Ian walked up to where Carlie was lying; he bent over and patted her pockets. Finding the bulge in her left pocket, he reached in and pulled out her handkerchief. Tossing it into the air, he listened as it made a satisfying jingle when it landed in his hand.

Slipping Carlie's money into his jacket pocket, Ian walked away, whistling as he stuck the gun back into his waistband.

Carlie lay in the dirt staring at the stars in the night sky. She knew she was dying. She closed her eyes, and a single tear rolled over her cheek and into her ear.

The sun had passed overhead before Carlie opened her eyes again. The bright sun was still warm, but the late afternoon air was growing decidedly cooler. She gingerly touched her side. Her entire shirt and jacket were stiff with dried blood. Reaching her hand underneath her shirt, she could feel the hole where the bullet had entered her side. It was still oozing.

Rolling onto her side, she checked her back as far as she could reach. There was a gaping exit wound where the bullet had passed through her. She had been lying in a pool of her own blood the entire night and most of the day. Her muscles ached as if she had been in a fistfight, but there didn't seem to be any real pain from the bullet wound itself.

Checking her chest, she found the hole where the bullet had entered. She was reasonably sure that it hadn't passed all the way through. Somewhere inside of her was one of Ian's bullets. It must have done some serious damage; when she coughed up a mouthful of phlegm, she spit it into the dirt and discovered that it was stringy with black ribbons mingled with bright red blood.

She tried to stand, but wobbled and dropped to her knees. The jolt from the landing sent lightning bolts of pain through her side and back, nearly causing her to pass out.

She needed to move. Ian would be back for her body, maybe not today but surely by tomorrow.

Walking on all fours was a slow, uncomfortable process. It was better than trying to walk and then falling down, and it was decidedly better than crawling on her belly, grinding rocks, sticks, and dirt into her open wounds.

It was after midnight by the time Carlie made it back inside the barn. She was dehydrated and exhausted, and every inch of her body was racked with pain. Crawling across the manure-laden floor, she stopped when she reached the water pump and pulled herself to her feet.

Pumping the handle slowly to prevent any unwanted sound, she shook under the strain and nearly succumbed to her lightheadedness. She had lost so much blood; her slightest movement caused her head to rush and her knees to buckle underneath her. She braced her weight against the side of the wooden water trough to prevent herself from falling. Cupping her hands, she sucked down mouthful after mouthful of cool, clean water.

Hanging on the wall overhead, she found a feeder bag with a handful of sweet oats. Pulling it down, she sat on the hard dirt floor under the water trough and began to eat. She had finished almost the entire bag before she felt at least a small part of her strength returning. She drank a few more handfuls of water, then sat back down, leaned against the wall, and closed her eyes.

She had been sleeping for almost an hour when the slamming of the screen door brought her fully awake and ready to run. She couldn't run far or very fast, but she knew hiding places inside the barn that Ian would never find.

When Ian went back inside a few moments later, Carlie wondered what was going on. Had he already been out to the cornfield and not found her body where he thought he had left it? That could explain why he was still awake. Or perhaps he was just anticipating what he would have to do before the sun came up.

Watching the house through a knothole in a barn slat, Carlie followed Ian's movements by the light of his lantern as he made his way up the stairs to the second floor to his and Edith's bedroom.

Carlie made her own way in the dark through the barn to the tack room. It was a torturous trip in her condition. There were so many heavy, sharp implements hanging on the walls and ceiling; one false move and she would set off an alarm that Ian would be able to hear in the next county. She was feeling somewhat better, but she was still a long way from being steady on her feet.

In the far corner, she found Ian's ax. No matter how hard she tried, though, she couldn't lift it over her head. More throwing it than lifting, she tried to get it over her right shoulder. After three attempts, she was able to lift it high enough, except something inside her tore open, racking her body with agonizing pain. Dropping the heavy implement on the floor, Carlie fell to her knees and threw up. She was running out of time; the puddle between her hands was black as pitch. She was slowly bleeding to death.

Crawling to the corner, she ran her hands over the tools lying on the floor. She needed to find something she was capable of handling. She ran her hand along the side of a piece of curved wood lying half-hidden under a blanket. She could feel its sanded and lacquered surface against her fingertips. It had to be at least four and a half feet long and three inches in diameter at its widest point. It was the brand-new handle for Ian's old, worn ax. It had been hand-carved from a solid piece of hickory. If she hit someone with it—even in her weakened state—it would be like being hit with a steel bar. Lifting it with one hand, Carlie found that she could maneuver it with very little effort.

Lifting the handle over her head with both hands, she slammed it down on a bale of hay. The impact was resoundingly solid and perfectly balanced; there was no reverberation through the wood at all. After catching her breath from the exertion of swinging the wooden handle, Carlie picked up a pair of nail pliers and walked to the house, dragging the ax handle behind her.

Ian had locked the screen door to the back porch, just as Carlie had expected. In her entire life, she couldn't think of a single time when Ian had locked the back porch—or the back door, for that matter. It meant that Ian was worried about something. It made Carlie smile when she pictured Ian lying in bed staring at the ceiling and reacting to every little sound.

Taking out her penknife, she slid it between the door and the frame and quietly lifted the hasp. When the hook was out, she pulled the door open. Once inside, she let the door come to rest without a sound. Pulling out the nail pliers, she crimped the hook, locking the door permanently. She pulled off her boots and set them next to Ian's in front of the steps.

Turning the door handle, she found it locked.

During one of Ian's temper tantrums, he had smashed one of the windowpanes in the back door. Carlie had seen him replacing the glass and was positive that the sealer would still be pliable enough to re-move the glass without breaking it.

Sliding her penknife between the glass and the sealer, she cut out a ribbon completely around the window, allowing the glass to fall forward into her hand.

Reaching inside, she unlocked and unchained the door.

Carlie was surprised to find Ian and Edith's bedroom door standing wide open. She stood silently in the hallway and listened to the couple breathing. They were both sound asleep.

Inside the room, Carlie waited for her eyes to adjust to the darkness. She could see Edith in front of her, asleep on the right side of the bed, and Ian's massive bulk on the left. Once she could discern where Ian's head was, she reached out with the ax handle and touched his leg.

Ian moaned slightly and swiped at empty air.

Reaching out again, Carlie brought the ax handle down on Ian's elbow, bringing him straight up in bed. Before Ian even realized what was happening, Carlie swung the ax handle like a baseball bat, connecting the blow squarely across the bridge of his nose.

Ian let out a howl like a wounded animal as blood sprayed in a geyser across the bed.

Carlie readied the handle once again and waited. Ian's face, distorted from surprise, pain, and swelling, met Carlie's eyes.

Edith sat up in bed. When she saw the broken and bloody boy standing at the foot of her bed, she unleashed an earsplitting scream Carlie never imagined a human could make.

Taking her attention off Ian for even a second nearly proved to be fatal. Spinning around in bed, Ian threw off the covers, exposing the gun in his right hand, which he was already moving in the direction of Carlie's face.

Carlie swung the ax handle again, this time with every ounce of energy left in her body. The barrel of the gun flashed an instant after Carlie connected the handle with the side of Ian's head. The bullet whined past her left ear and buried itself in the bedroom wall.

Ian slumped forward; a massive gash opened up across the side of his face and left temple. Before he could recover, Carlie lifted the handle one more time and brought it straight down on the top of his head. Ian didn't make another sound; his arms jerked out to his sides, and he fell backward onto the bed.

Carlie stood dispassionately and watched as Ian's body convulsed in its death throes.

Edith was still screaming, but her voice had lost most of its shrillness.

Walking to the nightstand on Ian's side of the bed, Carlie picked up the lantern. She shook it and found it completely full. Back at the foot of the bed, she stared at Edith, who was now silently staring back at her. Carlie searched her soul to find even the slightest bit of compassion for the woman who had brought her into the world. She was shocked to see how Edith had aged. Her once dark red hair was now completely gray. Worry lines etched deep valleys in her smooth, almost childlike face. Carlie wondered how she could have missed noticing what life with Ian had cost this poor woman.

Carlie looked at Edith in hopes of finding redemption in the woman's eyes. When she couldn't, Carlie said to her, "I told you that this was my farm and my home. I offered you the chance to stay here as long as you wanted. Now I insist that you and your husband remain here with me. I will show you how to create the family you couldn't manage on your own."

Carlie lifted the lantern and threw it against the wall beside Edith's head, spraying kerosene over Edith and the prone body of Ian. Taking out the box of matches she had found in Ian's jacket pocket, she struck one and threw it on the bed.

The blue and yellow flame crept slowly across the bedspread like a wind-driven ripple on its way to shore.

Edith could only watch in horror.

Carlie was watching Edith so intently that she didn't notice the flames as they moved in waves across the floor and up the walls.

Edith's screaming brought Carlie back to the moment. Carlie noticed that the flames weren't hot at all—in fact, they actually felt ice cold. She was shaking uncontrollably, but it didn't really matter anymore.

Carlie watched as the flames completely consumed the woman that was her mother. Edith's body went rigid for a few moments and then began to writhe spasmodically across the bed as the flames stripped the flesh from her bones. Her screaming had long since stopped; a sound similar to bacon sizzling had replaced it.

Carlie knew she had only a few moments left; a searing pain so unbelievably excruciating it was beyond comprehension had replaced the cold.

Carlie held her breath, closed her eyes, and waited.

~

The brilliance of the sun in the crystal-blue morning sky nearly blinded Carlie when she opened her eyes. Standing in the front yard, she took a long, satisfying look at her home. She vaguely remembered something about a fire, but there was no trace of it now, and the memory was rapidly fading. This was her home—her farm—and it was perfect.

Closing her eyes, she let the warmth of the sun radiate on her face and the gentle morning breeze play in her hair. When she opened her eyes again, she was standing in the kitchen.

Carlie sat straight up in bed. It took almost a minute before she realized that she was herself again, in her own bed and her own room.

# 42

Jon was in the shower when Carlie sat up. The clock on the nightstand showed that it was already 8:30 AM. She had planned to be in the office early that morning, but she needed to talk to Jon first; she needed to tell him what had happened to Ian and Edith. As much as she understood the reasons why Andrew did what he did, she still couldn't bring herself to believe that the boy had intentionally killed them both.

But he had.

Andrew had killed them all.

Carlie was lost in her thoughts when Jon walked into the bedroom.

"Well good morning, sleepyhead."

Carlie looked up at Jon and blinked in confusion; it was almost as if she didn't recognize him.

"Carlie, are you all right?"

"I don't know. . . . I think so."

Jon had seen the aftermath of her nightmares too many times before, and he was positive that this was what he was seeing now.

"Another nightmare?"

"Oh yeah!"

Carlie began her story on the day of Andrew's eighteenth birthday. Over the next couple hours, she described the events leading up to and including the horrible deaths of Ian, Edith, and Andrew.

Jon thought about what Carlie had told him before he started speaking. "Damn, that seems to explain why Ian and Edith are bound to this house. It makes me wonder why Andrew isn't haunting it too."

"Oh, he is, Jon. After Ian shot him, Andrew was going to die no matter what happened to Ian and Edith. It was just sheer willpower that kept him alive long enough to exact revenge on them—a revenge that didn't end with the death of the three of them.

"The last thing I remember was waking up in the front yard. I had closed my eyes in the bedroom, and a moment later, I was standing in the yard. I was alive again.

"I could feel the sun on my face—I even felt the morning breeze in my hair—and I didn't hurt. I think that is what really struck me the most. I can't tell you the last time I hadn't—Andrew hadn't hurt. I saw the house without any fire damage. The house and the farm were now *my* home—I earned it."

The look on Jon's face told Carlie that he didn't completely understand, not just about how she believed that Andrew was still alive, but also why Andrew had insisted that Ian and Edith become a part of his new reality.

"It's all very complicated, Jon. Don't believe for an instant that I have the answers, because I don't. But I think—and this is just me thinking out loud—that Andrew didn't really want Ian and Edith to be his family, but instead he wanted them to watch him create family after family. Only this time, these families would accept him as their equal and treat him with respect."

Carlie's assumption surprised Jon at how much sense it made. "That actually makes sense, and it would explain a lot, especially Edith's begging for our help to be released. What it doesn't explain is the *us*—or the how.

"Now, Carlie, this is just me thinking out loud too, but what I'm thinking isn't good. What if, after all these years, Andrew hasn't been able to find a family that would care about him, make him part of their life, and treat him with the respect that he feels he deserves?"

Carlie had no answer for that. As farfetched as both her and Jon's theories might have sounded, she could visualize the possible consequences—and those consequences scared the hell out of her.

Book Three

# NOWHERE TO RUN

# 43

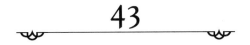

Jon had serious reservations when Carlie first suggested they have a Christmas party in Aunt Grace's house. However, these *were* Dexter's last few weeks before he left for Europe, and this would give all his friends one final opportunity to say goodbye and wish him well.

Jon remembered seeing a dozen large boxes in the attic when they first moved in some eight months earlier; some of them were marked "Christmas decorations." Armed with the brightest flashlight he could find, he pulled down and climbed the ladder in the bedroom closet. Once in the attic, he gingerly catwalked across the floor to the far corner. The boxes were exactly where he thought he had seen them.

When Jon finished wrestling them down the ladder, he returned to the corner of the attic. Opening each remaining box, he found an assortment of antique children's toys, old cast-iron pots and pans, and a couple boxes packed with vintage clothing.

Sliding these boxes out of the way, he found three smaller boxes tucked into the corner out of the way of prying eyes. These smaller boxes were not marked.

The first box was packed neatly with two hand-crocheted blankets. Running his hand in between and underneath the folds of the delicate thread, he touched something metallic—it was a small handgun.

Moving the box to the side, Jon opened the next one. This box was full of journals—there had to be at least twenty. They were more contemporary than Edith's.

Lifting the heavy box of journals out of the way, Jon opened the last of the small boxes. Inside Jon found a set of work clothes. Pulling out each piece, he found the shirt and jacket to be stiff and encrusted with something dark and foul-smelling. The pants were an old-fashioned pair of blue denim jeans. Sticking out of the left front pocket of the filthy pants was the corner of a red handkerchief. With the tips of two fingers, he pulled it out and held it at arm's length. The handkerchief was very heavy and knotted an inch below Jon's fingers. Giving it a quick shake, Jon could hear the sound of silver dollars as they rattled in their cloth confines.

Jon picked up the three smaller boxes, climbed down the ladder, and set the boxes inside the closet. Returning to Carlie in the bedroom, he found her staring at the enormous decoration boxes as if they might attack her.

Once downstairs, he opened the top of the first box. Jon could hear Carlie audibly sucking in her breath in anticipation. Packed tight to the top was string after string of colored lights.

In the middle of the box, he discovered boxes of garland and old-fashioned lead tinsel. Underneath that were an even dozen boxes of hand-blown glass ornaments. The contents of two of the boxes were breathtaking; neither Jon nor Carlie had ever seen anything like them. Someone had carved each of the ornaments out of wood and hand-painted a portrait of an adult's or a small child's face on each one.

"My God, Jon, these are beautiful. I've never seen anything like them."

"Me neither."

"Someone in town must have made these. They look like Renaissance paintings."

Over the next three hours, Jon and Carlie unpacked the remaining two massive boxes. There were hundreds of decorations in each box, and every item was from a different era long past. There were enough of them to decorate every room in two houses the size of Grace's.

# 44

Carlie had delegated the task of purchasing the perfect Christmas tree to Jon, a job he found daunting. Two hours and half a dozen tree lots later, he finally found and settled on a blue spruce that smelled terrific, was the perfect shape, and looked to be the right size for the corner Carlie had picked out. He paid the attendant and arranged for the tree's delivery that evening.

When the delivery truck arrived, Jon watched as two burly men hoisted the tree over their shoulders and walked across the drive to the front porch.

Without a word, the delivery men carried the tree up the steps, past Jon, and laid it down in the corner.

Lying on the floor, the tree somehow looked a great deal larger than he remembered it on the lot.

Resting her hand on Jon's shoulder, Carlie started laughing uncontrollably. "Jesus, Jon. All we wanted was a Christmas tree, not a friggin' sequoia."

Jon wanted to have the Christmas tree up and in place before Carlie awoke the next day, so he set the alarm for 5:00, rolled over, pulled the comforter up over his shoulder, and fell asleep—long before Carlie even closed her eyes.

The next morning it took Jon hours to get the tree ready to stand up. Wrapping his arms around and through the sharp branches, he pushed with all his might. With a full head of steam and momentum fostered by intense pain and pure determination, Jon pushed and shoved the monster tree into a standing position.

From the top of the stairs, Carlie watched as her husband disappeared into the foliage of the enormous tree. While Jon grunted and struggled to stand the tree upright, she made her way as quietly as possible down the stairs into the kitchen.

Within a few minutes, the front room fell silent. The only sound Carlie could hear was the cursing and heavy breathing of her husband as he walked into the kitchen. She couldn't believe her eyes. Gobs of sticky yellow tree sap and pine needles covered Jon from head to toe. He had deep gouges on his forehead, neck, and arms. He looked pathetic.

"The tree is up—sort of."

"That's wonderful. Go clean up. When you're not all sticky, you can help me decorate it."

Jon hung his head and walked out the back door.

# 45

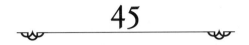

Stripped to his underwear, Jon quickly ran a cloth soaked in kerosene over his arms and face. Once the sap dissolved, he lathered himself in dishwashing detergent.

Bending over the laundry tub, Jon rubbed at his hair and neck with the kerosene rag. The idea of someone flipping a lit match right then sent a cold chill through him. He was completely alone in the barn, but he couldn't shake the feeling. Filling his hand with shampoo, he lathered his hair and scrubbed erratically at the remaining sap.

A chilly breeze kicked up, sending goose bumps across his neck and shoulders. Pulling his collar a little tighter against his neck, Jon hurried to get the soap out of his hair. As he moved to swing the faucet out of the way, a cold hand grabbed him at the base of his skull, forcing his head back under the water. Holding Jon's face under the stream of water, the ghostly hand squeezed hard enough to cause the bones in his neck to start popping. Yanking Jon's head back, the presence slammed him forward, smashing his forehead against the bottom of the concrete sink.

The harder Jon struggled, the tighter the grip became.

The hand yanked Jon's head back again, holding his face only inches from the mirror. The reflection of the face standing over his left shoulder almost stopped Jon's heart. With his lips pulled back so tight they looked as if they might tear, Ian screamed like a wounded animal as he slammed Jon's head against the steel edge of the laundry tub.

When Jon opened his eyes, everything was blurry, but he could vaguely make out a hazy form straddled him. Ian's face flashed through Jon's mind, causing him to scramble backward.

A gentle, cool hand touched Jon's cheek, immediately stopping his flight. Blinking rapidly, Carlie's face slowly came into focus. "Jon? *Jon!* Can you hear me?"

Jon nodded in reply.

"What the hell happened?"

Jon couldn't answer; all he managed to do was stare at her.

"Can you stand?"

Taking Jon's hands, Carlie slowly pulled him into a sitting position.

The shadows in the barn made it difficult for Carlie to determine how seriously her husband had been hurt. The blood seeping from the gash on his forehead clearly indicated something had happened, and she wasn't sure if she should even try to move him.

Jon shifted to his knees and slowly rose on rubbery legs. Carlie steadied him as he tried to stand. Once he was on his feet, Carlie led him out of the barn and toward the house. Stopping occasionally to let Jon try to focus and catch his breath, they finally made it to the steps of the back porch. Dropping down on the top step, Jon hung his head and held it in his hands. The sun was brighter than he had ever seen it; he had to shield his eyes to keep them open.

Jon felt like he had been sitting on the porch for hours when he heard a car drive up.

A door slammed and he heard footsteps walking across the gravel drive.

"Well, well. Let's take a look here," said a deep, gravelly voice.

A massive hand reached down and gently pulled Jon's hand away from his forehead. Cupping his hand over his eyes to block out the sun, Jon looked up into the weathered face of Doctor Tremmel.

With two fingers, Tremmel pulled Jon's eyelids apart. Shining a light back and forth across Jon's left eye, he hesitated a moment and then repeated the process on the right eye.

"Well, I don't think there's any permanent damage. You have a slight concussion—and, I imagine, one hell of a headache. It's a good thing you have a hard head."

Reaching into his black bag, he pulled out a syringe, which he filled from a small vial of clear liquid. With Jon staring down at his feet holding his aching head, Doctor Tremmel poked the needle deep into the gash on Jon's forehead.

"Son of a bitch!" Jon screamed.

"You big baby, sit still," Tremmel said. "You need a few stitches."

Doctor Tremmel left explicit orders for Carlie to keep Jon awake for at least another three hours.

Once the doctor was gone, Carlie sat down on the edge of the couch next to Jon. Most of the color had returned to his face, and he was no longer clammy. "Jon," Carlie said, "can you tell me what happened?"

Jon started to feel icy fingers tightening like a vise around his neck as he thought about Ian's face in the mirror. "I guess I fainted. I vaguely remember being dizzy and then waking up on the floor of the barn."

"Then why didn't you tell Doc Tremmel you were dizzy? He should know about it."

"I didn't tell him because I didn't think it was a big deal. I have to assume that it was a residual effect of breathing in the kerosene fumes." Touching his head, he ran his finger across the gauze pad covering the gash. "I just wish I had turned away from the laundry tub before I passed out."

～

Jon didn't hesitate at Carlie's offer of a pain pill. Swallowing it with a mouthful of water, he laid his head back and waited for it to take effect.

～

The grandfather clock showed that it was 8:45 PM. He had been asleep for almost eleven hours. He was surprised that he had slept so long—he was also surprised that he no longer hurt.

Spinning around, Jon stared aimlessly at the tree. He knew that eventually he would have to tell Carlie what had really happened in the barn. Jon suspected that she already had a fairly good idea that it hadn't happened the way he said.

# 46

Carlie and Loretta had spent all night and most of the day cooking and preparing for Dexter's party. They had invited over a hundred guests, and remarkably, ninety percent had RSVP'd.

Even Jon was looking forward to the party. Since the incident in the barn earlier in the month, the house had taken on a new atmosphere of calm and serenity. For the first time since setting foot on the property, Jon felt at peace. Carlie was actually sleeping soundly through the night, and Jon hadn't had a single recurrence of seeing or being accosted by Edith's or Ian's spirit.

The guests started arriving a few minutes before 5:00 PM. By half past, everyone was there except Dexter. Jon flashed back to the day Paul had found the old man lying face-down in the driveway.

When the grandfather clock chimed at 6:15, Jon felt that he had waited as long as he could. After putting on his coat, he wandered around the kitchen trying to remember where he had left his car keys. He was about to yell for Carlie when the doorbell rang. He could tell by the excitement that Dexter had finally arrived.

Dexter hadn't even taken off his coat before everyone in the room formed a line to shake the man's hand and wish him well. The old lawyer deserved every bit of the adulation he was getting.

The dinner was just shy of gourmet, and everyone raved about it. Afterward, the guests mingled with drinks in hand, reminiscing and telling stories. Of course, not every story was a case of hero worship. Old Dexter had made a few mistakes in his days, but no one held them against him, and enough time had passed that everyone could have a good laugh about it now.

By 11:30, the guests were pretty much gone. The few that remained behind were helping Carlie and Loretta clean up. The front room was peacefully quiet, and Jon and Dexter were nursing their brandies when Dexter sat forward and said, "I don't want to impose, but would you and Carlie mind if I spent the night here tonight?"

"Of course we don't mind."

Dexter gave Jon a casual smile. "I've moved up my plans. I'm leaving tomorrow morning for Europe. I'd appreciate it if you could take me to the airport."

"Why so early?"

"There's nothing keeping me here anymore. I have a cousin outside of London; we figured we would live out the rest of our lives together in the British countryside. I hear it's quite beautiful there.

"I do want to talk to you and Carlie before I leave, and the ride to the airport seems like a perfect opportunity."

With Carlie out of the room, Jon placed his finger across his lips and motioned for Dexter to follow him upstairs. Jon opened the closet door and pointed inside. "I found these upstairs in the attic."

Dexter leaned in and saw the cardboard box lying on the floor. "What's in it?"

Jon gently moved the man aside and stepped in. There was only one box on the floor. Opening the top, he found that it was the box containing the journals. In a panic, he started throwing blankets and shoes. "They're gone!" he exclaimed.

Looking perplexed, Dexter asked, "What's gone?"

"There were three boxes in here this morning. One had a gun in it, and the other a set of bloody clothes. Now they're gone.

"I think they belonged to the McPhersons."

As they walked back down the stairs, Dexter said, "Mmm, that's interesting. That's one of the things I wanted to talk to you about—not the McPhersons specifically, but this house. It can wait until tomorrow though—when we're far away from here."

Carlie, Jon, and Dexter thanked Loretta and Cecil for everything and walked them to Cecil's pickup truck. The snow had started falling and the wind was picking up at a steady pace. The forecast had called for snow late. The wind whipping the snow around was going to make their trip to the airport in the morning a nightmare.

Carlie had been so busy during the party that she never got the opportunity to spend more than a few minutes with Dexter, but looking at the man, she could see that he was exhausted. His eyes were red and unfocused—even the skin on his face seemed to droop. "Follow me and I'll show you to the guest room."

Dexter followed Carlie; when she opened the bedroom door and turned on the light, Dexter leaned down and gave her a gentle peck on the cheek. "I can't thank you enough for everything, Carlie. It was a terrific party."

~

The next morning, Jon pulled Dexter's Mercedes onto the main highway. "I wanted to talk to you two about the house," Dexter said. "Carlie, I know you don't want to hear this, but please listen. I won't ever have the chance to tell you again.

"Something inside that house killed both your Uncle William and your Aunt Grace. I can't tell you how many other people it has killed, run off, or driven insane, because I just don't know. But I do know that I can't stand by and watch anything happen to you. I have to try to convince you to leave.

"My house is empty now, and it's yours if you want it. I want you to think about what I have said. I'm telling you that I want to see you walk away from that house. Leave it and never give it a second thought. You both will be so much better off if you do."

"I appreciate your offer, Dexter, but we'll be all right—I promise."

"Carlie, my dear, you are making a promise you cannot keep.

"Jon, please try to persuade her. If you don't, maybe the next time you're attacked, you'll end up dead."

Jon spun around in the front seat and glared at Dexter. He couldn't believe the old man would say that in front of Carlie.

"Jon, we have seen all of this before, many times. I can tell you this: it is only the beginning. Things are going to get a lot worse for the both of you."

The three of them rode in silence until Jon pulled to the curb in front of the British Airways terminal. Once Carlie pushed the button for the trunk, a skycap loaded Dexter's luggage onto a cart.

Jon shook Dexter's hand but couldn't think of anything appropriate to say, so he pulled the man close and gave him a hug. "Take care of yourself, Dexter," Jon whispered.

Carlie didn't want to cry—she had even promised herself that she wouldn't—but she started sobbing all the same. Throwing her arms around Dexter's neck, she buried her face in his jacket. "I'm going to miss you so much. Please take care of yourself."

Wrapping his arm around Carlie's back, he pulled her tight and whispered, "It's not me you need to be concerned about. It's you and your husband who are in danger."

Pulling away, she gave him a weak smile. "We're going to be just fine."

"No—no, you're not. But don't say I didn't warn you."

# 47

"Sir," the flight attendant said as she wrestled Dexter straight up in his seat. "Sir, are you all right?"

A second flight attendant moved next to his partner. "Is everything all right here?"

"I don't believe so. He's not breathing and I can't find a pulse."

"I'll notify the captain."

# 48

Jon and Carlie stood on the tarmac as the KLM 747 carrying the remains of Dexter Simmons landed. They watched the massive airplane as it taxied down the runway toward the empty hangar where they stood waiting. After it came to rest, a group of men in blue jumpsuits rushed out and opened the cargo door.

A black hearse slowly pulled into view and parked alongside the door. A silver-haired man exited the passenger side and walked around the vehicle. After opening the back door, he waited patiently. A few minutes later, an airport employee rolled up the gurney carrying Dexter's coffin. The two men carefully slid both the coffin and the gurney inside the hearse and locked it in place.

In less than ten minutes, Jon and Carlie were back on the interstate following Dexter to the funeral home.

As the funeral director read the directions in Dexter's will for the interment of his remains, Carlie sat stoically and listened. These people were so matter-of-fact, Carlie wanted to reach across the table and slap them.

Suddenly Carlie realized she had been wrong—she *could* cry. Picking up her purse, she ran to the top of the stairs and out the door.

When the funeral director ran out of add-ons to pitch, Jon signed the contract.

He stepped out of the dreary funeral home into the bright afternoon sun, and spotted Carlie sitting on the park bench across the street.

Squatting down in front of her, Jon took her hands in his and waited until she made eye contact. "Everything has been taken care of. We really should go home."

Carlie looked over at Jon and said, "Before we go, I want to stop by Dexter's house. We won't be long, I promise, but I want to make sure the house is locked up and secure."

As they rode across town, Carlie read the coroner's accompanying letter. In it, he explained that Dexter had suffered from a congenital weakness in his carotid artery. When it ruptured, he suffered a brain aneurism. Because these ruptures occur so quickly, Dexter would have experienced a rapid decline in oxygen to the brain, mobility restrictions, shortness of breath, and maybe even hallucinations. This type of aneurism is incredibly fast, virtually painless, and always fatal. The last section of the letter gave her pause. The coroner had found a small vein that had ruptured inside his brain a year or so earlier. Its symptoms would have been identical to a stroke; however, such ruptures are rarely ever fatal.

~

Inside the house, she found it deathly quiet, as if somehow the house knew that Dexter was dead. She wondered if a house could mourn; if it could, this house was in mourning.

Carlie sent Jon to check the windows on the second floor, and she started in the living room. Opening the drawers to Dexter's desk, she discovered a large manila envelope addressed to both her and Jon. She folded the envelope and slid it into her purse. She then proceeded to check the first floor to make sure that Dexter had locked all the doors and windows. Secure in the knowledge that he had, she made her way up the stairs to join Jon on the second floor.

She found him standing transfixed in the doorway to Dexter's bedroom. Someone had completely ransacked the room, scattering books and papers everywhere. The broken bed lay stripped and shredded against the far wall. Every remaining article of Dexter's clothing lay in a pile in the center of the room.

Jon looked over at Carlie and said, "Let's get the hell out of here. Is everything locked up?"

"Everything is locked as tight as a drum."

"Good. Then we're out of here."

~

By mid-afternoon, the weather had changed dramatically. Moderate to heavy snow was predicted by early evening. When Sheriff Duncan pulled into Jon and Carlie's drive, the wind was whipping the heavy snowfall into whiteout conditions. The snow was coming down so hard, no one saw the pickup truck as it followed the sheriff into the driveway.

Jon answered the door and invited the sheriff in.

Duncan stood in the middle of the front room with his hands on his hips, looking very pompous and official—and just a little suspicious.

Before the sheriff could take a seat, the back door opened and closed, causing both men to look toward the kitchen. A few moments later, Loretta and Carlie entered the room.

Walking up to Sheriff Duncan, Loretta said, "Sit down, Wilbur. Quit acting like such an ass."

Carlie couldn't help but snicker, and Jon smiled at Loretta's bluntness.

The sheriff glared at Loretta for a few seconds before he smiled and apologized. Taking his seat, he looked at Jon and said, "I got a report of a break-in at the Simmons house. I assume it was you who made the call."

Jon explained what they had been doing that morning—how they had driven by Dexter's house to make sure he had locked all the doors and windows before he left.

Up to the point where Jon explained what condition he had found Dexter's bedroom in, the sheriff had shown no sign of interest. When Jon threatened to notify the state police of Duncan's unwillingness to investigate, the sheriff finally agreed to see what he could do. "Well, all right. I'll look into it." Standing, Sheriff Duncan zipped up his jacket and put his hat back on. "Good evening, folks—you too, Loretta. If the weather lets up, I'd appreciate your meeting me at the house in the morning, say 10:00 or so."

Jon extended his right hand; however, the sheriff hesitated before accepting it.

Neither Jon nor Carlie followed Duncan out the door. As soon as the sheriff was on the porch, Jon closed the door behind him.

The snow was falling more heavily than it had been earlier. The wind had also picked up, blowing the sugar-fine powder in swirls and forming five- to six-foot drifts across the road.

~

As Sheriff Duncan passed a clearing in the trees, the wind-driven snow whipped itself into a solid wall of white crystal, obliterating the world around him.

Straining his eyes to locate the centerline, he looked up just in time to make out the shadowy figure of a man standing in the roadway. Yanking the steering wheel hard to the left, Duncan steered his cruiser directly into the path of the massive blade of a snowplow as it bore down on him through the wall of white. An instant later, the blade sliced a gaping hole through the cruiser's fender and buried itself deep into the driver's door, spinning and wedging the cruiser underneath the raised dump bed.

Sheriff Duncan screamed briefly as twenty tons of steel and road salt crushed and twisted what was left of his vehicle. He watched in silence as the rear tires of the massive snowplow cut through the roof directly over where he sat.

## 49

The snow had yet to let up for any significant period of time. For over two straight weeks, it had screamed down the jet stream out of northern Canada in wave after wave. The weather bureau was predicting one of the worst winters for the Midwest in recordable history.

During Dexter's funeral, the sun broke through the clouds for the first time in almost a month. Carlie hoped it was Dexter's way of letting her know that he was all right.

When Jon finished giving Dexter's eulogy, a solemn procession passed his gravesite, heading toward the far end of the cemetery. Preceding the silver hearse, a motorized police escort passed with their lights flashing mournfully. Nearly one hundred uniformed officers on foot followed closely behind the late Sheriff Duncan.

~

The house was eerily silent when Carlie and Jon walked through the kitchen door. It felt like someone had again sucked the life out of it. Carlie had refused to take down the Christmas decorations after learning that Dexter had died. In her mind, they retained a certain amount of cheer in a miserably depressing situation. Today, however, they looked like cheap, lifeless pieces of wood, porcelain, and paper.

Jon had just finished stoking the fire and adding a new log when Carlie called to him from the kitchen. "Sweetheart, I hate to ask, but would you mind bringing in the long folding table from the barn?"

"Not a problem." Putting on his coat and gloves, Jon headed out the kitchen door.

The snow had started in earnest the minute they left the cemetery. Jon hoped that everyone would make it safely to the house for Dexter's wake—or better yet, that they would stay home. It looked like it was going to be a bad night.

In the corner of the barn, Jon located the table hidden underneath a heavy green canvas tarp.

After folding the tarp and putting it on a shelf, Jon wiped off the table and started maneuvering it toward the house. It was easy enough to slide across the barn floor, but it was going to be an entirely different story carrying it in the wind to the back door. Jon could picture a gust of wind lifting him and the table like a glider, and dropping them somewhere in the cornfield.

Stepping out of the barn into the wind-driven snow, he heard a familiar voice, "You need a hand with that, Mister Summers?"

Looking toward the side of the barn, Jon watched Smitty as he stepped out of the shadows and approached him. "Wind'll probably catch it and rip it out of your hands. Hold on a second, I'll help you."

Jon couldn't believe his luck. "I appreciate it." When Smitty got closer, Jon couldn't help but wonder what the kid was doing out there. "You mind my asking what you're doing all the way out here on a day like this?"

"Just on my way home. Been kind of busy lately.

"I really like what you did with the old house, Mister Summers. It's been quite a few years since anyone put up decorations. It makes it feel like a real home."

Jon wasn't sure how long the boy wanted to talk, but he remembered how sensitive he was and didn't want to offend him, so he waited patiently and listened.

"It was a shame indeed about old Lawyer Simmons. I heard his funeral was today."

"Yes, it was. Carlie and I just got home from it."

"A sad thing indeed. He should have listened; I warned him."

"What do you mean, you warned him?"

"Hell, that old duffer had been trying to scare you and the missus off this property since the first day you came out here. I warned him back at the beginning—before you even moved in—to leave it alone. He just wouldn't mind his own business."

Without another word, he picked up the back of the table, and he and Jon began walking it toward the screen door. "Better get this in the house before the missus thinks you up and had another accident."

Jon wanted to laugh, but deep inside he knew that this was no laughing matter. Something was seriously wrong with this boy—and the sooner he got away from him, the happier he would be.

Just inside the screen porch, he thanked Smitty and told him he could take it from there.

Smitty just smiled, tipped his hat, and walked away. Jon watched him until he disappeared into the wind-whipped snow.

Once he was out of sight, Jon wrestled the table through the back door and into the kitchen.

Dropping the table on the floor, he made a dash upstairs to the closet and pulled out the box of journals he had found in the attic.

Racing downstairs, Jon started screaming, "CARLIE! CARLIE, HURRY—I NEED YOU DOWNSTAIRS!"

Rushing into the front room, she found Jon sitting on the couch staring at the box on the coffee table. He didn't appear to be hurt—there was no blood, just Jon sitting on the couch staring off into space.

"Okay, I'm here, Jon. What the hell are you screaming about?"

Jon looked up at her. When he did, she saw something reflected in his eyes that she couldn't begin to fathom.

Taking a seat next to him on the couch, she placed the back of her hand against his cheek. He wasn't hot; he apparently didn't have a fever. But something was definitely wrong—his eyes were distant and he could barely focus on her face.

"Sweetheart, did you hit your head again?"

When Jon's eyes began to focus, he shook his head almost imperceptibly.

"Then tell me what's wrong."

In a whisper, he answered, "I'm not completely sure yet, but I think we're in serious fucking trouble, Carlie.

"Jesus, Jon, you're scaring the hell out of me."

"Please, Carlie. We need to read these journals."

Before Carlie could answer, Loretta stuck her head in the front door. "Hi, y'all. Can we come in?"

Jon turned and smiled. "Of course. Get in here out of the cold."

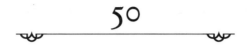

# 50

It took Carlie and Loretta almost an hour to set up the buffet. The weather seemed to be cooperating; it had stopped snowing and the wind had died down to a gentle breeze. Jon prayed that it would stay that way, at least until everyone made it back home.

As the guests started arriving, Jon couldn't stop himself from keeping an eye on the shadows by the barn. He felt as if someone were watching him and the house, but he couldn't prove it. He didn't see any movement anywhere—and then he did. Someone was standing just inside the barn. Whoever it was seemed to be watching the guests as they arrived.

Loretta was standing just inside the door when Jon walked back into the house. Gently tugging his sleeve as he walked by, she stopped him and moved with him to the side of the room. In a whisper, she said, "Carlie told me about the new journals. She also told me that you believe something really important might be in them. I'm not positive what's going on, or what I can do to help, but I'll be here if you need me."

Jon leaned down and gave the older woman a kiss on the cheek. "Thanks, I appreciate that."

Dexter's wake broke up at around 6:30, and by 7:00, the house was empty. Loretta and Carlie were completely finished cleaning up by 8:00.

After Carlie and Loretta were finished, they brought three cups of coffee into the living room, where they found Jon sitting on the couch staring at the box of journals.

When everyone had settled in, Jon lifted the lid from the box. He had a good idea who had written the journals, but he needed to be sure.

Taking the first journal out of the box, he handed it to Carlie for confirmation. "Is this your Aunt Grace's handwriting?"

It took her about five minutes to answer. "Yes, this is her journal—it is her handwriting."

The faraway look in Carlie's eyes told Jon that this discovery was going to take a heavy toll on her. "During all the time I lived with them, I never once saw her writing in a journal. I didn't know she even kept one."

Jon had no idea where Grace's journals were going to take them. However, considering his last conversation with Smitty, he had an idea—and it wasn't going to be good.

"Jon, I think it would be best if I was the one who read these. It's nothing against you or Loretta, but she was my aunt and I'm not sure what she may have written."

Jon nodded. "What would you like for us to do?"

"Maybe just go to bed and get some sleep."

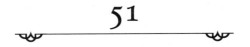

# 51

Jon woke up when he heard clanking and clinking in the kitchen below. Rolling over, he looked at the clock on the nightstand; it was still hours before the sun would come up. He tried to go back to sleep, but his eyes popped open again as if they were on spring hinges.

At the bottom of the stairs, he saw Carlie and Loretta sitting at the kitchen table. As he walked around the corner into the kitchen, he said, "Good middle of the night, ladies."

Carlie looked up at him and smiled. "Everything I'm about to tell you took place over a seventeen-year period of time. During that time, I lived here for three of them. I don't know how I missed it, but I didn't know any of it was going on.

"My father never could understand why Uncle William and Aunt Grace bought this place to begin with. It was huge; it had thousands of acres to take care of. All Uncle William ever wanted was to become a gentleman farmer, not a real farmer.

"When it came time for Uncle William to plant his crops, he found a young man by the name of Andrew Smith to help him."

"Are we talking about Andrew Smith—Edith and Ian's Andrew Smith? You're telling me that Andrew has been haunting this house for a hundred and thirty years?"

"Actually, I'm thinking ninety. Remember, when I woke up from the fire—or should I say, when Andrew woke up from the fire—there were no traces of fire damage.

"According to Aunt Grace's journals, Mister Smith's family knew the McPherson family. According to Mister Smith, Ian and Edith were found in the charred remains of the master bedroom, with their only son lying at the foot of the bed.

"Aunt Grace had no reason not to believe him. She had no idea who Edith and Ian McPherson even were.

"I find this next part very disturbing. I always thought Uncle William died in a car accident—at least that was what my parents told me. But according to Aunt Grace's journals, he was killed when a tractor slipped off a jack. He was pinned underneath, and his chest was crushed. Poor Uncle William lay out in the driveway and suffocated.

"This took place a couple days after Uncle William told Andrew that they were going to lease the land to a third party, and they would no longer need his services.

"After Uncle William's death, Aunt Grace decided to sell all the property back to the county, except for what we have here, of course.

"Andrew had a fit when he heard about Aunt Grace's proposed sale. He tried to convince her that he could run the farm just fine without William, but she had her mind made up. I think she gave him a sense of false hope by keeping him on for several months after the sale. He cleaned and repaired all the machinery and groomed what livestock they had left—pretty much what he had done for Ian before *his* planned sale of the farm.

"Then one morning, Grace told him about her plan to auction those off as well. Andrew went ballistic. He actually became physically abusive with her. Then he started destroying everything in sight. She ended up calling Sheriff Duncan."

Jon looked up and asked, "What happened to Andrew then?"

"He just disappeared. Duncan and his men searched for him for days." Carlie set down the journal and said to Jon with a sigh, "You were right, Jon—Andrew was looking for a family. Aunt Grace never even realized what she had done."

Jon looked at Carlie. "With the knowledge of Andrew that we have, we're in a very dangerous situation here, maybe even more so than Grace was. I don't believe for a second that your Aunt Grace died in an accidental electrical fire. I believe that Andrew killed her, and why not? So far he's killed everyone else.

"That boy Smitty, the one who helps me around here, knows way too much about what goes on in this house. After what he said yesterday, he gives me the creeps. He went so far as to tell me that he had warned Dexter to leave Carlie and the house alone.

"There have been too many unexplainable occurrences, and he seems to be involved in or know about each one. If I'm right—and I'm not saying that I am—we might consider getting the hell away from this house—for good."

Carlie stood and looked at Jon. "Jesus, I almost forgot." Leaving the room, Jon could hear her opening the drawer to the roll-top desk.

When she returned, she held two large manila envelopes. Dropping them on the table, she took her seat.

The first envelope she opened was the one with "Baxter" in large black letters across the front. Inside was a letter from Grace addressed to Carlie, a recorded deed for a piece of property, and a document of some kind from the county.

Carlie began to read.

*My darling Carlie,*

*After you left for college, your uncle and I wanted to leave you something special beyond what is in our will. At first, we had no idea what it could be. Then the nice young man who works for your Uncle William told us about a beautiful piece of property. It sits at the westernmost edge of the farm. I drove out with your uncle and looked at it, and it was everything and more the boy had promised it was.*

*We had Dexter divide this five-acre piece of property out of the balance of the acreage and create a separate deed for it. I had it fenced off and had a large monument placed on it. What William and I hope is that when you read this, you will be grown and married and will consider having your baby exhumed and moved to this new location. It is a much more appropriate burial site than in the garden.*

*Please consider it. Just ask Dexter where the old McPherson property line is located. This beautiful piece of land is yours now; I hope you find it as special a burial place for your baby as it was for your uncle and me when we saw it.*

*With much love,*
*Aunt Grace*

Carlie set the letter and the other papers aside and opened the second envelope. Dexter had addressed this letter to both Jon and Carlie. She read the letter to herself before reading it aloud.

*My Dearest Friends,*

*I have tried my best to convey to you the seriousness of your remaining in your Aunt Grace's house. Evidently I didn't do it well enough, or I wouldn't be writing this final plea.*

*I implore you to pack up and leave immediately. I stood by and watched as that house destroyed your aunt and uncle. Over the years, I have seen it destroy many families and many lives. In your Aunt Grace and Uncle William's case, I feel almost complicit. I feel that it was within my power to avert the tragedy that befell them, yet I did nothing.*

*Please, my dears, leave that house.*

*With sincerest concerns,*
*Dexter*

Carlie looked at Jon and Loretta and read it again.

Looking across the table at Jon and Loretta, Carlie asked, "Well, what do you think?"

Loretta answered first. "I'm not an expert, by any stretch of the imagination, but I do know this. There are two ways for a spirit to remain earthbound to a location. The first is free will. I'd consider Andrew's haunting to be of his own free will. The other is that there has to be something physical on the property to keep a spirit attached. When I say physical, I mean something tangible; it could be anything—a watch, a toy—something that belonged to and had an attachment of real significance to the person during their life."

Jon's face turned pale. "Carlie, there is something I need to tell you. The boxes I brought down from the attic—the three small ones I put in the bedroom closet ... "

Carlie had to think for a minute. It finally dawned on her. "The ones you wouldn't let me look in?"

"Yeah, those boxes. In one box I found Andrew's bloody clothes and his handkerchief full of money. The second box had Ian's gun and some of Edith's hand-crocheted baby blankets. The third box held Grace's journals."

Carlie gave Loretta a curious look. "Do these tangible belongings have to remain on the property to keep the spirit attached here?"

"If they're not here of their own volition, then I believe so, yes."

Carlie stood and walked to the window. She found that sometime during the night, the snow had quit falling. There were drifts across the back yard that looked to be six feet deep or better. "Do you know where the stand of trees my aunt referred to is located?"

"Sure, it's out at the end of Breckenridge Road."

"Do you think we could drive out there?"

"Not in your cars, we couldn't. Breckenridge is one of the last roads the county clears, if they clear it at all. There's not a soul living on it, and it really doesn't go anywhere. We could make it in a four-wheel-drive vehicle. Cecil's truck could make it."

"Could I bother you to see if he would be willing to take us out there?"

～

Loretta was right—the road was almost impassable, even for Cecil's truck.

At the end of the road, there was a beautiful white wrought-iron gate and an ornate fence running out into the countryside as far as the eye could see. Not thirty feet from the road was a magnificently sculptured stone monument of Christ on the cross. It was just as Grace had described it.

Jon turned to say something to Carlie, but her eyes had that faraway look in them again.

As Carlie stood staring at the monument, she couldn't help but remember the connection she had felt to this place in her dreams—the connection Andrew had felt to this particular spot during his life. It was no wonder he had suggested it. She hoped that it had been Grace's idea and not Andrew's that it be a location for the interment of Carlie's baby, especially after what Loretta had just told them.

# 52

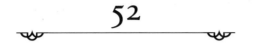

After his shower, Jon found Carlie sitting at the vanity brushing her hair. Walking up behind her, he placed his hands on her shoulders and began gently massaging. "Sweetheart," Jon said, "I'm serious; I think we really should consider moving away from here."

Carlie never moved her head, just her eyes. When she saw Jon looking at her in the mirror, she answered, "You know I can't do that, and you know the reason why. I wish you would stop asking."

"But you can now. Aunt Grace unwittingly made it possible. We can move the baby to the memorial she built for her. You see, that piece of property is no longer part of this farm. If your baby were there, she would finally be free of this house's hold on her. I feel we owe it to her. She deserves to be free.

"You deserve to be free."

Carlie thought about what Jon had said. He was right—if she moved her baby off the farm, they would both be free. "I'll tell you what, Jon. Tomorrow I'll call the funeral home. If it's possible to move her to the property on Breckenridge Road, I'll arrange to have it done. After it's over—and only after—will I consider moving."

"That's all I can ask."

The sun was warm on her exposed face and arms. From her vantage point underneath the three ancient oak trees, she could watch and hear the children as they ran, laughed, and played games in the yard.

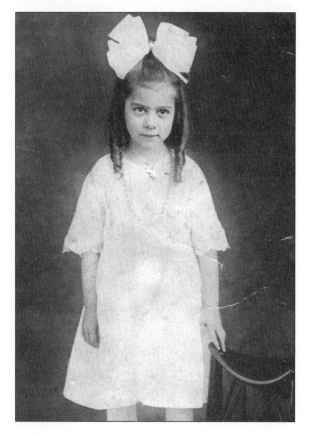

*Lisa. (Date and location unknown.)*

The grass had yet to dry out from the early summer sun. It was so soft and comfortable; Carlie lay down, closed her eyes, and in a moment, was sound asleep.

The soft buzz of the children's talking gave way to the sound of hushed laughter. Opening her eyes, Carlie found herself encircled by children of varying ages and dress. Three of the children stood out from the rest.

The oldest was a beautiful young girl. She wore her raven hair pulled back into a ponytail. A massive white bow accentuated her hair's natural blue-black highlights.

The others were twin boys—one only slightly taller than the other—and they moved to the front of the group. Taking up their positions on either side of the young girl, they each took her hand and stood silent like identical bookends.

Carlie sat staring at the trio. She sensed that they wanted to tell her something.

"Please come. Sit with me," Carlie said.

The boys were the first to react. The taller of the two boys pulled gently on the girl's hand as he took the first step. The young girl hung her head slightly and giggled softly under her breath. She reluctantly shuffled forward at their insistence until the three were directly in front of Carlie.

"Please sit down," Carlie said. "Talk to me."

The trio sat down and crossed their legs Indian style. Carlie couldn't remember the last time she had seen anyone sit that way. Wrapping her arms around her legs, she pulled her knees up under her chin and waited.

The girl lifted her head and fixed her gaze deep into Carlie's emerald eyes. "I am Lisa," she began. Turning her head to the taller boy, she introduced him as Clinton, and his younger brother as Clifford.

"What can I do for you?" Carlie asked.

"Help us!"

The young girl's request baffled Carlie. "How can I possibly help you?"

Turning around, Lisa looked at the other children standing behind her. Each made an indication that she needed to continue. "Release us," she said.

Silently, the two boys nodded in agreement.

"How can I release you? Release you from what?"

"Release us from here," Lisa said. "Take us with you. Please, we're begging you."

"I'm sorry," Carlie said, "I don't understand. How can I take you with me? I'm not going anywhere."

A dark shadow passed over Lisa as her face began to change. Her childlike grin quickly distorted into something depraved and wicked, exposing black, rotten, and missing teeth. She no longer possessed the radiance of youth; her eyes were sunken and hollow, cataract-opaque.

Her pristine white dress seemed to unravel before Carlie's eyes; ragged holes appeared out of nowhere. As the girl got closer, Carlie could not only see that patches of mold and dirt covered her entire dress, she could smell them. The air reeked of fresh dirt and the dusty aroma of mold spores. The beautiful white bow that had held her raven ponytail was now limp, yellowed, and half-detached and secured scattered thatches of what remained of her gorgeous hair.

Carlie stared at the children in disbelief. Watching the rest of the group as they moved silently toward her, she saw that all their clothes were tattered and filthy. Where fresh, young faces had smiled at her a moment earlier, ugly, hollow, decomposing masks glared down at her now.

The children's splintery, dry-rotted fingers scraped across Carlie's face and arms, leaving a trail of dust and detached skin as they grabbed at her.

The lifeless, rotting corpses of close to one hundred children quickly swarmed and overpowered Carlie, pinning her to the ground.

She wrestled desperately to escape their grasp. Forcing herself upright into a sitting position, she screamed "*STOP!*" at the top of her lungs.

Opening her eyes, Carlie found herself sitting on her own bed. But standing at the foot of the bed were Lisa, Clinton, and Clifford, staring down at her. Pushing herself against the headboard, she tried desperately to escape.

When the light on the bedside table turned on, the apparitions disappeared into the warmth of its yellow glow.

Jon wrapped his arm around Carlie's shoulder and pulled her close. "My God, Carlie, are you all right?"

Up to that point, Carlie's breathing had been fast yet still reasonably under control. But at the sound of Jon's deep, resonant voice, she began crying hysterically. Burying her face into his shoulder, she said, "Get us out of here, Jon, please ... before we end up dead."

# 53

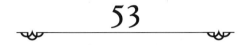

It was day twenty-seven and the snow had yet to let up. Every day since the beginning of the storm, Cecil had gone out of his way to make sure Jon and Carlie could get out of their driveway. The county, however, was not quite so concerned about an isolated road leading to an old farmhouse on the outskirts of town.

Jon, Carlie, and Cecil were just finishing their coffee when the phone rang. Jon looked down at his wristwatch and wondered who could be calling this early in the morning.

Excusing himself, he walked across the kitchen and picked up the receiver. "Hello? Oh, good morning. . . . Yes, yes I did. . . . I should be in town in about an hour. . . . That's fine. I'll meet you there. . . . Yes, and thank you again. Goodbye."

Carlie sat waiting for Jon to explain the conversation.

"That was Lester Jenkins. He's the man I hired to clean and repair Dexter's house. It seems the county finally got around to plowing him out, so he will be ready to start work today. I need to meet him at the house in an hour, so I guess I better get ready to go."

Cecil stood up and stretched. "I better get going too. I still have a half-dozen drives left to plow. Damn, what a winter."

As Cecil drove away, Carlie took Jon's hand and walked him back into the house. "Can I drive into town with you?"

Carlie gave him a big hug, and the two of them headed up the stairs to get ready for the day.

~

Carlie couldn't imagine for the life of her just how she was going to help these children, but if it was at all possible, she had to try.

Lester was already waiting when Jon pulled up to the curb. He had most of his supplies already on the porch, which impressed Jon to no end. Rarely had Jon found a contractor of any sort who was ready, willing, and able to start work when they said they would.

Walking up the sidewalk, Jon extended his right hand as he approached Lester.

"Good morning, Mister Jenkins. I'm Jon Summers."

"No need to be formal with me, Mister Summers. My daddy was Mister Jenkins. Everybody just calls me Lester."

"All right, Lester. Please call me Jon."

Jon unlocked the front door, pushed it open, and waited. The house was as quiet as a tomb. He didn't have any idea what he was expecting to happen, but almost everything he did these days caused a knot to form in the pit of his stomach. Even this generated an all-consuming sense of doom.

"Well, Lester, it looks like everything is still in order down here. Let's go upstairs. Dexter's bedroom is on the second floor, first door on the right."

Following Lester up the stairs, Jon stepped back as the contractor turned the handle and opened the door.

"Whew, quite a mess in here, Jon."

"Lester, you do whatever needs to be done. Start this room from scratch; strip it to the bare walls and floor. I'll leave a check on the table by the front door."

"No problem, Jon. When are they delivering the new furniture?"

"If the weather holds out, next Monday morning."

~

For the first time in months, Carlie seemed comfortable and at peace. She was openly excited about Lester working on Dexter's house and having it finished by the beginning of the following week. Jon wasn't sure if she planned to move in when it was finished, but he was surprised to find that she was genuinely excited.

Carlie and Jon stopped by the café and picked up lunch to take home. Carlie and Loretta laughed and giggled in the corner while their lunch was being prepared. Cecil kept Jon occupied with tales of his daring and heroism. It seemed that Clarence the barber's 1957 Cadillac had slid off the main highway on his way to work that morning. Cecil had just happened to pass by and rescue the old man before he froze to death.

Cecil knew how to embellish even the most mundane of stories. He had just started telling Jon about the giant wolf he had seen running up the highway outside of town when the bell in the kitchen notified Loretta that Jon and Carlie's lunch was ready.

After Loretta boxed up their lunch, she winked at Carlie and told her she would see her around 3:00. On the way out to the car, Jon's curiosity got the best of him, and he asked what the two of them had planned for the rest of the day.

"Oh Jon," Carlie said, "you are a very suspicious man. That's why I love you—nothing ever gets by you."

Jon waited for an answer, but the expression on Carlie's face told him that he would be waiting a very long time. She had said all that she was going to say.

The snow started falling again when Loretta pulled into the drive.

Their mood had changed considerably from when they were at the café. Neither Carlie nor Loretta was laughing or giggling anymore. Carlie found the attic dark, cold, and a tad bit scary. She had never been up there before, and when she was finished, she would make a point of never going up there again.

Loretta had brought an electric lantern from their farm. It was at least ten times brighter than any flashlight Carlie had around the house.

Turning the lantern on, Carlie could see all the way to the far end of the attic. On her knees, she spun the light in a 180-degree sweep around the room. There were boxes everywhere. She saw the boxes of Christmas decorations; they were the closest to the opening in the floor. At the far end were three large wooden boxes; those must be the ones Jon had referred to when he came down with the decorations.

On her hands and knees, Carlie made her way across the floor to the boxes. Standing, she was glad that Jon had already opened them; it made looking inside easier.

Jon was right. One of them was full of vintage-era clothing, and another was full of pots, pans, and antique toys. Jon hadn't opened the third box, and she had no way to open it now. It took her almost an hour to maneuver the heavy boxes to the opening and lower them down to Loretta.

At Loretta's suggestion, Carlie opened the decoration boxes in the attic and rummaged around in them until she located the hand-painted memorial decorations. Handing them down last, she climbed down the ladder and allowed it to collapse back up into the ceiling. Standing just outside the closet, Carlie couldn't believe how big the boxes really were now that they were sitting on the bedroom floor.

Carlie frowned at Loretta. "This is going to take forever, Retta. I can't believe this is the only way we can identify the children."

Loretta gave her friend a weak smile. "I know. I think the first thing we should do is move them downstairs, then separate the toys, memorial decorations, clothing, and journals by age."

"There are still a dozen or so smaller boxes and a steamer trunk in the attic. I don't know if they contain anything useful, but I think I'll have Jon go up after them. That is, after I explain to him what we're doing with these."

∼

Walking into the living room from the kitchen, Jon tripped over a metal fire truck lying in the middle of the floor. "Holy crap, what the hell are you two doing now?"

"God, I'm sorry, Jon!" Carlie exclaimed. "Sit down and I'll explain."

Jon sat silently as Carlie explained what she and Loretta were doing. It took a little longer for the two of them to explain the *why* to him.

Once he was fully up to speed, he asked, "Is there anything I can do to expedite this? I'd kind of like to have my living room back."

Carlie smiled at him. "I wish there was a way to hurry it along, but I can't think of one. However, you can help us if you want."

Together, Carlie and Loretta moved a pile of journals, toys, clothing, and the box of county records next to Jon. Carlie opened the first journal and set it in his lap. "If you find something, set it aside until we make a positive identification."

## 54

Jon watched as Carlie tapped on the glass of the kitchen window to get the attention of her family of cardinals. Jon was amazed at how they took to her. They literally followed her like puppies around the yard.

"Carlie?"

"Yes?"

"I really admire what you and Loretta are trying to do. I honestly do. But this could take months—even years. As Dexter warned, things have gotten progressively worse around here. I don't believe we have the time to accomplish what you want to do."

"I know, but I can't abandon them. I'll just find a way to do it faster."

Setting his coffee cup in the sink, Jon watched as the cardinals on the flower box ate their breakfast.

Carlie gave her husband a big hug and sent him upstairs to get ready. As soon as she finished doing the dishes, she followed him to get ready to go herself.

~

When Carlie arrived at Bannerman Funeral Home, Phillip Bannerman was already waiting for her. It took Carlie well over an hour to explain to the funeral director what she needed to have done.

She worried that the frozen ground would hamper what she wanted done, but Phillip assured her that with their equipment, her request would be no more difficult to accomplish now than if they did it in the middle of summer.

After Carlie agreed on a price and a starting date, she wrote him a check. Shaking her hand, he promised that his men would be at her home the following Monday.

She was relieved to find that the storm the weather forecasters had predicted for early that morning had managed to hold off—at least until she had finished with the funeral director. All the storm had to do now was hold off for one more hour, until she could get back to town.

The first snowflakes started to fall when she was less then fifteen minutes from the funeral home in Des Moines. The wind picked up, and before Carlie realized what was happening, the snow had obliterated the white lines on the highway. She slowed to a near crawl as the wind gusts buffeted the car back and forth from lane to lane.

The threat of oncoming traffic made her blood run cold. She had seen the aftermath of Sheriff Duncan's accident, and the last thing she wanted was to have a semi or a snowplow suddenly appear out of the blinding snow and run over her.

The right shoulder of the roadway was less than five feet wide in most places, but it was wide enough for her to park until the whiteout passed. She maneuvered her car until she could feel the gravel crunching beneath her tires, but she was scared to death to stop for fear that a car or truck behind her might rush headlong out of the snow and hit her.

She wished Jon were with her; she had never been good at driving in inclement weather. Rain made her nervous, and ice and snow terrified her, but this—this was different. She couldn't see two feet in front of her car or anything at all behind her.

Another gust of wind rocked and buffeted the car, causing Carlie to lose control for a moment. Looking in the rearview mirror, Carlie expected to see a set of headlights ready to plow into the back end of her. What she didn't expect to see was Lisa's smiling face in the mirror.

"Oh God no," Carlie pleaded. "Not now, please!"

"Shhhh," Lisa whispered. Reaching across the back of the seat, the girl rested her hand on Carlie's shoulder. "Just close your eyes. It will all be over in a second."

Carlie's voice hit a high-pitched squeal. "For God's sake, I'm trying to help you! Can't you see that?

"I'm going to take all of you with me, just as you asked. If I die, you'll stay on that farm for eternity."

Glancing back in the mirror, Carlie saw that the smile on Lisa's face hadn't wavered, but she saw a growing concern in the girl's eyes.

"*Please,*" Lisa whispered with urgency. "*You have to trust me. Close your eyes.*"

Carlie didn't believe for an instant that she could trust the girl. After what she had put Carlie through the other night, trust was not a commodity Carlie had an abundance of at that moment.

Lisa touched Carlie's shoulder again; her touch was even gentler than before. Her fingertips brushed Carlie's hair back and caressed her neck. Carlie found that she couldn't help herself; her eyes were growing heavy. A faint smile creased Carlie's lips as she leaned her head back and closed her eyes.

After what felt like a second, Carlie opened her eyes again, this time in a full-blown panic. How long had she been asleep? Was she flying headlong into another car—or worse? She blinked frantically to clear her vision as she slammed her foot down hard on the brake pedal.

It took a few seconds to register—her car wasn't stopping. She screamed loud enough to shatter glass, expecting to slam into something. It took at least thirty seconds for her to realize that she wasn't even moving. She was parked with her engine idling.

The flashing neon-red sign in her windshield read "Duffy's Truck Oasis." She had no idea where that was or how she had even gotten there. As the storm raged outside her windows, she looked hesitantly into the rearview mirror. The only things she saw were massive snowflakes melting against the heated window and running down in liquid droplets.

As with any storm, the whiteout conditions were just temporary. Within thirty minutes, the snow had slowed to a flurry. Carlie sat in her idling car until she heard the snowplows pass by on the highway outside her window.

Twenty feet before the stop sign leading onto the highway, there was another sign showing that she needed to turn right into town. It was still forty-five miles away—she couldn't have driven even a mile with her eyes closed. How on earth had she found this crossroad?

Once back on the highway, Carlie hadn't driven a mile before the cars in front of her came to a stop.

Every few minutes she inched forward, one car length at a time. Twenty minutes later, she could see the cause of the delay. There was a semi blocking the northbound lane. The state police were taking turns routing the lanes of traffic around the behemoth blocking half the roadway.

As she sat waiting her turn, a giant wrecker passed on her left. She watched as it turned around in the narrow lanes until it was facing the opposite direction. Once it was in position, the police began to let the cars pass again.

As Carlie pulled to a stop at the direction of the traffic control officer, she could see exactly what the commotion was all about. There was a black BMW sedan exactly like hers wedged underneath the front end of the semi—and not just wedged, but buried up to its rear bumper underneath the truck.

The police had wrapped the top of the car in a yellow tarp to keep curious eyes from seeing what was left of the driver. Carlie didn't want to look, but she couldn't help herself. Had it not been for Lisa, that surely would have been her covered in a yellow tarp—and her car ground into the pavement.

Once she was beyond the accident, it only took some thirty-five minutes before she was pulling into the parking lot of her offices. She hadn't stopped shaking during the entire drive into town. She needed a stiff drink—which Dexter had always kept hidden in his desk.

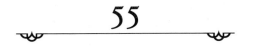

# 55

The snow was falling heavily again as Jon walked across the quad to the faculty parking lot. The wind was blowing hard enough at times to drive the white crystals sideways, stinging his face and eyes. The snow-covered lumps in the parking lot were all that was left of the faculty's cars.

As Jon approached the lot designated for morning classes, he thought he saw a black shadow standing next to the space where he believed he had parked his car. The closer he got, the larger the shape appeared.

A gust of wind came out of nowhere, almost blowing Jon off his feet. Turning his back to the driving snow, he braced himself against the wind. In front of him, the wind swirled and blew at least a ten-foot plume of snow into the air.

When the wind finally subsided, Jon turned toward his car again, and the shadow was gone. Jon wanted to run as fast as he could to the shelter of his automobile, but the brutally cold wind and snow made that impossible. They literally sucked the air out of his lungs. He wished he had brought a scarf to cover his mouth and nose, but it was too late now.

Pulling his jacket up over his head, he resembled the Headless Horseman, but he could see again—and most importantly, he could breathe. Moving at a trot, he guided himself through the wind and snowdrifts to where he had parked his car.

He worried about Carlie in this weather. She really couldn't drive in this or any kind of snow. He wondered if he should drive into town or drive home. Maybe she had already gone home before the brunt of the storm hit. Either destination was the same distance, and in this storm, it would take him over an hour. The snow lightened up just enough to allow his windshield wipers to keep up, so he chose to head toward Carlie's office in hopes that she might still be there.

As he made his way southeast from the college, the snow and wind picked up dramatically. He was heading right back into the storm that had just passed.

He was glad there was little to no traffic on the road; he could barely even see the road. The weather was so bad at one point that he missed his turnoff. It wasn't actually a turnoff; it was more a fork in the road. It really didn't matter what it was, because Jon had completely missed it.

Jon was hanging over the top of the steering wheel, straining to see the white line, when he thought he saw a gas station up ahead. There were flashing red and amber lights reflecting through the diffused white haze.

As he negotiated the hills, he would lose the lights temporarily, but then he would see them again off in the distance.

The closer he got, the steeper the hills were. He fought to keep control of his car. As it lost traction, spinning and fishtailing, he tried desperately to make it up the hills.

Jon was so fixated on maintaining control of his car that he completely missed the snow-covered "Road Ends" signs when he passed them.

As his car crested an almost impassible hill, he could see the lights flashing some two thousand feet ahead and below him. He touched the brakes, and the back end of his car immediately slid to the right. Taking his foot off the brake, he countersteered to correct the drift.

His palms were sweating, and the steering wheel quickly turned slippery. Gripping it with all his strength, he made minute adjustments to keep the car going straight.

Picking up speed at an incredible rate, Jon repeatedly tapped his brakes to stop at the bottom of the hill. However, every time he did, the back wheels locked, sending the car sideways.

Jon had never been this scared in his life.

He considered opening the door and jumping out, but he was afraid the car would run over the top of him if he did.

In the corner of his vision, he saw movement at the edge of the road approximately seventy-five feet in front of him. With a quick jerk of his head, he saw what appeared to be an enormous black dog. With his eyes back on the road, he kept the animal in his peripheral vision. *Fuck,* he thought, *this is all I need right now.*

Jon just knew that the animal would walk right out in front of him. That was how his day was going, and running over a helpless animal would be the icing on the cake.

The animal hunched its back and raised its hackles at the sound of Jon's approaching car. That was when Jon realized that this was not a dog—it was a wolf—and a really big one. This had to be the wolf Cecil had started to tell him about the other day. He wanted to kick himself; he hadn't believed Cecil at the time. If he lived through this, he would never make that mistake again.

Jon was right—the huge animal stepped into the roadway. It looked as if it were deciding if it should cross the road or not.

"NO, NO, NO, DON'T DO IT!" Jon screamed.

The wolf turned as if it had heard him and looked directly into Jon's eyes.

Jon touched the breaks again, sending the car sideways. He couldn't help but laugh as he thought to himself, *Insanity is doing the same thing over and over and expecting a different result each time.*

Jon had no sooner finished his thought than the wolf loped onto the roadway and started running directly at his car. Jon couldn't believe his eyes. He was free sliding at almost seventy miles per hour. He was less than the length of a football field from the bottom of the hill, and this wolf was attacking his car.

There had to be somewhere he could maneuver his car to. He had to find a way to avoid the huge beast. It was as he was exploring his possible escape routes that he realized the flashing lights were not a gasoline station. They were steel construction barriers.

*Crap,* he thought, *I'm going to crash through them.*

Now Jon was trying to keep an eye on both the wolf and the end of the road. As fast as the car was moving, the wolf seemed even faster. Jumping, the animal cleared the front end of the car and was about to crash directly through the windshield into Jon's face.

Survival instincts overrode Jon's common sense. Covering his eyes with his arm, Jon yanked the steering wheel and slammed on the brakes at the same time, sending the car spinning out of control.

In less than a second, a steel barrier exploded against Jon's door, sending the flashing light and shattered glass into his face and temporarily blinding him.

The back end of the car was the first to drop off the ledge. Jon's head snapped back so hard, it sent pinpricks of light flashing in front of his eyes.

Jon felt the passenger side of the car lift into the air. A moment later, the car spun ninety degrees, ripping off his door.

Jon was holding onto the steering wheel so hard, he didn't even realize it had broken off in his hands.

The windshield exploded seconds after the car slammed into the side of the ravine.

As the car tumbled and bounced down the hillside, Jon found himself suspended in midair outside the car. A moment later, the excruciating pain forced him to blink back tears. The left side of his head ricocheted off one rock and came to rest against another. A shard of glass imbedded itself deep into his left eye. When he finally stopped tumbling and rolling, his arms and midsection were pinned under the edge of the car's roof. His back, shoulders, and the side of his head were ground into the razor-sharp edge of a boulder the size of a dishwasher.

The snow seemed to be coming down harder now, and the temperature was dropping like a stone. Blowing and shaking his head, Jon was doing everything in his power to keep his mouth and nose from freezing and filling with snow.

"You don't listen very well, do you, Mister Summers?" said a voice from behind Jon.

Jon looked around frantically for the source of the voice, but he stopped as a leg crossed over the top of him. Straddling Jon's chest, Smitty lowered himself until Jon could make out his face with his one good eye.

"That better, Mister Summers?" Smitty didn't wait for an answer. "I gave you every warning I could think of. I started the very first day you arrived. I know you understood—you said you did the day you refused Dexter's offer to sell my house. You really seemed to get the message. But in reality, all this time, you were actually scheming and plotting to take Carlie away from where she belongs.

"Don't you understand? None of this had anything to do with you. You were never more than a necessary evil. Carlie belongs to me and to the house. My house and everyone in it belong to her. It's your fault that she wants to leave. I showed her my life—she understood and cared about what had happened to me. You were the one who made her fear the very thought of me."

Smitty started laughing. "You know, old Edith was right. It *was you* who allowed me into your lives. I guess I should thank you—but I won't.

"I'll tell you this, Mister Summers. With you gone, Carlie will never leave. She and I will finally be the family we were meant to be."

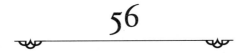

# 56

The afternoon was going by so slowly, Carlie felt that she could actually hear the seconds pass. Jon should have been home hours earlier.

Loretta and Cecil were trying to remain calm for Carlie's sake, but their concern was turning into panic, and it showed in their eyes. Loretta gave up trying to keep Carlie's mind occupied with other thoughts. She couldn't think of anything but Jon, either. Neither of them wanted to consider the worst-case scenario, but it was nearly dark and no one had heard a word from Jon since that morning.

Carlie called the college only to find that, according to the parking lot's automatic entry system, Jon's car had left school property at 10:45 AM.

Cecil retraced Jon's possible routes home from the college. First he drove into town, and then he reversed his route back to the college. Then he drove from the college to the house. Although there were cars and pickups stranded everywhere along the roadside, none of them was Jon's.

All three of them had run out of plausible excuses hours earlier as to why Jon was so late.

As the sun began to set, Carlie stood in the driveway and watched the cars pass by on the main highway. *Jon, where the hell are you?* she wondered.

When she finally couldn't stand the cold anymore, she turned to go back to the warmth of the house. The screeching and cawing of the blackbirds stopped her in her tracks. She saw them perched on the edge of the barn's roof. There must have been a hundred of them preening and flapping their wings. On the ground, there appeared to be at least fifty more. Carlie couldn't remember the last time she had seen this many birds out this close to sunset.

Directly in front of her, one blackbird stood out from the rest. It was larger, bolder, and much more aggressive. The feathers around its neck stood straight out and glistened in the setting sun—and it was staring at her. The bird's eyes were as black as polished obsidian. They were so clear and alert, Carlie swore the bird was thinking.

As Carlie watched to see what the blackbird would do, it stood perfectly still staring at her. It appeared to be sizing her up; for what reason, though, Carlie had no idea.

Walking toward the house, Carlie couldn't help but feel the bird watching her every move. It gave her an unsettling feeling, almost as strong as the shadows had the day of Dexter's stroke. Needing to see where the blackbird had gone, she turned around when she reached the steps. Carlie almost passed out when she found it following her less than three feet behind. It tipped its head and stared at her with one blue-black eye. It felt to Carlie as if it were trying to read her mind.

Loretta opened the door to see what was keeping Carlie. When she did, the blackbird took to the air. In less than a second, there was a cacophony of screeching and flapping wings as the entire flock took flight, disappearing into the night sky.

Night turned into day, and day turned into night, and still, no Jon. It was as if the universe had simply swallowed him up.

Carlie met with the state police the next morning. After convincing the officer that Jon didn't have a girlfriend and that they weren't having marital problems, the officer took a description of Jon's car. He explained that because of the storm, there were hundreds of stranded motorists—Jon was more than likely sitting on the side of a road somewhere, waiting for help.

When the officer left her standing in the empty driveway, she almost believed him.

By sunrise, the blackbirds had returned. They were not anywhere as vocal as they had been the evening before. They simply ruffled their glistening black feathers and watched.

By noon, the original two hundred had turned into a thousand. They were everywhere—on the roof, in the trees, on the ground. They were getting bolder; they barely moved when Carlie walked by.

At the bottom step, the largest of the birds was waiting for her, as it had the evening before. She bent down and reached out her hand. It looked at her inquisitively, showing absolutely no fear. Turning its head sideways, it blinked once and struck. Before Carlie realized what was happening, it bit her again, this time drawing blood.

Jerking her hand out of the way, she was about to kick the bird, but the look in its eyes, and the way the other birds were reacting, gave her pause. Looking around, she saw that every bird was staring at her. The large bird never gave an inch, not even when she shooed it and ran at it, clapping her hands. With ruffled feathers, it squatted in the snow, watching—and waiting.

Frustrated not only at the bird but at the situation in general, she looked down at it and said, "Fuck you, bird. Eat shit and die."

She didn't even look back as she slammed the door, leaving the birds outside.

Staring out the kitchen window at her cardinals as they ate, Carlie wanted to scream; moreover, she wanted to cry, but she knew that crying was the same as saying that Jon was gone forever. She couldn't give up hope.

In the distance, Carlie saw a dark triangular shape on the snow-covered hill, one she had never seen before. It was too far away to make out clearly, but it resembled a dog sitting on its haunches. If it was a dog, it was huge—and it appeared to be staring at her.

As she watched, it stood up and turned its head as if someone had called it. When it turned to leave, it stopped and looked back one more time.

In a second, it was gone. Carlie watched for a few more minutes, but it didn't return. The cardinals were finished eating, so she went into the living room.

To keep her mind off the clock as it ticked off every minute that Jon was still gone, she sat down on the floor and separated the clothes, pictures, and toys.

Dumping the entire clothing box on the floor, she was shocked to find a huge white bow on the very bottom. Separating the clothes one piece at a time, she found the tan corduroy overalls the twin boys were wearing in her dream, and finally, the white dress that belonged to Lisa.

Scooping all the pictures into a pile, she went through each one until she located the pictures of Lisa and the twins. She even found the boys' favorite toys in one picture, which sent her across the room to the boxes of antique toys. After a half hour of searching, she was able to find only one of the trucks the boys were playing with in the picture.

All she could find for Lisa was a black and white photo of her posing in her white confirmation dress, with the white bow in her hair.

She didn't find any of the three on a memorial, so Carlie figured that she had found everything there was for them. She placed their personal belongings in individual cardboard boxes.

When the front door opened behind her, Carlie spun around expecting to see Jon standing there. She was so positive that it would be Jon, she didn't even recognize Loretta.

Carlie's heart sank when she discovered it wasn't Jon. She felt that this was one less opportunity for him to walk through the door.

As Loretta sat down, Carlie told her what she had been doing. Before she told her what she had found, she asked if Loretta knew where the county had buried Ian and Edith.

Loretta looked at Carlie as if she were speaking Portuguese. "Why on earth would you want to know that?"

"I'm just curious, I guess. Do you know?"

Standing, Loretta took Carlie by the hand and led her into the kitchen. Pointing out the window, she said, "You see those three oak trees? That's where all the McPhersons are buried—even Andrew."

It was the same spot as in her dream and also where Carlie had seen the animal. "I thought it might be."

"I can't figure for the life of me why you would want to know. They're way off your property—isolated—exactly where they belong."

Turning and walking back into the living room, Carlie thought aloud, "Maybe . . . I hope so anyway."

Refocusing her attention, Carlie told Loretta what she had found. She had actually located the belongings and identities of three more children, making a total of ten.

By laying out the children's clothes, Carlie figured, she might be able to recognize them from her dream. If she could, maybe she would be able to remember the face that went with the outfit. There were a lot of ifs and maybes, but she needed to get this done so they could leave this house forever.

Together, Loretta and Carlie began to make significant progress. They were able to find clothing and/or toys that matched a part of a memorial, a photo, or a description in a death certificate. Loretta had brought hundreds of empty boxes from the café, so they placed what they pieced together in separate boxes.

When there was a knock on the door, they both jumped. Carlie's head spun toward the grandfather clock. It was 11:45 PM. *Could it be Jon?* she wondered. *If it is, why is he knocking on the door? Because he's hurt, that's why!*

Jumping to her feet, Carlie almost fell down. Her legs were sound asleep.

When the blood started to return, she raced across the living room and threw open the front door, expecting to find Jon standing on the front porch, broken and bleeding but very much alive.

She took three steps back when she saw the uniform of the highway patrol officer standing in front of her.

There was still a glimmer of hope that Jon was all right, but it was fading fast. Maybe he was hurt and in the hospital. Wouldn't the hospital call? Of course they would. There was only one scenario that required sending an officer to her door. Just the thought of it was too much for her. Her head began to swim, and her ears started ringing. The next thing she knew, the highway patrolman was kneeling beside her and Loretta was leaning over her.

They helped Carlie to Jon's chair and lifted her feet up. The patrolman sat down on the side of the ottoman and held her hand. He didn't need to say a word; Carlie knew that Jon was dead. She didn't need nor did she want to know all of the particulars. Nevertheless, the officer had a responsibility to let them know the how, when, and where of the incident. He was almost finished with his canned speech when he mentioned something in passing that immediately caught her attention.

"I beg your pardon?" Carlie said.

The patrolman sat in silence, waiting for her to be more specific.

"You said something about a large animal—possibly a dog?"

"Oh yes … I did. Next to your husband's body, we found some very large paw prints in the snow. I simply wondered if maybe you had a large dog. Do you? Have a dog, that is?"

"No, we don't."

"It's of no consequence. I just thought you should know."

"Thank you for telling me."

Loretta walked the officer to the door. Turning back to the older woman, he asked, "Are you going to stay with her tonight? I wouldn't leave her alone."

"Yes, I will. I have no idea how to contact her parents, but I'm going to be here with her."

Once the officer's tail lights turned onto the highway, Loretta closed the door and picked up the telephone.

"Cecil, I need you here. Jon's been found—he's dead. … She's just sitting here; she hasn't moved or even changed her expression. … Okay, I'll see you in a little while."

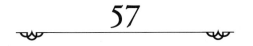

## 57

After pouring a cup of coffee, Carlie sat down across from Cecil and Loretta.

"It was Andrew," she began. "I don't know how he did it, but I know it was him. He's killed every single one of them, and now he's killed Jon too. I still have a few things left to do. But when I'm done—fuck Andrew, and fuck this miserable house—I'm going to burn this place to the ground."

Reaching across the table, Carlie took Cecil's hand in hers. "I need a huge favor."

Cecil looked down at the table and blushed noticeably. "Anything you need—just ask."

"I need a shotgun. I know nothing about guns, so I'm relying on you. I need at least two boxes of shells designed to take the top off that oak tree in the yard. I also want a box of shells powerful enough to take out that nasty animal, if I ever encounter it. I don't want to just take it out—I want to dismember it."

Looking over at Loretta, Carlie said, "Listen, you know Andrew is going to come after me. I don't know when or how, but he will. I want you two out of harm's way."

Loretta was about to complain, but Carlie waved her off. "Now you two need to run along. I'm going to take a shower and get going. I have a million things I need to do. If it's all right, I'll swing by the café and pick up the shotgun later this afternoon."

After Carlie walked Loretta and Cecil to their truck, she stood in the drive and watched them leave. When they stopped before entering the highway, she waved. Cecil honked the horn three times in response.

The house was as quiet as a tomb. Sitting down in Jon's chair, Carlie wanted to cry, but she knew she would never stop once she started. There would be a time to cry later. Right now, she had things to do.

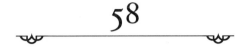

## 58

Carlie's first stop was to trade in her BMW. The day before, Carlie had spotted exactly what she was looking for sitting on a showroom floor.

As she entered the showroom, her eyes went immediately to the brand-new pickup with four-wheel drive sitting in the middle of the floor.

The owner of the dealership stepped out of his office to take care of Carlie personally. He knew her, and he knew Dexter; their firm had represented him and his dealership since he opened the doors.

"Carlie, I'm so sorry to hear about Jon. If there is anything I can do, don't hesitate to ask."

"Well, Peter, you can sell me that truck."

As Carlie was paying the cashier, Peter handed her the keys.

Carlie kissed him on the cheek and left him standing in the door scratching his head.

Pulling to the curb in front of Dexter's house, Carlie shut off the engine and waited. She didn't have to wait long. Lester opened the front door with his arms full of scrap paper and folded painter's tarps. Setting them on the front porch, he blocked the sun from his eyes and watched Carlie as she stepped out of her new truck.

As Carlie made her way across the front yard, she extended her right hand and introduced herself.

"Well, Missus Summers, I am very pleased to meet you."

"It's very nice to meet you too, Lester. Please call me Carlie. I just stopped by to see how you were doing."

"I heard about Mister Summers. I am so sorry. He was a nice man."

"Yes, he was. Are you still planning on being finished by Monday?"

"Yes, I sure am."

"Well, I was wondering if you could possibly do me a favor."

"Anything—you just ask."

"On Monday, they're going to be delivering the new furniture for the bedroom. I was wondering if you could meet the delivery men and show them where to set everything up. I'll gladly pay you for the extra time."

"I've been more than compensated. I'll be here first thing Monday. Don't you worry, Missus Summers."

Shaking his hand again, Carlie thanked him and walked back to her truck.

Carlie checked her watch; it was still early enough to make it the forty-five miles to East Des Moines before Bannerman Funeral Home closed for the day.

~

Phillip Bannerman was sitting in his office when one of his associates escorted Carlie to an empty conference room.

Carrying two cups of coffee into the room, Phillip's expression told Carlie that he was both curious and concerned about why she had returned so soon.

Carlie knew that the longer it took her to get to the point, the harder it was going to be. She had to face the fact that Jon was actually gone. Making his funeral arrangements was just about as real as the situation was ever going to get.

Phillip listened in sympathetic silence as Carlie told him about Jon's recent death.

"Phillip," Carlie said, "I understand that with the inclusion of Jonathon, you will not be able to start Monday morning as you had originally planned. I really hope that, weather permitting, you will be able to start by the end of next week."

"That will not be a problem, Missus Summers. You can be confident that I will handle all the arrangements. Please don't concern yourself."

Standing, Carlie shook the funeral director's hand. "Thank you, Phillip. I brought you ten boxes; they're in my truck."

As Carlie stood to leave, Phillip stood to escort her out. Stopping for a moment, he opened a cardboard box that was sitting on the entrance hall table. Pulling out a smaller box, he opened it for Carlie's inspection and approval. Taking the bronze urn in her hands, she turned it around and nodded in approval.

"This will be fine. Make sure you don't forget the concrete vaults. I want one for every grave."

Without another word, Carlie shook the director's hand again and left.

Carlie pulled into the parking lot of the café just after 1:00. The lunch rush was over, and Cecil's truck was the only vehicle besides Carlie's sitting in the snow-packed lot.

They were both surprised to see Carlie so early. When they stood to meet her at her and Jon's usual booth, she waved for them to sit. It was an unconscious action, but she understood that she was starting an era in her life where she would be sitting alone from now on.

Carlie ordered lunch, and for the first time in over twenty years, she ordered something that she and not Jon enjoyed eating.

For the next three hours, Loretta kept the conversation light and refrained from mentioning Jon or his impending funeral. Carlie broached the subject first by telling them that she had arranged for Jon's funeral services to be held on Thursday or Friday of next week, depending on the weather.

Standing, Carlie looked down at Cecil. "Well, I'm ready for my weapons lesson."

Cecil stood and Carlie followed him outside to his pickup. On the front seat was a black rifle case. Next to it was a large plastic sack from the local sporting goods store.

Taking the shotgun out of the case, Cecil pulled the ejector back to make sure it was empty. He opened one of the boxes from the sack and pulled out five shells. Tipping the shotgun onto its side so Carlie could watch, he slid each shell into the recessed slot on the right side.

"This particular shotgun will hold nine shells. It should take down anything that flies, from a turkey to a pterodactyl. All you have to do is hit it.

"Keep this padded piece tight against your shoulder. If you don't, the gun will jump, and you'll not only miss what you're shooting at, but the gun will more than likely hit you right in the chin.

"One last thing: this shotgun is fully automatic. It will eject the shell the second it fires. Since you're left-handed, try to keep your face out of the way—the shells are very hot. To eject shells on your own, simply pull the handle on the bottom toward you. Keep doing it until the shells stop coming out.

"Any questions?"

"I think I have it. I can't thank you enough, Cecil."

"Listen, I just want to remind you that you don't have to do this alone. Anytime you feel overwhelmed, don't give it a second thought—call me."

Carlie could barely hold back her tears. She stood on her toes and gave Cecil a kiss on the cheek. Without saying a word, she got behind the wheel of the truck and started it up.

Cecil stood in the parking lot and Loretta just outside the café door as they watched her drive away.

Pulling into the front yard, she stopped at the front steps. Shutting off the engine, Carlie took the shotgun out of its rack.

The blackbirds were back and sitting silently on the edge of the barn roof. The barren limbs of the giant oak trees were alive with the black, squiggling masses. As Carlie opened the truck door, she spun around, sitting on the edge of her seat. With her feet resting on the roll bar underneath the door, she watched the birds as they began to gather. Almost as if on command, a handful of birds dropped to the ground from their perches on the roof. Shaking and ruffling their ebony feathers, they squatted in the snow, tipped their heads to one side, and watched her.

Carlie searched the ground, the barn, and the trees, but she didn't see the larger bird that had bitten her. She had a surprise for him. Taking the shotgun in her left hand, she turned the key and locked the pickup's door. As she turned to walk up the front steps of the house, she saw the large bird standing on the top step, staring down at her. *Crap*, she thought, *I'm going to have to shoot a hole in my front door to kill this thing.*

Taking the shotgun, Carlie pointed it into the air and pulled the trigger. It exploded with an almost deafening roar. The impact of the gun's recoil slammed against her left shoulder, sending a wave of pain coursing down her arm.

Swinging the barrel back toward the porch, Carlie found she was a little too slow. The bird was already in flight and heading right at her face.

Ducking her head at the last instant, the bird managed to only graze her forehead and tangle its talons in her hair. Screaming, Carlie waved her free arm frantically. Hitting the huge bird in the side, she freed the frenzy of flapping wings and razor-sharp talons from her hair and scalp, sending her attacker and most of the flock into the air in a state of confused hysteria.

Picking up her purse and the plastic bag of shotgun shells from the snow, Carlie walked up the steps. Then she stopped, turned around, and looked to see if the bird had returned. A cold panic set in as she watched the black airborne wave descending on the power lines, barn, and snow-packed drive. She threw open the front door and ran into the house, slamming the door behind her.

Dropping the gun, sack, and purse on the floor, Carlie pulled the curtain back to find thousands of preening birds hopping and pecking at each other. A sea of black bobbing heads and flapping wings completely covered her driveway.

When three birds flew directly into the picture window, Carlie fell backward off the couch and threw the curtain closed as she did. A series of sharp thuds, followed by a softer, more subtle thud on the wooden porch, told her that the birds weren't completely finished committing suicide yet. She was glad that Jon had replaced the original window with a double-pane safety glass. It would take a bird the size of Rodan to break that window.

Sitting down on the edge of the couch, Carlie leaned over and put her head in her hands. "FUCK, FUCK, FUCK!" she shouted. "This is un-fucking-believable. My life is turning into an Alfred Hitchcock movie."

Standing, she kicked the shotgun out of the way as she walked to the kitchen. "You worthless piece of shit," she said under her breath.

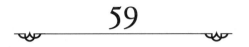

## 59

The sun coming through the kitchen window woke Carlie from one of the best night's sleep she had had in months. She needed to get dressed and get going; morning Mass started in less than an hour.

The blackbirds were back. Armed with her shotgun, she walked straight through them. After unlocking and opening the truck door, she stepped to the side and turned toward the huddled masses sitting in the snow. Carlie didn't even aim; she just pulled the trigger, unleashing seven hundred pellets rocketing through the freezing morning air at over eighteen hundred feet per second.

Before the shiny mass of screeching feathers could react, Carlie pulled the trigger again. Hundreds of birds took to the sky. Dozens more lay dead or dying in the snow. The frozen morning air hung heavy with the smell of burnt cordite as Carlie pulled her door shut. Starting the truck's engine, she waited a few moments for it to warm up before putting it in gear. She backed into the driveway and headed out to the highway.

Turning toward town, she never looked back.

It took almost two hours to arrange with the local parish priest to bless the property where Jon and so many others would soon be laid to rest. Satisfied that she had done all she could for the time being, she headed for home. She still had so many things to do, and she was running short on time to get them accomplished.

She spent the evening working on indentifying children. She needed to put a name to as many of the children as she could before the workers from Bannerman Funeral Home arrived the following week.

After three hours on the floor, she needed a break. Turning on the bathroom light, the reflection looking back at her in the mirror almost scared her to death. Her worn and haggard face looked twenty years older. Deep creases ran down both sides of her mouth, and her heavy eyelids drooped at the corners. White streaks had taken over her once-beautiful auburn hair.

What had it been, four, maybe five days since she had eaten more than a sandwich? She couldn't remember. If she didn't start taking better care of herself, Bannerman's would be burying her right along with Jon.

Standing over the kitchen sink, Carlie ate boxed macaroni and cheese out of the pan.

She was full after three bites; her stomach had shrunk to the size of an orange. Even after eating, she found that she didn't have any energy. She could barely lift the pan.

Pouring a cup of tea, Carlie returned to the living room. Looking at the mess on the floor, she was comfortable with her progress; she had accomplished a lot. She had located the names of three more children and placed their belongings in boxes.

Lowering the volume on the stereo, she wrapped her shoulders in a shawl. She sat down in Jon's old chair and took a sip of tea. Closing her eyes, she drifted into a shallow, restless sleep.

~

At the sound of the chimes, Carlie reluctantly stood and answered the door. Backlit in the moonlight was a redheaded, freckle-faced young man of about eighteen.

With his hands stuffed casually in his jacket pockets, the boy said, "Missus Summers?" He continued without waiting. He seemed to already know the answer. "I'm the caretaker of this property—and I have been for a very long time. Everyone calls me Smitty. I guess it's because my last name is Smith, but you can call me Andrew if you'd like."

Stopping for a second, he looked at the ground as if he were try-ing to remember something important. Quietly, he started again. "Oh yeah, by the way, I'm very sorry to hear about your husband's accident. I was surprised when I heard that you two might be moving away. I tried to warn him. I told him that he didn't want to leave. This is a very special house, but things happen here, especially if someone angers the spirits.

"I can't tell you how glad I am that you chose not to move away.

"I'm sure we'll get things back to normal around here in no time. We'll be just like a family, you and me."

With that said, the boy turned and walked away.

Carlie stood just inside the door and watched as the boy walked into the shadows. Slamming the door closed, she awoke from her dream when she heard someone beating on the door. As she opened her eyes, she heard someone beat on the door a third time.

Opening the door, Carlie almost passed out from shock. It was Jon. She knew that it was, but his misshapen head and the ungodly amount of blood made him almost unrecognizable. He stood in the frigid night air shaking and dripping mud, debris, and diluted blood on the porch. Dried blood matted his blond hair to his scalp.

Carlie couldn't believe her eyes; she wondered how he had made it all the way home in this condition. All along, she had known he wasn't dead—she just knew it. However, he would be soon by the looks of him. She had to do something quick; she had to help him or he would die.

With his eyes fixed on Carlie's face, his mouth moved incoherently, as if controlled by an unseen puppet master.

Carlie flipped the switch to turn on the porch light. Stepping onto the porch, she saw that something besides the obvious was horribly wrong. Jon had the appearance of a broken marionette. His hips jutted backward, and his spine seemed to be completely detached. His misshapen body rocked, jerked, and twitched spasmodically as he tried to speak.

Carlie couldn't take her eyes off his face. His left eye was milky white. It had a thin shard of glass almost an inch long protruding from the center of it, and a translucent white liquid ran down his cheek. But it was his right eye that drew her attention; it begged for her to listen—he wanted to tell her something.

Even though she was horrified by his appearance, Carlie knew in her heart that this was the man she loved—the same man that she had vowed to spend the rest of her life with.

As she reached her arms out to hold him up, Jon tried to raise his own, throwing him off balance. There was an audible crunching as she lifted his left arm over her shoulder. The bones separated in his forearm, dropping the front half of it down the center of her back.

Carlie felt an icy chill permeate her robe when Jon fell into her arms. Twisting his good arm around her waist, he pulled her tight up against where his chest used to be.

His voice was raspy, and his breath reeked of raw meat, formaldehyde, and alcohol when he whispered in her ear, "I've come...to take you with me."

Carlie pushed him away, tearing off the two buttons holding his shirt closed. Staring at his grayish skin and a hastily sewn Y that started at both shoulders, met in the middle of his sternum, and ended below the waist of his pants, she screamed at the top of her lungs.

Carlie awoke and found herself sitting straight up in the chair. No longer screaming, she was, however, panting like a dog. Staring at the front door, she realized she was on the verge of a complete meltdown. All she needed was one more nightmare like that one.

As she dropped her head on top of her knees, she made a vow that she would never sleep again.

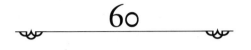

# 60

By the end of the fourth day, Carlie couldn't even find the courage to walk from one room to another without carrying her shotgun. She was completely losing it—she knew it—but she didn't know how to stop. Andrew could get to her anytime he wanted.

The workers from Bannerman's would be there the next day, or the day after at the latest. They would complete the burials as agreed, and then she could get the hell out of the house forever.

If everything went all right, tonight Carlie would finish identifying the children that she had personal items for. She merely needed to finish going through the steamer trunk from the attic. A few days earlier, she had managed to wrestle it down the ladder and empty everything out that belonged to a child. Then she had dragged the old trunk out to the barn. She had nearly thirty new boxes completely finished and waiting for Bannerman's crew.

Carlie almost jumped out of her skin when the telephone rang. It hadn't rung in almost a month. She actually had to stop and think where she had left it. The portable was lying exactly where Loretta had left it the night of the storm, but the battery was dead.

Rushing into the kitchen, she managed to pick up the receiver before it switched to the answering machine. She was about to say hello, but she stopped and held it away from her ear as if it were a snake. She could still hear Jon's raspy voice reverberating in her head. As she stared at the receiver in her hand, she could hear a man's voice on the other end. "Hello? Hello—Missus Summers? This is Bannerman Funeral Home. Hello?"

Still a little apprehensive, Carlie put the receiver to her ear. "Hello?"

"Hello, Missus Summers?"

"This is Carlie."

"Hello, Missus Summers. This is Phillip Bannerman."

"Oh hello, Phillip. How can I help you?"

"Well, actually, I'm calling to tell you that my men will be there by 7:00 AM tomorrow. Is it all right if they meet at your house and then you show them where the property is?"

"That will be fine, Phillip. I'll be expecting them."

Hanging up, Carlie stood in the kitchen going over everything she could think of that she needed to have finished by morning.

It was almost lunchtime, but she still didn't have an appetite. She forced herself to eat something at least once a day.

When she took a shower now, she averted her eyes from the mirror. She looked like an Auschwitz survivor.

She only ate to keep herself alive.

She could work on identifying the children later that night. Right at the moment, she needed to find one last item. She wasn't positive where she would find it, but she had a good idea where to start looking.

Carlie headed out the front door to the barn with her shotgun resting over her left arm. The blackbirds were pecking and ruffling their feathers when she walked out the door. The minute she reached the bottom step, the birds stopped what they were doing and started staring at her.

"Good afternoon, you little assholes," Carlie said. Lifting her shotgun, she fired two shots in quick succession at the barn roof and one more at the top of the oak tree. As birds, dead leaves, and small branches fell to the ground, the rest of the flock took to the sky. She knew they would be back, but it really didn't matter to her anymore.

Reloading, she walked toward the barn.

The crowbar was hanging on the wall exactly where she had left it. Taking it down, she carried the heavy tool back to the cellar door. Kicking the snow away, she jammed the hooked end under the hasp and pushed down with all her weight. There was a creaking sound as the wood began to give, but the lock and its mount didn't budge.

Carlie stepped on the end of the crowbar with her heavy work boot. As the crowbar settled to the ground, the hasp made a sharp cracking sound—and then a loud, distinctive pop as it released from its wooden mounting and flew across the yard.

After prying open the heavy cellar door, Carlie returned to the barn for the electric lantern. Hanging up the crowbar, she took down the lantern and returned to the cellar. As she shined the light down the stairs, she was glad to see that it had enough power to eliminate any shadows.

At the bottom of the stairs, she saw boot prints. They weren't hers, and Jon didn't have a pair. She followed them around behind the staircase. Tucked into the corner out of sight were two boxes.

Carlie opened the top of the first box and shined the light inside. The clothes inside were filthy, and there was a crusty dark brown substance coating almost every inch of them. The pants were stiff with the same substance, as were the front and back of the shirt. In the bottom of the box was a handkerchief full of what felt like money. Carlie knew she had the right boxes.

In the second box she found a beautiful hand-crocheted baby blanket. Carlie doubted that Edith had made it for Andrew, but she might have. Taking it out of the box, the revolver wrapped inside fell to the floor. This had to be the same gun Ian had shot Andrew with. It was the only explanation that made any sense. Andrew had destroyed every other personal item Ian and Edith had owned in the fire.

Carlie put everything back in the boxes, then picked them up and walked toward the bottom of the stairs. Taking one last look around the empty cellar floor, she leveled her shotgun in front of her and started up the stairs.

She had taken no more than three steps when a dark shadow at the top of the stairs blocked the light. Carlie waited for less than a minute before the massive shadow started moving quietly down the wooden steps. The only sound it made was a gentle clicking as it moved from one step to the next.

The small slit of daylight behind the enormous shadow disappeared with an audible thud. Dropping the boxes, Carlie flicked on her powerful lantern to see a pair of green eyes reflecting back in the pitch-black cellar. Someone had closed the cellar door after letting this beast in to kill her. She tried to steady the light on the approaching animal as she rummaged in her jacket pocket to retrieve a handful of the deer slugs Cecil had bought for her.

She dropped two on the floor, but she managed to hang on to three, and fed them into the shotgun. Cocking the gun, she fed the first shell into the chamber; bracing herself, she waited.

Slowly the beast made its way down the stairs.

Carlie wasn't sure what to expect next. Would it leap at her when it got close enough? Perhaps it would simply run down the stairs and attack her at ground level.

The glowing eyes seemed to have stopped moving. Carlie could hear its breathing; it sniffed repeatedly at the stagnant cellar air, getting her scent. Carlie figured that if it were searching for the scent of fear, it wouldn't have to search very hard.

Carlie leveled the shotgun at the sound of its breathing. The electric lantern was heavy and cumbersome when holding it under the barrel of the shotgun. Its light danced crazily between the wall and the handrail of the cellar stairs. As the light crossed the beast, she briefly made out its size and general appearance. Its elongated face and hunched shoulders definitely didn't look like any dog Carlie had ever seen.

"Listen," Carlie said aloud, "we can do this one of two ways. I can blow you into bite-size pieces, or you can get out of my way and simply let me go by."

The huge animal cocked its head as if it were listening.

"Well, what's it going to be?"

Slowly the animal walked down a few more steps Stopping, it again sniffed the air.

Carlie stepped back and lowered the barrel of the shotgun. As she did, the animal moved down a couple more steps.

Carlie backed herself against the cellar wall as the animal made its way to the bottom of the stairs. She trained the light on the beast as it sniffed the floor and the air. Carlie had never seen a wolf up close before—it was bigger than she ever could have imagined. It stood almost to her waist.

Carlie watched as it sniffed the boxes lying on the floor. She needed those boxes, and she couldn't let this animal stop her from taking them. "Okay, you. Back the fuck up. Those are mine."

Again, the animal cocked its head, listening to every word Carlie said. It remained perfectly still until Carlie began to move toward the boxes. When she did, it dropped its head and gave a deep guttural growl. Carlie planned to take the boxes with her—even if she had to shoot the animal. As Carlie took one more step forward, the wolf bared its teeth. It didn't turn toward her or make an overt move to attack, but it kept its head lowered over the boxes—moving only its eyes to watch her.

Carlie moved forward again. She was close enough to grab at least one of the boxes. The animal growled again, deeper and more threatening. Reaching out her hand, the beast turned toward her. It dropped its haunches and lunged at her hand, snapping its teeth as it did.

As fast as the creature moved, Carlie knew she couldn't raise the shotgun, aim, and shoot before the animal would tear her apart. As long as she didn't attempt to touch the boxes, she felt relatively safe.

Standing perfectly still against the wall, she couldn't help but smell the animal in the enclosed confines of the cellar; it had a wild, gamy odor underlying a different scent—a more pleasant one. Its fur smelled like newly harvested wheat. The gaminess had to be from when it exhaled its fetid breath.

With the barrel of the shotgun lowered in the most nonthreatening manner she could manage, she hung her head in submission and skirted the animal as she walked toward the stairs. At the bottom, she turned around to find the large animal still watching her. Moving backward, she took one step at a time, keeping her light trained on it, waiting to see if it still planned to attack her. Evidently it didn't—as long as she left the boxes where they were.

At the top of the stairs, she turned and pushed on the cellar door. It flashed through her mind that Andrew might have locked it.

Again, she pushed on the door, and this time it started to move. Standing straight up, she pushed with all her strength. The door swung past the halfway point and fell open with a soft thud onto the snow.

After throwing the cellar door closed behind her, she ran as fast as her legs would carry her into the safety of the house.

She started sobbing and shaking. Dropping to her knees, she wrapped her arms around herself and rested her head on the hard wooden floor.

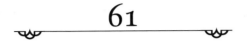

# 61

Opening the front door and sticking her head inside, Loretta found Carlie lying motionless in a fetal position on the living room floor. "Oh my God, *Carlie!*" Loretta screamed.

Looking up at her friend kneeling at her side, Carlie asked, "What are you doing here?"

"I'm here to help. I've had a sick feeling in the pit of my stomach for days. I knew something was wrong—I just didn't know what it was."

Helping Carlie into a sitting position, Loretta picked up the shotgun lying on the floor and stood it in the corner. By the time she was done, Carlie was already standing and moving toward the couch.

Sitting down on the coffee table, Loretta placed her finger under Carlie's chin and lifted her face until they were looking into each other's eyes.

Before Carlie could say anything, Loretta put her finger to Carlie's dry, cracked lips. "Shhhh, I don't want to hear another word. It's time you listen to me for a change. This hero crap is not working out at all. I don't know what's going on here, but by the looks of the carnage in the front yard, you're having real problems."

Carlie couldn't help but smile. "I really am glad to see you. I just don't want you hurt."

"I'm not going to get hurt, and I'm going to do everything in my power to make sure you don't get hurt either. What do you have left to do before you can get the hell out of here?"

"I have maybe a half-dozen children left to identify."

Taking Loretta's hand, she led the older woman into the kitchen. As she put on a pot of coffee, Carlie told her about her encounter with the giant black wolf in the cellar.

"We don't see many wolves around here," Loretta said. "I can't remember hearing of a wolf getting this close to the population."

"This beast was huge—bigger than any wolf I've ever seen. It came into the cellar to protect those boxes. I hate to say this, but Edith is on her own. I'm not going to die to help her."

"That sounds like the best idea you've had in months."

Picking up their coffee cups, the two moved into the living room. Carlie figured it would only take them a couple hours to identify the rest of the children. There just wasn't that much left to go through.

A little after midnight, Carlie and Loretta loaded the back of her pickup with the finished boxes. They had done all they could to identify the children that Carlie had seen in her dream.

After hearing Carlie's story, Loretta kept the shotgun leaning against the side of Carlie's truck. Neither of them moved more than a foot away from it unless the other was there to take her place. It took longer to move all the boxes from the house, but they didn't intend to allow anyone or anything to get close enough to hurt them.

Loretta wondered if Carlie would survive to see the end of this nightmare.

～

There was a knock on the front door at exactly 6:45 the next morning. At the sound, Carlie sat straight up in the chair and looked over at Loretta, who was sound asleep under the comforter on the bed. The second knock came almost a minute later and was a little more forceful. It was much too reminiscent of her dream for her liking. When the third knock came, the door chimes followed it immediately. Carlie's stomach tied itself into a knot.

A soft voice came from under the comforter. "Are you going to answer the door, sweetie, or should I?"

Realizing that she wasn't dreaming, Carlie felt foolish overreacting to a simple knock on the door. Standing, she pulled on her robe and tied the sash around her waist. "I've got it."

Opening the door, Carlie was surprised to see her entire driveway filled with excavation equipment, pickup trucks, and a dozen men in work clothes. Phillip Bannerman's assistant was standing on the porch in the gray early morning light. He was dressed in his customary black suit and an expensive black overcoat. Looking down at what she was wearing, Carlie blushed and apologized.

"I'm so sorry," she said. "I forgot you were coming so early. Please come in."

Stepping back, she allowed the man inside the house.

Stopping just inside the threshold, the man extended his right hand. "I'm Harold, Mister Bannerman's assistant. Phillip will be here a little later, but right now, I will be in charge of the removal of the coffin in your garden. If you will show me its location, my men will get started."

"Give me five minutes to get dressed. Please have a seat. I'll be down as quickly as I can."

Loretta was dressed and tying her boots when Carlie walked into the bedroom.

"It's the workmen from Bannerman Funeral Home," Carlie told her.

"I'll keep them company while you get dressed," Loretta said as she passed Carlie on her way out the bedroom door.

Carlie listened as Loretta made her way down the stairs. When she heard conversation, she quickly dressed in a pair of jeans and a heavy long-sleeve shirt.

Carrying her boots in her hand, Carlie followed the sound of voices into the kitchen. Loretta was pouring three cups of coffee. Harold had taken off his overcoat and unbuttoned his suit coat. He looked like he was actually comfortable sitting at the breakfast table. Loretta had a way of making people feel right at home.

Carlie took a sip of coffee as she tied her work boots. Her baby's grave lay underneath at least three feet of new snow, and the drifts were up to six feet deep in places.

Putting on her Uncle William's old jacket, Carlie looked down at Harold and said, "You might want to stay here. I'll find the man in charge and show him where the gravesite is."

"I'll go out with you; my men will clear a path. I need to get my automobile back there anyway."

Harold pulled on his overcoat and followed Carlie and Loretta to the front door.

Outside, his men had already plowed a large circle at the end of the drive. When Carlie walked up to the man in charge, he crawled out of the machine and introduced himself. Carlie pointed to where the gravesite was located, but she needed to make sure he wouldn't fall through the cellar door. Walking across the yard, Carlie stopped and showed him where the door was located. She was surprised to find the door closed. She figured Andrew would leave it open after letting out the wolf and retrieving his boxes.

As three of the crew members dug carefully in the garden, Carlie and Loretta sat in Carlie's idling pickup.

The blackbirds had returned at sunup. There were more birds today than Carlie had ever seen. They not only lined the edge of the barn, they covered the entire roof of it. Every tree was alive with sound and movement, as were the power lines running from the highway to the house.

Loretta looked at the flock in amazement. "How long have they been here?"

"They started about the time Jon died."

Just as Carlie caught a glimpse of the larger bird, Bannerman's silver hearse pulled up behind her truck. Indicating they were ready to go, Carlie backed into the drive and led the convoy out onto the highway.

No one had cleared Breckenridge Road since the beginning of the storm. The snow was almost as deep as a car in places. The crew had brought digging equipment, but only the tiny Bobcat had the capability to clear a path.

It took a little over an hour for the convoy to make it to Grace's monument.

Once on the property, the little Bobcat immediately started clearing the snow. The rest of the men unloaded the pickups and started laying out tent poles. Harold told Carlie and Loretta that they would be ready to start digging just after lunch. If they wanted to come back then, it would be fine. There was little sense in them waiting in the cold for three or four hours.

Carlie walked through the gate into the tiny cemetery to tell Harold that they would be back later when she noticed movement outside the fence. Someone was watching what was going on. She wasn't sure if there were any neighbors around, but if there were, they didn't have to lurk in the shadows; she would be more than happy to explain to them what she was doing.

Harold touched her sleeve, causing Carlie to jump.

While telling him her plans, she kept the location of the movement in her peripheral vision.

Back in the truck, she pointed out the area where she had seen the movement. She and Loretta watched and waited; it took only a few minutes before they both saw two shadows just outside the stand of trees. As they watched, the dark figure led a large dog away into the valley.

Just before they were completely out of sight, the shadowy figures stopped and turned. Carlie was positive they were looking directly at her.

# 62

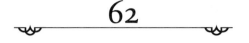

Carlie and Loretta parked the truck on the side of Breckenridge Road just as the backhoe scraped back the first few inches of grass and dirt.

The white tent that Bannerman's crew had set up was large enough to cover the entire cemetery. However, the sides were rolled up, allowing Carlie to see exactly what was going on inside. She watched as the big yellow tractor took another bite of the dirt.

Looking over at Loretta, Carlie asked, "Do you want to come with me?"

Grabbing her coat, Loretta nodded, opened the door, and stepped out into the frigid afternoon air.

Harold had backed the Bannerman hearse inside the enclosure. Both Phillip and Harold were standing next to its open back door. As Carlie walked up to the men, she noticed the little coffin sitting on the floor of the hearse. She was amazed to find that they had taken the time to clean and cover it before they transported it to its new location. Sitting next to it was the cardboard box that held the urn with the remains of her husband. Just looking at the box gave her an empty, sinking feeling.

This was it—this was the end of her life with Jon. Just the thought of never seeing his crooked smile or hearing his infectious laughter again broke her heart. She wanted to say something inspirational, something that might give the utter absurdity of this entire situation a higher purpose in the grand scheme of things. But she couldn't. When Loretta touched her sleeve, Carlie turned and looked at her friend. With tears forming in her eyes, she said, "A life as wonderful as the one I shared with Jon could never end any other way than tragically. This is

*Carlie's baby's coffin just before reburial.*

*Carlie's cemetery on Breckenridge Road, circa 1985.*

entirely my fault, Loretta. I'm the one who wanted this house enough to sacrifice everything to keep it. Jon's dead because of me."

As soon as the backhoe was finished, Harold backed the hearse closer to the newly dug grave. Phillip and Harold each took hold of a side of the white homemade coffin. Reverently they carried it to the side of the grave. Setting it down, they asked if Carlie cared to say a few words before they lowered it. She didn't.

After they lowered Carlie's baby into her new resting place, they placed Jon's urn in a concrete burial vault and sealed it. Setting it at the bottom of the little white coffin, they looked to Carlie again for some kind of eulogy. When none was forthcoming, two men with shovels began to fill in the hole.

Loretta took hold of Carlie's hand as they stood at the graveside. They watched in silence while the men filled it in. Carlie's hands and feet were so cold, they had lost all feeling, but neither of them moved until the men were completely finished.

After the workmen left, Carlie just stood staring at the newly formed mound of dirt. Her mind was wrapped in an impenetrable black shroud.

"Excuse me, Missus Summers?" Phillip Bannerman said.

Carlie looked in his general direction, but she had escaped to a world where there was no pain or loss—one where the sun would rise in the morning.

Loretta looked at Phillip and shook her head slowly.

"It's nothing that can't wait. We'll be here for at least three days."

Still holding Carlie's hand, Loretta led her back to her pickup.

Carlie didn't pay any attention to anything that was going on around her; she just stared at the ground as Loretta opened the passenger door and urged her inside, out of the cold. She complied almost robotically.

At the end of Breckenridge Road, Loretta looked over at her friend, who was still sitting motionless, staring at the floor with her hands folded in her lap. Instead of turning left to Carlie's house, Loretta turned right, heading to the opposite end of town.

Twenty minutes later, Loretta pulled into her own driveway. Cecil was in the yard playing with the dog when the strange pickup turned into his drive. Throwing the ball as far as he could, he crossed his arms and waited. When the truck was close enough for him to see that it was Loretta driving, he loped to the edge of the yard. Loretta pulled up next to him and parked.

Cecil looked in through Loretta's window to see Carlie sitting like a carved granite stone in the passenger seat.

"Don't just stand there like a lump—help me get her inside."

Cecil hobbled around to the passenger door and opened it. Loretta helped spin Carlie's legs around until they were outside the truck. Once Loretta had Carlie's coat zipped, she led her across the yard and into the house.

Inside, Cecil put on a kettle of water for tea, while Loretta led Carlie to the spare bedroom. Carlie stood like a statue in the middle of the room while Loretta found a pair of pajamas and a robe for Carlie to change into. Carlie put up no resistance while Loretta dressed her in the clean nightclothes. Just as she finished, Cecil knocked on the door. "Come on in. We're decent."

"How is she doing?" Cecil asked.

"Not too well. I think it finally hit her—Jon is really dead. If she survives it, she can actually start to grieve."

Cecil stood in the middle of the room holding two cups of tea. "Do you think she can drink this?"

Loretta sat with Carlie on the edge of the bed and helped her drink almost half of her tea. When she started to resist, Loretta handed the cup back to Cecil. "Thank you."

Sitting at the kitchen table, Loretta reached over and took Cecil's hand. "This is the worst day of Carlie's life. I imagine it feels like her whole world collapsed in on itself today."

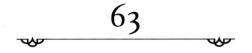

# 63

"CECIL! CECIL, SHE'S GONE!"

Cecil dropped the can of coffee and hobbled as fast as he could to the sound of Loretta's voice. Turning into the bedroom, he found Loretta standing next to an empty bed. Not only was it empty, but someone had made it up to look as if no one had even slept in it.

Bending over the bed, Loretta patted the covers as if Carlie might be hiding.

Loretta didn't wait for Cecil to say anything; she just turned and ran by him toward the kitchen. Cecil hobbled after her as fast as he could, but slowed when he heard the kitchen door slam.

By the time he made it into the kitchen, Loretta was back and closing the door behind her. "Her truck is gone."

"Get your coat on, woman—we'll go find her."

Loretta looked at him as if he had lost his mind. "Do you have any idea where she might be?"

"Unless she is out driving around aimlessly—which I doubt—she is in one of three places. We'll start with the most obvious."

Loretta was zipping up her coat as Cecil lifted his truck keys off the hook.

"Damn," Loretta said, "I should have kept her truck keys in my pocket."

"Hell, she was practically comatose when she got here. How could you have known she would get up and leave?"

As they turned onto Breckenridge Road, the trucks and equipment parked on both sides made passage slow and dangerous. When they pulled to a stop in front of the entrance to the burial plot, one of the workmen walked up to Cecil's open window and asked if he could help them.

"I was just wondering if Missus Summers was by here today."

"No, I haven't seen her. Mister Bannerman asked me the same thing not an hour ago."

Thanking the man, Cecil turned around and made his way back to the main highway. Turning left, he headed toward Carlie's house.

In just under twenty minutes, they pulled into Carlie's drive. Her truck wasn't in front of the house, so he drove to the circle Bannerman's crew had cleaned the morning before. He breathed a sigh of relief when he found her pickup parked behind the house.

Turning the door handle, Loretta discovered that the door was unlocked. She opened it very slowly, then stuck her head inside and looked around the empty living room. She was about to yell Carlie's name when she heard someone in the kitchen.

As she walked across the living room, she announced her presence. "Carlie? It's Loretta and Cecil. Are you decent?"

When she didn't get an answer, Cecil stopped where he was and Loretta called out again, "CARLIE?"

"I'm in the kitchen, Loretta."

Cecil took a seat on the couch, and Loretta went into the kitchen.

Carlie looked worse than the day before. "Sweetie," Loretta said, "have you even been to bed?"

"No."

"Why did you leave?"

"For some reason, I felt I should be here."

"Why?"

"I'm not finished yet. I need to get everything out of here that belonged to Jon, Aunt Grace, and, if possible, every family that ever lived in this place."

"I can't believe I'm saying this, but you could just burn the place to the ground."

"I'm not sure that it would do any good."

For the first time since they had been talking, Carlie looked directly into Loretta's eyes. "I'd like you to call me every morning and every night until I'm out of here. If you don't get an answer, come by and check on me. If I need you, I promise I won't hesitate to call."

Carlie stood up and walked the couple into the living room. Opening the roll-top desk, she pulled out a large manila envelope and handed it to Loretta. "If anything happens to me, I'd like for you to open this. There are provisions in it to finish what I've started. I'd like you to oversee it."

Loretta stood there for a moment holding the envelope. Without a word, she and Cecil closed the door behind them as they left.

# 64

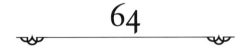

It was a little after 2:00 in the morning when Carlie had the first load in the bed of her pickup. As hard as it was, she managed to get every article of clothing, piece of jewelry, and incidental that Jon owned packed into suitcases and boxes and loaded. Just the scent of his aftershave lingering on his shirts sent her into crying fits.

She was exhausted. She hadn't slept in almost three days. Her legs felt like rubber as she walked up the stairs to the bedroom. As she sat on the edge of the bed, she looked forward to a long, hot soak in the tub.

Carlie never stirred when the side of her bed compressed. She turned slightly onto her side when a touch as gentle as a summer breeze moved her hair out of her face. Opening her eyes, she saw Jon smiling down at her. Turning onto her back, she reached out and touched his face. It was the same face she had touched, kissed, and even helped shave after his accident in the barn, but something about it didn't feel the same.

Jon leaned down and whispered in her ear, "I love you so much, Carlie."

She recognized Jon's voice instantly. "God, Jon . . . I love you too—so much."

She shuddered with excitement as his lips brushed against the hollow of her throat. She pulled his head tighter against her.

As his hand traced a path up her inner thigh, she arched her back in anticipation. She could feel his weight shift in bed as he slid her nightgown above her waist. Spreading her legs in surrender, she waited for the moment when they would again become one.

Breathlessly she whispered, "Take me, Jon. Make love to me. I've missed you so much."

"Oh, I'll take you, you bitch."

When Carlie's eyes snapped open, her face was mere inches away from Ian McPherson's. She no longer smelled Jon's intoxicating aftershave, but only rotting flesh. Pushing her into the mattress, he burned a hole deep into her soul as he ravaged her half-naked body with his eyes; as fast as a cobra strike, he was on top of her, biting and snorting into her ear like a rutting pig.

Screaming at the top of her lungs, Carlie pushed at Ian with all her might. She tried to sit up in bed, but she couldn't budge the dead weight on top of her.

Rolling onto her side, she pushed again and slid off the bed and onto the floor. Lying helpless with her nightgown hiked up around her waist, she struggled desperately to catch her breath.

Ian stood over her with his hands on his hips. Staring down at her, he cracked a greasy, solicitous smile. Carlie waited to see what he intended to do next. He faded until she could barely make out who, or what, was standing over her. In another moment, he was gone.

Carlie pulled herself up onto the bed and turned on the bedside light. Wrapping the comforter around her shoulders, she lifted up her nightgown and examined herself. She found fresh bruises the size of fingertips on the inside of her thigh. She was positive that they would become sizable black and blue marks by morning.

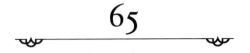

# 65

The sun was glaring through the kitchen window when Carlie opened her eyes again. The clock over the stove showed that it was 10:00 AM; she had slept for six hours.

As she sipped her coffee, the telephone rang. Reluctantly, she picked up the receiver. "Hello?"

"*Where the hell have you been?*" said the voice on the other end. "*I've been calling you for the last two hours.*"

"I'm sorry, Loretta. I was asleep. I didn't even hear the phone ring."

"Well, when you didn't answer, I sent Cecil out to your house. He should be pulling into your driveway any minute now."

"I'm fine, Loretta. I'll send him home as soon as he gets here."

"Don't bother. He'll just drive me crazy hanging around here all day. I'm sure you can find something for him to do to help you."

Carlie couldn't help but smile; she couldn't remember all the times she had tried to pawn off Jon just to have a few minutes to herself. "Not a problem. As a matter of fact, I can use him."

Loretta let out a roaring laugh. "Holy shit! I don't think anyone has ever said that about Cecil. Just don't let him be the supervisor, or he will be as much help as a lump of clay."

Carlie was just about to promise that she wouldn't when she heard the report of a gun. "I'm going to let you go now. Cecil is playing GI Joe with the birds in the front yard."

"I hope he's wearing his glasses. If not, you'll probably be replacing all your windows."

Carlie put on her jacket, picked up her shotgun, and took one last look to see if she had forgotten anything in the kitchen. "Oh hell, I almost forgot." She pulled out the coffee can full of birdseed from under the sink. Scooping out a cupful, she opened the kitchen window. As she brushed away the snow from the planter box, her finger touched something about four inches long and as hard as a rock. Picking it up, she started brushing it off but stopped the second she saw the brilliant red coloring. Bringing it inside the house, she laid it on the kitchen table and gently wiped it off with a damp paper towel. Picking it up again, she gently rolled it over in her hand. Every part of it was stiff except its neck, which lolled over the side of her hand.

Laying it back down on the table, she walked back to the window and ran her hand through the planter box again. It took less than a minute to locate the rest of her little family. Each had a broken neck.

Carlie couldn't control her emotions any longer. Screaming, she started crying uncontrollably. She was hurt and she was grieving their needless deaths, but most of all, she was mad. Picking up her shotgun, she loaded it and stormed out the front door. She didn't even look to see where Cecil was. She figured that he was a big boy and could get out of her way.

Pointing at the edge of the barn, she fired five times in quick succession. As the birds took to the sky, she fired four more times at the top of the trees and at the birds in flight.

Knowing that the birds would circle around and land again, she reloaded and prepared herself for their return.

She assumed Cecil would join in after she eliminated as many blackbirds as she could, but he didn't. While she waited for the birds to return, she looked around the yard and found him sitting on his tailgate with his back to her.

Walking up behind him, she saw his shotgun lying on the ground next to him. His head was resting on his chest, and he was holding himself up with both hands on the tailgate. Blood covered his left hand; something had shredded his jacket sleeve.

Walking around to the back of his pickup, Carlie couldn't believe her eyes. Something had attacked Cecil while he was waiting for her. He had vicious bite marks on his face, arms, and legs. Along with the bites, he had several deep cuts and what looked like peck marks.

Touching his hand, Carlie found that it was still warm, and he had a pulse—it wasn't strong, but it was there. Climbing up into the bed of the truck, she put her hands under Cecil's arms, slid him inside the bed, and laid him down. Covering him with a stack of corn sacks and a heavy woolen blanket, she blocked him in, in preparation for a fast and rough ride to the hospital.

Twenty-five minutes later, Carlie was sliding to a stop at the emergency entrance. Honking the horn from the street, she had three inquisitive nurses peering out the window as she stopped at the door.

As Carlie dropped the tailgate, the nurses wheeled out a gurney before she could even ask.

In the waiting room, Carlie called Loretta at the café. When she answered, Carlie explained that Cecil had been hurt. Loretta thanked her and told her not to worry. Cecil was a tough old bird; he had survived a lot worse than this in his lifetime.

An hour later, Doctor Tremmel walked into the waiting room. Carlie and Loretta were the only two people in it, so it made sense that they were waiting for him.

"Cecil is doing fine. His injuries were mostly superficial. He did receive some nasty bites. We cleaned them up and sewed them shut. Unfortunately, to be on the safe side, I had to give him a series of rabies shots. I wanted to keep him overnight, but he's being a pain in the ass, so we're going to release him in a little while."

"Let me give you a ride back to the house," Loretta said. "I'll come back and wait for the old man."

"I can't apologize enough, Loretta. All of this is my fault."

"No, it isn't. It's that fucking house. The sooner you get out, the sooner everyone will be safe."

"I'll be out of there by morning—I promise."

Once they were back at the house, Carlie showed Loretta what someone had done to her little family of cardinals. As she touched them ever so gently, she couldn't help herself and started crying again. Loretta found a box of new work shoes on the floor of the kitchen pantry. Taking out the shoes, she tenderly wrapped the birds in paper towels and then wrapped them one more time with the tissue paper from inside the box. "We'll give these little guys a new home in Dexter's yard. No one will ever hurt them again."

Carlie kissed Loretta on the cheek and walked with her as she carried the shoebox to the door. Stopping, Loretta turned to Carlie. "I'll meet you at Dexter's in an hour and a half at the most. Get out of here now!"

## 66

Carlie had almost finished unloading when Loretta pulled up behind her truck. After setting the last four boxes on the ground, she waited for Loretta.

"Well, how is Cecil doing?"

"He's pissed. He only had birdshot in his shotgun. Birdshot ain't much good against a 150-pound wolf. He'll know better next time."

"God, I'm so sorry."

"Don't be. He's got himself one hell of a story to tell."

Picking up two boxes, Carlie could only shake her head and laugh.

When Carlie had finished unloading the boxes, she spotted Loretta in what would be an exceptionally beautiful spot in the backyard come summertime. Loretta had dug a hole deep enough to keep curious animals away and buried Carlie's beautiful little family of cardinals.

As Carlie approached her, Loretta was forming a makeshift cross out of two pieces of wooden fencing.

"I want to make sure we can find this spot in the spring. We'll make a proper marker after the snow melts."

Carlie knelt beside Loretta and ran her hand over the tiny mound of fresh dirt. Carlie started crying.

Putting her arm around Carlie's shoulder, Loretta pulled her close and just held her. Rocking her gently in her embrace, Loretta let her friend grieve.

~

Sitting at the kitchen table, Carlie finished making a list of everything they were going to move to Dexter's house. With Loretta's pickup, they would be able to finish in two trips.

It was late afternoon, and the sun would be going down soon. To give them the light they were going to need, Carlie made a trip out to the barn and turned on all the floodlights. Tonight, she wanted the farm lit up like a football stadium.

After Cecil's run-in with the wolf, they decided that they would take turns loading. Loretta would take the shotgun first.

The farm was deathly quiet; even the wind had stopped blowing. Carlie got a creepy feeling that moved from her spine to her stomach. Something wasn't right. Stepping back, Carlie tugged on the back of Loretta's jacket, making her follow her into the house. Slamming the door shut and locking it behind them, Carlie ejected the shells she had in the shotgun and reloaded it with deer slugs. "Something isn't right. The birds are gone."

Before Carlie was finished loading the shotgun, Loretta was on the telephone.

"Kenneth, we need your help.... I'm at Carlie's.... I don't give a damn. It's probably a rerun anyway.... Kenneth, get your dead ass off that couch and get over here, NOW, and bring your big rifle.... Yes, it might be the wolf again."

It was still light out, but after what had happened to Cecil, Carlie was very leery of moving the journals to her pickup bed until Kenneth arrived. They were heavy and cumbersome, and she was afraid that carrying them would make her and Loretta easy prey for any wild animal, especially a full-grown wolf.

The two women carried the heavy boxes and stacked them just inside the front door. As Carlie set down the last box, there was a loud knock on the door. Carlie pulled back the corner of the curtains and saw Kenneth and Cecil standing on the porch. Nodding her head, Loretta opened the door and pulled them both inside the house by the front of their jackets.

"What in the hell are you doing here, old man?" Loretta asked.

"Moral support. Figured you might need some."

316

Kenneth picked up his rifle and headed to the front door. As everyone except Cecil fell in behind him, he handed his rifle to Loretta and picked up four of the boxes of journals. Carlie unlocked and opened the door for him. Loretta moved out onto the porch first and scanned the driveway for any movement.

Kenneth made short work of the heavy boxes. In less than an hour, he had both Carlie's pickup and Loretta's completely loaded and ready to take to Dexter's house.

# 67

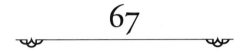

Kenneth and Cecil were sitting guard on the front porch while the women were upstairs packing. Cecil first noticed the movement by the barn. Poking Kenneth on the arm, he pointed toward where he had seen a dark shadow cross in front of the closed barn door. "Look over there," he said. "Did you see that?"

Kenneth strained his eyes to see anything through the blinding snow. Finally, he caught a subtle movement at the corner of the barn. "I think so, but it's not in the middle, it's at the corner now."

Cecil looked in the direction Kenneth was pointing just in time to see a dark sinewy shape as it appeared briefly and then slinked around the corner. Cocking their weapons, they watched and waited. There was more movement; however, it was not by the barn. This time it was by the oak trees. Cecil was positive he was looking at a man. He seemed to be leaning against the tree—and watching them. As Cecil watched the man, he could make out three different shapes as they moved restlessly in the dark.

As the wind began to pick up in intensity, the snow swirled and drifted in abstract shapes, providing cover for the shapes as they approached the porch undetected.

Kenneth was the first to notice their movement. Three emaciated gray wolves the size of small German shepherds stepped out of the raging storm onto the top step of the porch.

"Jesus, Cecil, those poor things are starving to death.

"After almost two months of below-zero temperatures and waist-high snow, their food source has burrowed in. It's no wonder they're roaming the countryside. They're looking for food. Hell, I would too.

"You're so full of crap, Cecil. There's nothing supernatural or even out of the ordinary about these skinny little creatures."

Of the three, one wolf stood out as a leader. It wasn't any larger, but it was decidedly more aggressive. Lowering its head, it raised its hackles, and from somewhere deep inside its chest, it started a low rumbling growl. Taking one cautious step at a time, the beast approached the two men.

Kenneth didn't even stand up; he pointed the barrel of his rifle over their heads and fired. The near-deafening roar of the weapon reverberated against the walls of the house. Lung-burning smoke and the odor of burnt cordite swirled inside the enclosure.

Within a few seconds, both Cecil and Kenneth realized that the shot had had no physical or psychological effect on the animals—they hadn't even flinched.

Taking aim this time, Kenneth fired just as the wolf jumped. Blood sprayed in a geyser across the wall of the house, and without a whimper, the beast flew backward off the steps and lay motionless in the snow. The remaining two wolves that had been standing shoulder to shoulder stopped moving forward and separated to a safe distance.

Cecil leveled his shotgun at the one on the left, and Kenneth, the one on the right. The men waited apprehensively. Seconds passed like hours, and neither of the wolves moved a muscle. With heads lowered, they stood like statues, their eyes never wavering from the two men sitting in front of them.

A spine-chilling howl from somewhere in the blizzard propelled both men out of their chairs. Kenneth swept his rifle barrel toward the barn and the oak trees, while Cecil remained immobile, steadying himself on his crutch. He leveled the barrel of his shotgun in the direction of the two wolves on the porch.

An enormous silhouette appeared out of the shadows. Standing next to the dead wolf, it bent down and sniffed. Lifting its head, it unleashed an earsplitting wail, and a hundred or more voices from somewhere off in the distance joined in its song of death.

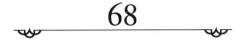

# 68

Looking out the window, Carlie couldn't see a thing. "I can't believe how hard it's snowing out there. I can't even see the back yard."

Carlie emptied the dresser and both nightstands onto the bed. She had packed all her clothes and the remainder of Jon's into three boxes when she noticed the gray velvet ring box.

Opening the box, she ran her finger over the shiny new wedding band inside. She had wanted Jon to have something special. Her birthstone was a sapphire, so she had had a perfect blue sapphire set into the center, with a diamond of equal size on each side. They had even made plans to renew their wedding vows on their next anniversary. She wanted to cry, but she had cried enough for one day.

Just as she set the ring box in with her underwear, there was a loud report from somewhere in front of the house. Carlie looked up at Loretta, who had heard the gun shot too and was already moving to the stairs.

"Don't worry, Carlie, they're both big boys. They can handle whatever comes along."

"Oh God, please don't let anything happen to them," Carlie said under her breath.

Just as Loretta threw back the curtain in the living room, Kenneth fired a second shot. Blood sprayed across the window, and the carcass of a skeleton-thin gray wolf sailed by, falling into a heap in the snow.

Loretta turned to Carlie, who was looking deathly pale after what she had just witnessed, and said, "We need to get finished so we can get the boys and ourselves out of here."

Loretta took Carlie by the arm and led her back up the stairs. They picked up the loaded boxes and carried them back down. As they slowly opened the front door, a wolf let out a howl the likes of which neither of them had ever heard. It stopped Carlie in her tracks, raising the hair on the back of her neck. Loretta passed her, her arms loaded with boxes. Snapping out of her momentary lapse, Carlie picked up four boxes and hustled them out the door and into the bed of the truck.

Slamming the door behind them, both women ran back up the stairs. With careless abandon, they literally threw everything else lying on the bed into empty boxes. As they finished each box, they taped it shut and set it outside the bedroom door.

# 69

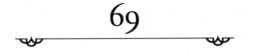

Kenneth let out an audible sigh as the giant black wolf stepped slowly out of the shadows and onto the porch. "Holy shit, where did this big fucker come from?"

"Just a guess," Cecil said, "but I'd say the depths of hell."

Kenneth pulled the bolt back on his rifle, making sure there was a round in the chamber, and said to Cecil, "From three."

"Three ... two ... one." Both weapons fired in chorus, sounding like one deafening roar.

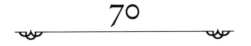

# 70

Carlie and Loretta grabbed all the clothes hanging in the closet and blindly staggered down the stairs as fast as they could without falling and breaking their necks.

Carlie reached the door first and turned the handle. As she slowly pulled it open, the loudest gunshot she had ever heard shook the walls and rattled the windows. Grabbing hold of the clothes she was carrying, she made a dash out the door and threw them into the bed of Loretta's truck. Turning, she ran headlong into Loretta, almost knocking her off her feet. Taking half of Loretta's armload, they threw the clothes in the truck and rushed back into the house.

Carlie picked up the remaining four boxes and carried them down the stairs. She had barely gotten them in the truck when she heard Loretta screaming at the top of her lungs.

Taking the stairs two and three at a time, Carlie noticed the pungent smell before she even reached the second-floor landing. She had smelled it before, but couldn't remember exactly where.

Just as she reached the second floor, Loretta ran by screaming in the direction of the bathroom. Her shirt and pants were ablaze, as was the carpeting behind her. Carlie recognized the smell now—it was kerosene.

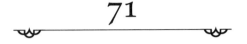

## 71

The giant wolf dropped to its stomach on the porch and didn't move. The two smaller wolves backed cautiously into the yard and melted into the shadows.

"Do you smell that?" Cecil asked. "It smells like smoke." Hobbling off the front porch, Cecil was surveying the entire house when he spotted a flicker in the second-floor rear window. Pulling on Kenneth's sleeve, he said, "Up there, do you see it?"

"Shit," Kenneth said. "What the hell is going on here?"

Kenneth made the front door in three strides, while Cecil limped along behind as fast as he could. Grabbing the door handle, Kenneth found the front door locked. "Wait here, Cecil. I'll go to the kitchen door."

Kenneth took off running as fast as he could. Reaching the back porch, he yanked on the screen door only to find it locked. Hitting the door with his rifle butt, it splintered and swung inward. Turning the back door handle, he found it locked, too.

Kenneth backed into the yard and looked up to find the second-floor windows dancing with yellow and orange flames. Thick black smoke was rolling out from under the eaves, spinning and swirling into the night sky.

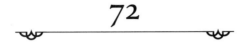

# 72

Carlie ran down the hall and caught up with Loretta just before she entered the bedroom. Ripping the comforter from the bed, she wrapped it around Loretta; pulling her to the floor, Carlie rolled on top of her, smothering the flames.

She needed to get Loretta out of the house—she needed to get her to the hospital. As Carlie held her tight, she heard the woman whimpering softly and could feel her starting to shake. Loretta was only moments away from going into shock.

Herding Loretta into the bathroom, Carlie opened the shower door and turned both handles on full force, soaking the comforter.

Turning around under the water, Carlie drenched her own hair and clothes.

The odor of kerosene was almost overpowering. Smoke and flames crept under the door, blocking their escape route. The blue and yellow flames consumed the saturated carpeting like a rolling wave, one foot at a time.

Taking Loretta's hands, Carlie squeezed them into a fist on the edge of the soggy material. "Hold this tight against your face—breathe through it," Carlie said to her. "Don't let it fall, or you'll suffocate."

Loretta nodded in understanding.

The flames had advanced into the room. Spreading up and across the bed, they ignited the wooden dresser, the nightstands, and, as Carlie watched, the headboard.

Carlie's eyes were watering so hard, she could barely keep them open; and even though she was breathing through her heavy wet shirt, her lungs burned as if they too were on fire.

Carlie hung on the drapes with all her weight until they broke loose and fell to the floor, seconds before they ignited.

Huddling Loretta under the protection of one arm, Carlie crashed through the window with her other arm.

Succumbing to the smoke and heat, Loretta dropped to the floor. Carlie had no time to waste. She smashed out the rest of the glass with the side of her right hand and arm, then bent into the flaming carpet and scooped Loretta and the comforter into her arms.

With strength she never realized she had, Carlie lifted and slid Loretta out the open window onto the snow-packed roof.

As Carlie started to follow, a voice from across the room shouted, "Wait!"

Stepping out of the heaviest smoke, the figure of a young boy stood in the middle of the burning room—the same boy Carlie had seen in her dream.

"You can't leave—we belong together. I did everything for you."

Carlie stood and listened to Andrew in shocked disbelief. Almost hypnotized by what she was seeing and hearing, she failed to realize that the flames had crawled completely across the floor and up the wall behind her. Her wet shirt, her pants, and even her work boots were beginning to smoke from the heat.

No sooner had she finished saying, "It's your house now, Andrew," than her shirt burst into flames.

Without giving Andrew or the house a second thought, Carlie jumped out the broken window onto the roof. The wind whipped the flames in every direction. Throwing her burning shirt into the wind, she took hold of Loretta's comforter and dragged her to the edge of the roof. Carlie gently lowered her down, then Kenneth and Cecil took the bottom of the comforter and let her slide into their waiting arms.

As Carlie jumped from the edge of the roof into the snowdrift below, Andrew, backlit by the raging fire, stood in the broken window watching as Carlie disappeared into the night. *"NOOOOOO!"* he howled. His desperate, wounded cry was instantly absorbed into the buffeting winds and swirling snow.

Carlie pulled onto the highway, driving as fast as she could through the blinding snow. Cecil held and gently rocked his wife. "Please, Retta," he whispered, "don't die—I can't live without you."

When the heater started blowing warm air into the cab of the truck, Carlie gagged at the overpowering stench of burnt flesh and chemical smoke.

Carlie hurt so bad, she could barely stay conscious. As much as she didn't want to, she surveyed the damage she had inflicted on herself. Her right arm, from the elbow down to her wrist, was shredded—some spots to the bone. Blood dripped from the bottom of her arm and her fingertips onto the leg of her pants and the floor. To make matters worse, there were large patches on both arms that the fire had burnt black, and the crusty surfaces had torn away with her shirt, leaving open, oozing wounds.

As they reached the emergency room entrance, Carlie slammed on the brakes, shoved the shift lever into park, and shut off the engine.

Reaching her arm from under the comforter, Loretta gently squeezed Carlie's hand. "We made it."

"Yeah, Loretta. Thanks to you, we did make it."

# Epilogue

### FIVE YEARS LATER

The frozen gravel crunches under my tires as Carlie and I approach the old McPherson house. As we get closer to the end of the drive, I can feel her beginning to tense and shift uncomfortably in her seat. She averts her eyes from the old house—eyes that plead with me to turn around—to run.

Parking next to the barn, I promise her that I will be back in a few minutes. I need to take one last look.

As I walk the grounds around this once magnificent house, I can still feel an oppressiveness that is beyond reason or explanation. Even in the middle of the day, I feel a dark, angry shadow hanging over the old house. To all outward appearances, it is nothing more than a vacant house, a house that someone abandoned long ago.

However, upon closer inspection, I can't help but notice that the truly violent nature of the house seems etched into its very existence. The second-floor windows are still dark and discolored—a permanent reminder of Carlie's brush with death. They are boarded up now with wood that has warped and grayed with age, a testimony to the cruel influence that the passage of time has had on the old house.

Rope tendrils still cling desperately to a rafter in the darkest recesses of the barn. Now the ill-fated victims of age and the elements, they may have at one time echoed the sound of laughter from a child's swing. On the other hand, they may tell a completely different story— a story of one child's abuse and indescribable suffering.

In their own subtle way, each tells the story of the McPherson house— a story with a past so dark and so cruel that the house has become little more than a scattered collection of broken lives, shattered dreams, and the deaths of its inhabitants.

While it is said that time heals what reason cannot, the true evil that is the McPherson house defies both time and reason.

As I climb behind the steering wheel, I hold Carlie's hand in mine. I thank her for sharing her story, and I apologize for the pain it has caused in its retelling.

As we drive toward the end of Baxter Road—and away from the old house for the last time—the untended "For Sale" sign still leans precariously in the front yard. Its faded letters on rusted hinges squeak gently in the afternoon breeze, beckoning anyone who might hear it, as a siren to an unsuspecting sailor.

Turning onto the main highway, I can feel the house, and the evil within it, watching us drive away.

Again, it patiently waits.

ANNIE WILDER

THE
TRUE
STORY
OF A
HAUNTED
HOUSE

HOUSE
*of*
SPIRITS
AND
WHISPERS

# House of Spirits and Whispers
*The True Story of a Haunted House*
### ANNIE WILDER

Annie Wilder suspected the funky 100-year-old house was haunted when she saw it for the first time. But nothing could have prepared her for the mischievous and downright scary antics that take place once she, her two children, and her cats move into the rundown Victorian home. Disembodied conversation, pounding walls, glowing orbs, and mysterious whispers soon escalate into full-fledged ghostly visits—provoking sheer terror that, over time, transforms into curiosity. Determined to make peace with her spirit guests, she invites renowned clairvoyant Echo Bodine over and learns fascinating details about each of the entities residing there.

Wilder's gripping tale provides a compelling glimpse into the otherworldly nature of the lonely spirits, protective forces, phantom pets, and departed loved ones that occupy her remarkable home.

978-0-7387-0777-8, 192 pp., 6 x 9                    $14.99

STEVEN LaCHANCE
with LAURA LONG-HELBIG

THE
UNINVITED

The True Story
*of the*
Union Screaming House

# The Uninvited

### *The True Story of the Union Screaming House*
### Steven LaChance
#### with Laura Long-Helbig

*Its screams still wake me from sleep. I see the faceless man standing in that basement washing away the blood from his naked body.*

Steven LaChance was forever transformed by the paranormal attacks that drove him and his family from their home in Union, Missouri. When another family falls victim to the same dark entity, Steven returns to the dreaded house to offer aid and find healing.

Paranormal investigators, psychics, and priests are consulted, but no relief is found. The demon's presence—screams, growls, putrid odors, invisible shoves, bites, and other physical violations—only grow worse. LaChance chronicles how this supernatural predator infects those around it. But the one who suffers most is the current homeowner, Helen. When the entity takes possession and urges Helen toward murder and madness, LaChance must engage in a hair-raising battle for her soul.

*The Uninvited* is a true and terrifying tale of extreme haunting, demon possession, and an epic struggle between good and evil.

978-0-7387-1357-1, 264 pp., 6 x 9                                   $16.95

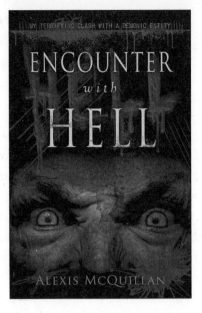

# Encounter with Hell
*My Terrifying Clash with a Demonic Entity*
### Alexis McQuillan

The events in this story are true, but the names and locations have been changed to protect the reader. Alexis is a psychic who never believed in demons until she came face to face with pure evil. This is her true story of battling a terrifying entity that was so powerful it turned her life upside down and put her in mortal danger . . .

Her nightmare begins shortly after she and her husband relocate to a small lakeside community. After hearing rumors about the nearby Matthews residence, Alexis investigates the nineteenth-century house and its spirit inhabitants. She soon finds herself caught in a demon's snare of violent fury—subjecting her to deep growls, a malevolent force attacking her in bed, and phantom apparitions, ultimately leading to a horrific spiritual battle with a demon hell-bent on her destruction.

978-0-7387-3350-0, 216 pp., 5³⁄₁₆ x 8                     $14.99